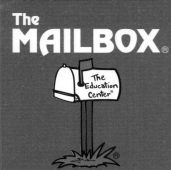

SUPERBOOK

Grade 5

Everything You Need for a Successful Year!

W9-DEF-418

- Language Arts
- Math
- Science and Health
- Social Studies
- Graphic Organizers

- Management Tips
- Centers
- Games
- Differentiation Tips
- Bulletin Boards

And Much More!

Revised and Updated!

Managing Editors: Debra Liverman, Thad H. McLaurin

Editorial Team: Becky S. Andrews, Kimberley Bruck, Sharon Murphy, Diane Badden, Peggy Hambright, Amy Payne, Gerri Primak, Kelly Robertson, Karen A. Brudnak, Juli Docimo Blair, Hope Rodgers, Dorothy C. McKinney

Production Team: Lori Z. Henry, Pam Crane, Rebecca Saunders, Chris Curry, Sarah Foreman, Theresa Lewis Goode, Greg D. Rieves, Eliseo De Jesus Santos II, Barry Slate, Donna K. Teal, Zane Williard, Tazmen Carlisle, Kathy Coop, Marsha Heim, Lynette Dickerson, Mark Rainey, Karen Brewer Grossman, Amy Kirtley-Hill

www.themailbox.com

©2007 The Mailbox®
All rights reserved.
ISBN10 #1-56234-738-1 • ISBN13 #978-156234-738-3

Manufactured in the United States
10 9 8 7 6 5 4 3 2 1

TABLE OF CONTENTS

TABLE OF CONTENTS

Holidays and Seasonal Activities

BACK-TO-SCHOOL

Not Just a Nametag!

Assist your students in learning about new classroom procedures with a little help from their nametags! Make one copy of the nametag pattern on page 7. On the boxed side of the nametag, list several procedures that you want your students to learn quickly. Next, make a class set of the programmed nametag on heavy paper. Write each student's name on a different nametag; then fold and place the nametag on a desktop so that the name faces the front of the room and the procedures face the student's chair. These nametags will not only help you learn your students' names quickly, but they can also help to remind your students about some very important classroom routines!

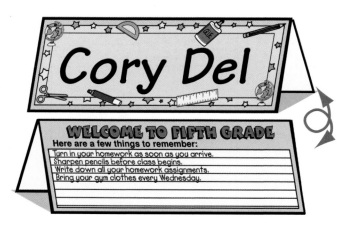

Cory Del

WELCOME TO FIFTH GRADE
Here are a few things to remember:
Turn in your homework as soon as you arrive.
Sharpen pencils before class begins.
Write down all your homework assignments.
Bring your gym clothes every Wednesday.

Sandra

GRAFFITI BOARD

Create a one-of-a-kind display with this quick and easy bulletin board idea. Cover your board with black bulletin board paper, rough side facing out. Place a box of colored chalk next to the board, and invite each student to visit the board during free time. Have him use the chalk to sign his name graffiti-style and add a colorful picture. When every student has signed his name, recognize the person who penned each signature; then share something that you have learned about that student during the first few days of school. What a great way to make each student feel special!

Alex   Devin

Creating a Model Student

Create a classroom full of model students with this novel idea! Draw a stick figure on a sheet of chart paper or poster board and label it "The Model Student." Have your students suggest the characteristics they think constitute a model student. Then draw a disproportionate feature on the stick figure that represents each suggested characteristic. For example, a student could say that a model student is a good listener. Then you could draw very large ears protruding from the stick figure's head. Students will love the ridiculous cartoon that results, and you'll be relaying important information about helping your students succeed.

A model student is awake and alert.

A model student is a good listener.

A model student raises his hand before he speaks.

A model student always has something to write with.

Get-to-Know-You Roundup

This icebreaker can help your students get acquainted in no time at all! Program one index card with a different question for every two students in your class. Divide your class into two groups and instruct them to sit in two concentric circles on the floor so that each student in the inner circle faces a student in the outer circle. Next, give each child in the inner circle a programmed index card; then allow him one minute to discuss the question on his card with the child across from him. Explain that both students need to share their thoughts during this time. After one minute, give a signal for each student with an index card to pass it to the child on his right and for each student on the outer circle to move one space to the right so that he faces a different partner. Continue in this manner until each student has answered all the different questions.

If you could visit anywhere in the world, where would you go? Why?

What is your favorite food? Why?

Of all the places you've been on vacation, which place was your favorite? Why?

Who is your favorite actor? Why?

What is the best book you've ever read? Why?

What is your favorite subject in school? Why?

What is your favorite TV show or video game? Why?

What's the most unusual thing that's ever happened to you at school?

Where were you born?

Tony Capland

Bethany Kiser

Owen Troy

POSTCARD EXPRESS

The next time one of your students does something worth bragging about, send the message home via postcard express! At the beginning of the year, give each student two large blank index cards. Instruct him to decorate one side of each card any way that he chooses. Have the student turn over each card and neatly print his home address on the right half of the card. Collect the cards and store them in your desk. When a student does something special, simply write a brief message explaining what he did on the left half of one of his cards and drop it in the mail. What a great way to get both a student and his parents to feel very proud!

Jonathan Jones
8 Harbor Way
Jonesville, KS 12345

Trading Cards

Your students can feel like stars with this getting-acquainted project! Instruct each student to bring in a recent picture of herself. Then give each student one unlined index card. Direct the student to paste her picture onto one side of her index card and write her name underneath the picture. Then have her use a black ink pen to write information about herself—such as her birthdate, height, place of birth, favorite food, hobbies, and so on—on the back of the card. Paper-clip each card to a length of string stretched across a wall as shown so that students can remove one card at a time and read the back. What a fun way for students to learn about their classmates!

Student Cubes

Looking for a creative back-to-school activity to help your students get acquainted? These student-made cubes should do the trick! Give one copy of the cube pattern on page 8 to each student. Instruct each student to illustrate each side of the cube pattern. Then direct the student to follow the directions for assembling the cube. Use the completed cubes as desktags, story starters, or simply as an attractive display.

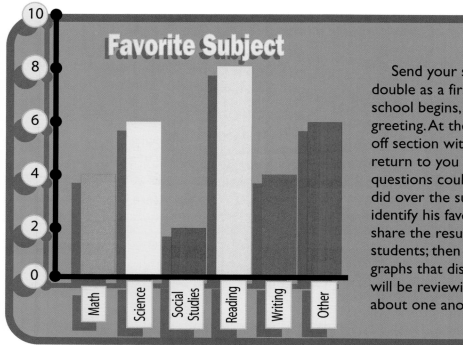

The Survey Says!

Send your students a welcoming letter that can double as a first-week graphing activity! Before school begins, mail each student a short, personal greeting. At the bottom of the greeting, include a tear-off section with a mini survey that the student should return to you on the first day of school. The survey questions could have the student list five things he did over the summer, name his favorite movie, and identify his favorite subject. On the first day of school, share the results of each survey question with your students; then have each student create a set of graphs that display the different data. Your students will be reviewing an important math skill and learning about one another at the same time!

WHAT'S IN A NAME?

Help each student learn more about her own name as she learns the names of her classmates. Check out from your local library a book of baby names. Assign each student the task of finding out the origin and meaning of her name as well as the possible reasons why her parents chose that name for her. Next, have each student use her findings to write a name poem that tells the story behind her name. Display the completed poems on a bulletin board titled "What's in a Name?"

Deborah is a Hebrew name.
The English changed it to Debra.
It means "the Bee."
My paRents liked the name and now it's mine,
But All my friends call me Debi.

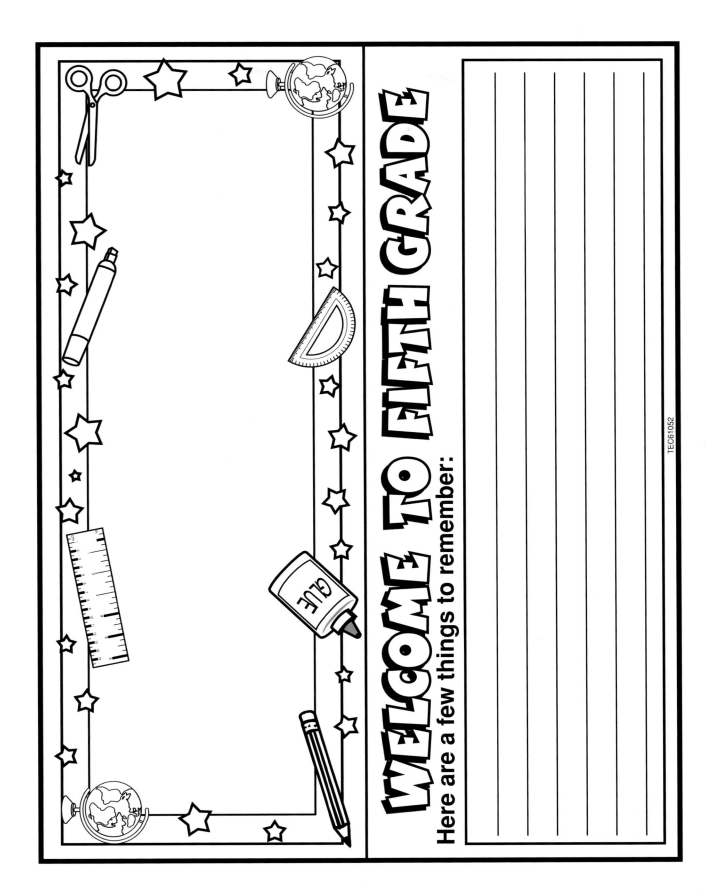

WELCOME TO FIFTH GRADE

Here are a few things to remember:

TEC61052

Cube Pattern

Use with "Student Cubes" on page 6.

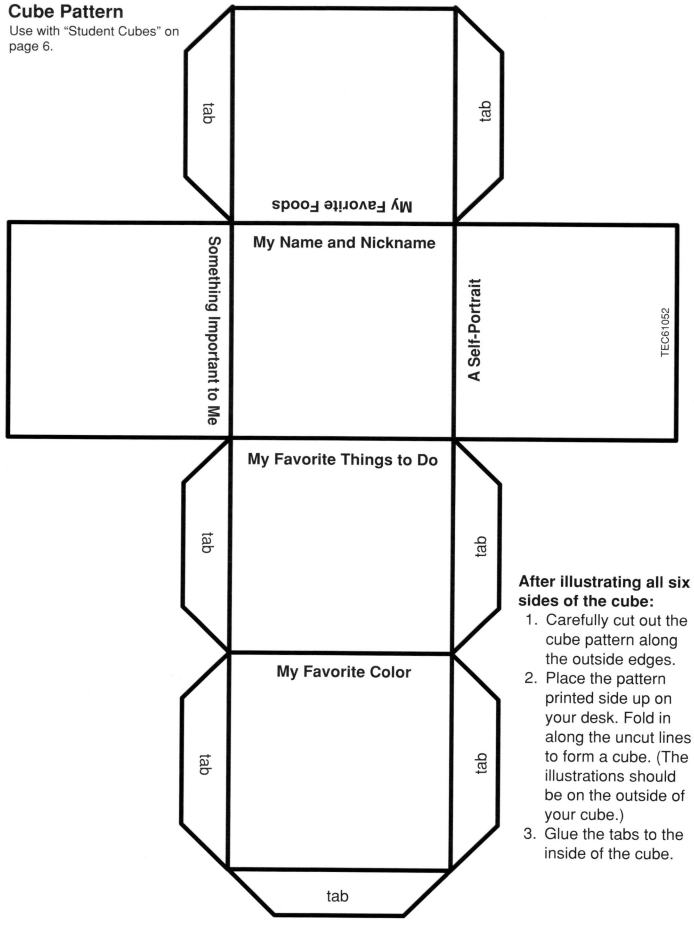

tab

tab

My Favorite Foods

Something Important to Me

My Name and Nickname

A Self-Portrait

TEC61052

My Favorite Things to Do

tab

tab

My Favorite Color

tab

tab

tab

After illustrating all six sides of the cube:

1. Carefully cut out the cube pattern along the outside edges.
2. Place the pattern printed side up on your desk. Fold in along the uncut lines to form a cube. (The illustrations should be on the outside of your cube.)
3. Glue the tabs to the inside of the cube.

THE FIRST DAY!

Can you believe your first day in fifth grade is almost over? Read the heading for each illustration below. Then use the lines provided on each shape for your responses.

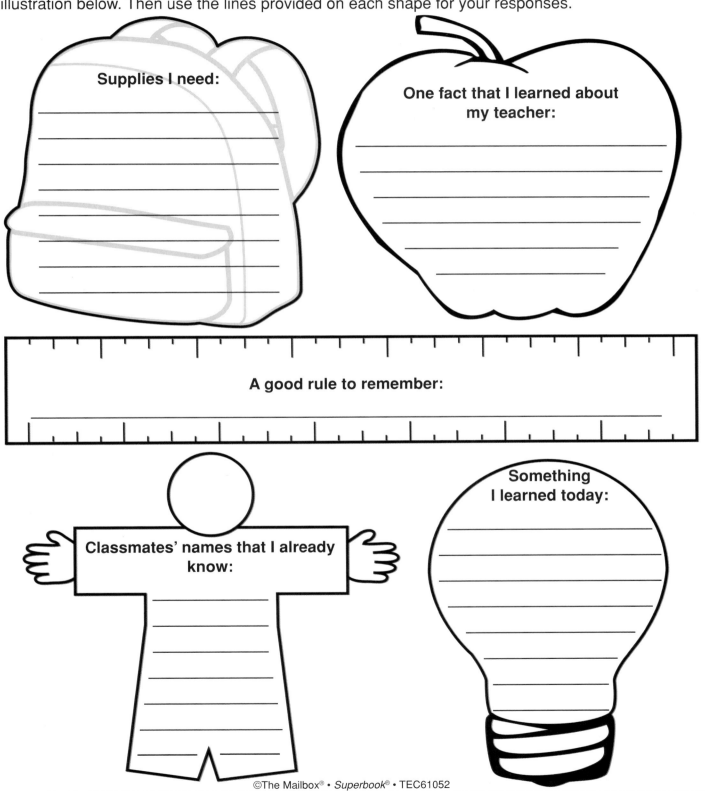

Supplies I need:

One fact that I learned about my teacher:

A good rule to remember:

Classmates' names that I already know:

Something I learned today:

Note to the teacher: Give each student a copy of this sheet at the end of the first day of school. Instruct him to complete the sheet as directed and take it home to share with his parents.

Reading Comprehension

Get the Idea?

Turn tissue boxes into handy sorting centers for practice with spotting main ideas and supporting details. Attach a pocket labeled with a different main-idea sentence to each side of an empty tissue box. Label a supply of tagboard strips—at least three for each main idea—with different detail sentences. Store these strips in the box. Place the box at a center along with an answer key. Have each student who visits the center pull out the strips, place each strip in the correct pocket, and check his work with the key. For additional practice, have each child complete a copy of page 26 as directed. **Main idea**

Learning a new hobby can be a lot of fun.

The Seven Natural Wonders of the World are incredible sights to see.

The Great Barrier Reef of Australia is the world's largest coral formation.

Disappearing Details

Looking for a quick way for students to practice identifying the main idea of a paragraph of expository text? Display a transparency on which you have written a selected paragraph. Remind students that a topic sentence is not always the first sentence of a paragraph. Have them read the paragraph together and decide which sentence is the topic sentence. After verifying their choice, underline the topic sentence and wipe away the rest of the paragraph. Then challenge students to recall the missing supporting-detail sentences—verbally or in writing—to rewrite the paragraph! **Main idea**

Getting to the Point

Use this visual activity to help your readers determine the topic of a particular selection of text. Divide students into groups of four and have them read a passage of your choice. Next, give each group a copy of the arrow patterns on page 27. Have each member of the group summarize one or two of the selection's paragraphs by writing a phrase for each sentence on an arrow cutout and then gluing it on colorful paper as shown. Once all of the arrows have been glued to the paper, have students identify the topic related to the phrases and record it in the space the arrows are pointing to. **Main idea**

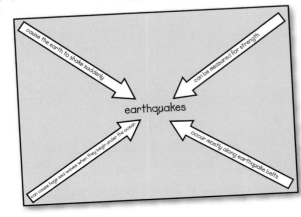

cause the earth to shake suddenly

can be measured for strength

earthquakes

can cause huge sea waves when they begin under the ocean

occur mostly along earthquake belts

What's the Big Idea?

Showcase students' growing comprehension skills with this umbrella-making project. After reading any informational text, guide each child to identify its main idea and three supporting details. Next, have the child cut an umbrella shape from a colorful sheet of construction paper and label it with the selection's main idea. Then have him cut three raindrop shapes from blue construction paper, label each one with a different supporting detail, and suspend the details with string or yarn as shown. Allow students to share their mobiles before displaying them around the classroom. **Main idea**

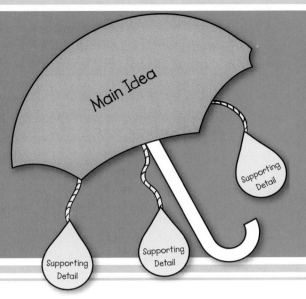

Hot off the Press

Check students' understanding of main idea and supporting details with this easy-to-make center. Cut short articles from the newspaper. Number each headline and remove it from the article. Mount the article on a sheet of paper and give it the same number as its headline. After laminating the articles and headlines, place them in a center along with wipe-off markers. To use the center, a child reads each article to determine its main idea and writes an appropriate headline in the space above it. Then he compares the headline he wrote to the one written by the actual journalist! **Main idea**

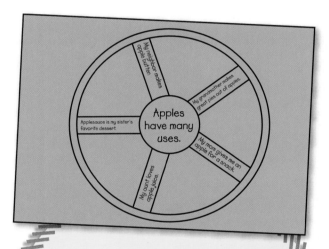

Let's Roll!

This anytime strategy can "wheely" help students strengthen their comprehension skills! After students read a story or selection of informational text, have each child draw on a sheet of paper a wheel with five spokes. Have her write an event or important detail from the selection on each spoke and then trade drawings with a classmate. Instruct her to read her partner's details, determine what they have in common, and write it in the hub as the main idea. When each child has gotten her drawing back, have students share their wheels and identify the main ideas together. **Main idea**

Index Card Storyboards

Write on the board in scrambled order several important events from a story students have read. Have each child copy the events on separate unlined index cards and add an illustration to each card. When he is finished, have him number the cards to show the order in which the story events occurred. Check the order of his cards. Then have the student create a storyboard by gluing his cards to a colorful sheet of construction paper!
Sequencing

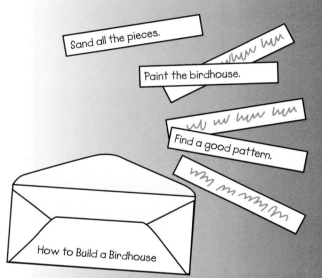

Sequencing Strips

All you need to do to generate the materials for this self-checking center is have your students read how-to articles! After each child reads her article, have her write six to eight steps on separate paper strips and lightly number the backs to show the correct order. When she's finished, have her place the strips in an envelope labeled with the article's title and then attach the envelope to the article with a paper clip. After checking students' work, place one envelope at a time in a center. To use the center, a child reads the article, arranges the strips in the order he thinks is correct, and then turns the strips over to check. **Sequencing**

Sequence in a Snap!

Put your classroom computer to work helping students understand more about what they read. Use a word-processing program to type the steps of an activity in scrambled order. Have each child using the computer use the Cut and Paste functions to put the events in the correct order. When he's finished, have him print a copy of his document and close it without saving it (so that the original scrambled list will be saved for the next student to sequence). **Sequencing**

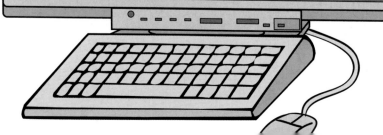

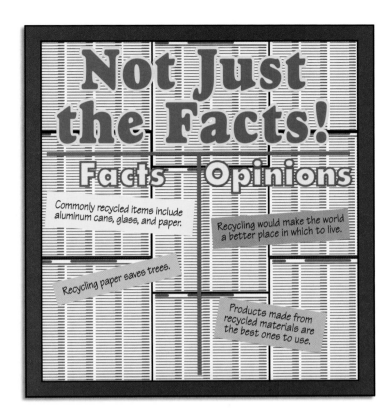

Not Just the Facts!

Cover a bulletin board or wall space with sheets of newspaper. Label one side of the board "Facts" and the other side "Opinions." Then find one statement of fact and one statement of opinion in a newspaper article. Write each statement on a different sentence strip. Share the sentences with your students and have them explain the difference between a fact and an opinion. Place the sentence strips on the appropriate sides of the bulletin board.

Next, give each pair of students a marker, a section from a newspaper, and two sentence strips. Direct each pair to search its newspaper section for statements of fact or opinion to write on separate sentence strips. After each pair shares its examples, post them on the appropriate side of the bulletin board.
Fact and opinion

Cereal Box Battle

How much truth is there on a product's packaging? Have students find out by bringing in empty cereal boxes or other product containers. Give a box to each pair of students. Have the partners look at their box to find examples of facts and opinions and then copy the examples on a sheet of paper in separate columns. As students share their findings with the class, they may become smarter shoppers!
Fact and opinion

Says Who?

Transform students into cartoonists with this simple activity. Instruct each child to draw a large rectangle on unlined paper. In the left half of the rectangle, have him draw a large book and label it "Encyclopedia." Opposite the book, have him draw a person or an animal. Then have him add speech bubbles to show the drawings talking to each other, with the encyclopedia sharing a fact and the character responding with a related opinion. If the student wishes, allow him to create an entire strip of boxes with related conversations! **Fact and opinion**

Take the Challenge!

Follow up the reading of a story or selection of informational text by dividing students into groups of three or four. Assign each group a specific part of the selection to reread. Next, have the team write three facts and one opinion on separate index cards and then label the backs of the corresponding cards with the appropriate category. Check the cards for accuracy; then have one group read its statements aloud to the other groups. Challenge each group to tell which statement is the opinion and why. After each group has given an answer, award the groups that answer correctly a point. Offer each winning group a chance to earn an additional five points if its members can change that opinion to a fact using information from the text! **Fact and opinion**

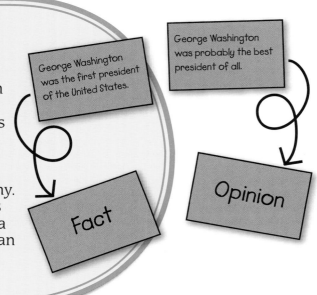

What'll It Be?

This game has students practicing fact and opinion as they review different topics. Label ten to 15 cards "Fact" or "Opinion," varying the number of each type, and stack them facedown in a pile. Next, divide students into two teams. Have a student from each team take turns drawing a card and giving a fact or an opinion about the topic, depending on the card drawn. Continue in this manner, shuffling the cards as needed, until the topic has been reviewed. If desired, change the topic after each round, or stick with one topic and see how long students can provide corresponding facts and opinions! **Fact and opinion**

Staged Scenario

In advance, arrange for a coworker to pound on your classroom door at an appointed time and then leave. Go to the door and act puzzled when no one is there. Ask students to write a report to inform the principal about this interruption. After everyone is finished writing, collect the reports and read them aloud. Students will notice obvious differences. Guide the listeners to point out which statements in the reports are facts and which are opinions. Then confess that you asked someone to knock loudly at the door in order to set the stage for the lesson! Fact and opinion

Why Don't You?

Think of all the different excuses for not completing an assignment you've ever heard from students. Then follow the steps below to offer your students a chance to give you some truly creative excuses!

1 Explain that a cause and an effect go together—whenever there is a cause or reason, there is a result or an effect.

2 Write lists of sample effects and appropriate connecting words like the ones shown on the board.

3 Discuss how some connecting words signal a cause, and others signal an effect. Give examples, such as "Because I looked for my dog after he ran away, I didn't study for my science test" or "My little sister spilled chocolate pudding on my homework last night, so I don't have it today."

4 Have student volunteers use the lists to create several cause-and-effect sentences.

5 Afterward, give each child an 8½" x 11" sheet of white paper. Challenge her to come up with a clever cause for one of the effects listed on the board.

6 Next, have her write a cause-and-effect sentence on her paper, draw an accompanying illustration, and share her resulting—and entertaining—excuse with the class. Afterward, if desired, give each student a copy of page 28 to complete as directed.

Cause and effect

Effects
- don't have my homework
- was talking
- forgot to study for a science test
- didn't finish my book report
- don't have a pencil
- got sent to the principal's office
- was running in the hallway
- can't remember my multiplication tables
- missed the bus
- am not sitting in my own seat

Connecting Words

Causes: because, since, as, whenever, if

Effects: resulted in, as a result, consequently, for this reason, therefore, so, so that

---

Give Me a Reason!

Begin by writing on the board one of the sentences shown. Read the sentence aloud and explain that it represents an effect. Next, have each child write a sentence that includes an interesting cause for that effect. Continue in this manner until students have written a sentence for each of the effects. When everyone is finished, read aloud one effect at a time and invite students to share the creative causes they wrote for it. Then have students vote for the most interesting or creative cause for each effect! *Cause and effect*

1. The picnic was canceled.
2. All the lights went out.
3. Mom's car was out of gas.
4. Grandpa watched only half the TV show.
5. There was no money in the drawer.
6. The cat ran under the bed.
7. There was no ice cream in the dish.
8. Ants were everywhere in the kitchen.
9. Dad missed having dinner with the family last night.
10. My sister yelled, "Stop!"

My sister yelled, "Stop!" because a dog was about to run in front of our car.

Who Gets the Last Word?

Divide students into two teams. Next, say a phrase related to a topic of study, such as food chains. For example, say, "Planting a bean seed." Challenge Team 1 to think of the stated phrase as a cause and to respond with a sentence that names an effect of that cause, such as "Planting a bean seed can cause it to grow." Have Team 2 respond by using Team 1's effect as a cause to state a related effect. For example, the team could say, "Because the bean seed grows, it produces food." Continue having the teams respond to each other's statements in this manner until one team cannot come up with an appropriate response. Repeat the activity as time allows, using either another topic-related phrase or a silly one! **Cause and effect**

What If...?

To prepare for this game, cut apart a copy of the sentence strips on page 29 for each team of four to six players. Fold the strips and place them in a separate brown lunch sack for each team. To play, one player on each team draws a slip and reads its question (a cause) aloud to his teammates. The player on the reader's left supplies the first answer (an effect). The next player on the left supplies a different answer. Play continues in this manner until every player has had a turn. Each player who is able to supply a new answer earns one point. To play another round, have a different player draw a new question! **Cause and effect**

The sky would match the grass.

No one would know when to stop at a traffic light.

What if everything in the world were green?

Spaghetti would look funny!

Artists would not have much fun.

One Thing Leads to Another

Provide each child with five large paper clips and one 3" x 3" sticky note. Have the student link her five paper clips together to form a chain. Next, instruct her to cut the sticky note into five strips and then wrap the sticky end of each strip around a different paper clip as shown. Have her write on her first strip an event that has recently happened in her life. Have her write on her second strip the effect caused by the first event. Then, on her third strip, have her write the effect caused by the second event, and so on until she has labeled all five strips. When she's finished, she'll have a literal chain of events that can help her better understand how events are connected to one another! **Cause and effect**

I forgot to study for my math test.

I didn't make a good grade on the test.

My parents were not happy.

I was grounded for a week.

I didn't get to go to Haley's birthday party.

Connections Chain

To make text-to-text, text-to-self, and text-to-world connections easier for students to understand, cut a supply of paper strips in the colors shown. As a child reads independently (or listens as you read aloud) and makes one of those connections, invite him to label a link with a sentence describing his connection and add it to a classroom chain. Challenge students to make the chain grow until it reaches a certain length. Whether they make one long chain containing all of the different connections or create one for each color, seeing the chain(s) grow will motivate students to stay alert! **Making connections**

Connection Colors
text to text = red
text to self = blue
text to world = green

Visual Prompters

Display cutouts that remind students to make connections while reading. Create poster board cutouts like those shown and post them in a prominent place in the room. As students read a short story or novel, have them briefly describe on sticky notes the connections made and then attach the notes to the appropriate cutouts. Set aside time to discuss the connections. Not only will students learn from their classmates' observations, but the visual prompters can be used again and again! **Making connections**

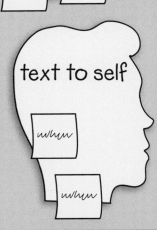

text to world

text to self

text to text

Stellar Connections

In advance, cut out interesting newspaper headlines that are small enough to fit inside the star on the shooting star pattern on page 30. Also, make a copy of the star pattern on yellow paper for each child. Next, have each student cut out the copy, choose a newspaper headline, and glue the headline inside the star on her cutout. Then have her make a connection to her headline—text to self, text to text, or text to world—and record it in the appropriate section. When everyone is finished, have students trade cutouts, read the headline on the new cutout they receive, and record a connection. Continue in this manner until all three sections are filled in. Invite students to share the connections with the class. Then showcase the cutouts in a display titled "Stellar Connections." **Making connections**

Text to Self
This reminds me of a time when I asked my brother to help me, and he didn't. I had to wash our dog alone. My mom was proud of me for getting it done.

Text to Text
In a story I just read, the main character did not get the help she needed from her friends. But in the end, she forgave them and shared her food with them.

Text to World
I don't think this is something people should think. Countries have to help one another. We all have to get along.

Don't Rely on Others

Facts From the Textbook
1. Photosynthesis is the way plants make their own food.
2. Photosynthesis occurs in a plant's leaves.
3. Leaves are green because they have chlorophyll.

Facts From Both Sources
1. Photosynthesis is how plants make their own food.
2. Leaves are green because they have chlorophyll.

Facts From the Encyclopedia
1. Photosynthesis is the way plants make food.
2. Green plants use the energy from light.
3. All our food comes from plants and photosynthesis.
4. Chlorophyll makes leaves green.

Text "Mobile-ity"

For practice with text-to-text connections, pair students and have each partner read a passage on the same topic but from a different source. For example, instruct one child to read a textbook passage and the other an encyclopedia entry. Next, direct each partner to trim and illustrate an index card so that it resembles a book and then list on it important facts from his passage. Have the pair compare the lists, checking off and copying the common facts onto a third trimmed shape and circling facts unique to each source. Finally, have the duo connect the cutouts with string or yarn and share the resulting mobile with the class. Display the mobiles around the classroom. **Making connections**

Use the Clues

Help your students develop a better understanding of making inferences with the following picture-perfect activity. Cut several pictures from magazines and share them with your class. As you share each picture, ask a question about it, such as "Where is this person going?" Have each student answer the question and list on a sheet of paper the clues in the picture that helped him infer the answer. After showing all the pictures, have each child share his responses. Explain to students that their responses were similar because of what they inferred from the picture clues and the similarity of their own experiences. Tell students that just as in the pictures, the stories we read contain information that may not always be stated directly. Explain that readers often have to use sentence clues and personal experiences to fully understand what is read. Follow up the activity by having each student complete a copy of page 31 as directed.
Making inferences

What's the Story?

Use wordless picture books to help students strengthen their inferencing skills. As you share each page of the book, ask students to study the illustrations and jot down notes about what they think is going on. Then have each child use his notes to write and illustrate his interpretation of the story. Post students' work along with the book that was shared on a display titled "Now the Story Has Words."
Making inferences

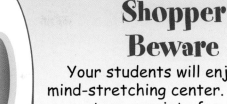

Shopper Beware

Your students will enjoy this mind-stretching center. Save your store receipts for several weeks. Ask students to also save and bring in receipts from the grocery store, drugstore, hardware store, etc. (Be sure that none of the receipts contain credit card numbers.) When you have a good number of receipts—and a wide variety—bundle them in groups of five or six. Make sure that each receipt within a bundle is from a different store. Instruct students at the center to examine a bundle of receipts carefully, noting the types of stores and the items purchased, and to use their notes to help them draw conclusions about what kind of shopper might purchase the items. Post a list of questions like the ones shown at the center. Then direct each child using the center to answer the questions about each receipt in the bundle.
Drawing conclusions

Shopper Questions
1. Do you think this person lives alone or with a family?
2. What do you think this person likes?
3. What do you think this person's job or hobby might be?
4. When does this person do his or her shopping?
5. What other conclusions can you draw based on the bundle of receipts?

Concluding Comics

Search through newspapers and cut out several comic strips with at least three sequence boxes. White-out the caption in each box. Add a new caption that gives a humorous clue about what is happening in the picture of each box, leaving the last box's caption blank. Do this for each comic strip. Next, glue each comic strip to a different sheet of construction paper and laminate it. Place these sheets at a center along with a wipe-off marker. Instruct the student to use the clues in the captions of each comic strip to write a concluding caption for the last box.

Extend this activity by having each child choose one of the comic strip characters and create his own concluding comic. **Drawing conclusions**

You're Invited!

Before students read their next book, have them design invitations to predict what the book will be about. Write on the board guidelines like the ones shown that direct each child through the process. Then have each child skim her book for clues that can help her complete the invitation. After she reads the book, have her share her invitation with the class and point out whether her predictions were accurate. **Making predictions**

You're Invited!
Time: Clues about the setting
Who: Clues about what the main character is like
What to bring: Clues about the tone
Date: Clues about how long it will take to read the book
Where: Clues about the plot
RSVP: An overall opinion of the book

What Will Happen?

Making predictions is a great critical-thinking exercise to incorporate with literature. Give a copy of page 32 to each student; then select a picture book of your choice. Show students the cover illustration and read the title. Have students make predictions about the story's plot by completing page 32 as directed. Invite student volunteers to share their predictions with the rest of the class; then read the picture book aloud so students can learn how accurately they predicted the plot. If desired, repeat the activity when beginning a new chapter of a novel. **Making predictions**

Just the Gist!

To summarize...

- Read the selection.
- Identify the main idea.
- List details (who, what, when, where, why).
- Decide which details are the most important.
- Write one sentence that combines the most important details.

Boil-It-Down Bookmark

Help students strengthen their summarizing skills by providing them with a handy bookmark that reminds them what to do. Make a copy of the bookmark on page 33 for each child. Discuss the bulleted tips on the bookmark with the class. After each child colors and cuts out his bookmark, laminate it for durability. Whenever he is asked to summarize something he has read, have him use the bookmark's tips to help him focus on writing one sentence that combines the most important details. **Summarizing**

Sticking to Business

In advance, gather nonfiction picture books with tables of contents related to a topic of study. Also gather a supply of small sticky notes. Pair students and give each twosome a picture book. Direct the partners to scan the book's table of contents and choose a section to summarize. Next, give each duo about ten sticky notes. Instruct the partners to read their section, write important details in their own words on the sticky notes, and leave the notes in order on the book's pages. Have the partners check each note to be sure it's accurate and written in their own words. As each duo shares its notes with the class, invite the rest of the students to suggest ways to combine the most important details into one sentence. **Summarizing**

Keep It Brief!

Have each pair of students fold a sheet of construction paper in half and cut handles so that it resembles a briefcase. Instruct the twosome to label the front with the topic of a passage of informational text and the pages to be read. As the students read the passage, have them decide on each paragraph's main idea and record it on a sticky note. Next, have the partners open up their briefcase and write "Important" on the left side and "Less Important or Not Related" on the right. Direct the duo to read each sticky note and decide under which heading it belongs. Once all of the notes are affixed, have the twosome fold its briefcase so that only the important details can be seen. Instruct the partners to arrange the visible notes in an order that matches the passage's sequence. Then have them write one sentence on the front of the briefcase that combines the most important details. **Summarizing**

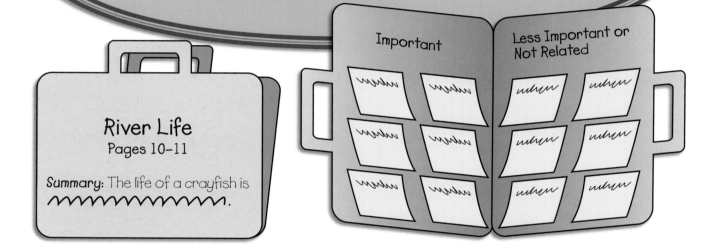

River Life
Pages 10–11

Summary: The life of a crayfish is

Important

Less Important or Not Related

Recap It!

For a center that gives students more practice summarizing and also creates a great reference for kid-recommended books, provide a three-ring binder and select a student volunteer to design a cover for it. Divide the notebook into sections by genre, such as mystery, adventure, realistic fiction, humor, fantasy, and science fiction. Also make a class supply of page 34. Then place the decorated binder and the copies in a center near your classroom library. Each time a student reads a book, have him complete a form and place it in the appropriate binder section. Should he need help deciding what book to read next, have him consult the binder! **Summarizing**

Book Review
I recently read a book titled
_____
This book had approximately _____ pages, and it took me about _____ days to read it. The main character is a _____ named _____
The first thing that happens in this book is _____

The next thing that happens is _____

This is followed by _____

You'll have to read the book to find out what happens next. The ending **will/will not** be a surprise. There **is/is not** another book that continues this story.
(circle one)   (circle one)
This book would be enjoyed by someone who _____

One sentence that best sums up the book is _____

I would/would not recommend this book to my classmates. I got this book from
(circle one)
the classroom library/the school library/home.
(circle one)

reporter _____

date _____

It Figures!

Share several forms of figurative language, such as those shown, with your students, giving an example of each form. Then give each student a 4" x 11" sheet of white paper and challenge her to find figurative expressions in her reading. Have the student write each expression in the form of an illustrated newspaper headline. Finally, have her share her headlines, explain the meaning of each one, and tell which type of figurative language it represents. Post the headlines on a wall or bulletin board titled "Hilarious Headlines." **Figurative language**

➤ **Idiom**—an expression that means something other than the usual meaning of the words
Example: Since it's raining cats and dogs, you'd better take your umbrella!

➤ **Simile**—compares two unlike things using *like* or *as*
Example: My mouth is as dry as a desert.

➤ **Metaphor**—compares two unlike things directly
Example: Her heart is an ice cube.

➤ **Hyperbole**—an exaggerated comparison
Example: Annie was so hot she melted.

You Don't Say?

Share with students the different devices that writers use to make their sentences sound more pleasing (see the examples). Then place a five-foot sheet of bulletin board paper, colorful markers, and various books on a large table. Challenge each student to skim the books to find a sentence that uses one of the devices you shared, write it on the bulletin board paper, and draw a colorful illustration to accompany his sentence. Display the completed banner; then invite each child, in turn, to share the sentence he recorded with the class. **Figurative language**

➤ **Alliteration**—the repetition of beginning consonant sounds
Example: The sidewinder snake slithers silently on the sand.

➤ **Assonance**—the repetition of vowel sounds in words
Example: Explain how rain makes the pavement dangerous.

➤ **Consonance**—the repetition of consonant sounds anywhere in words
Example: Remember to put the baby in the crib.

➤ **Onomatopoeia**—words whose meanings sound like their pronunciations
Example: A honeybee buzzes.

Amazing Animals

The sidewinder snake slithers silently on the sand.

A honeybee buzzes.

Ants are organized animals.

A three-toed sloth eats tree leaves.

Brushing Up

Make colorful copies of the paintbrush patterns on page 35 and store them near your class library, along with containers labeled with the different types of figurative language on which you wish students to focus while reading. Challenge each child to find examples of idioms, similes, metaphors, personification, and hyperbole as she reads. Each time she finds an example, have her fill in a shape, cut it out, and place it in the appropriate container. **Figurative language**

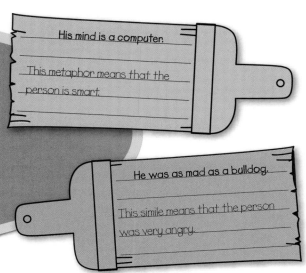

His mind is a computer.

This metaphor means that the person is smart.

He was as mad as a bulldog.

This simile means that the person was very angry.

Hats Off to Hyperbole!

Review with students that writers often use exaggeration to make their work more interesting. Have each child read a tall tale and look for examples of exaggeration in the selection. Then have him trim a sheet of light-colored construction paper in the shape of a hat that relates in some way to the main character. Instruct him to list one or more examples from his list on the front of the cutout along with what he thinks might have actually happened. After students share their findings with the class, post the hats on a display titled "Hats Off to Hyperbole!" Repeat the activity with other types of figurative forms. **Figurative language**

He grew until his head and shoulders busted through the roof that was over the porch.

John Henry may have been taller than most boys his age.

Fishing for Meaning

Use this team game to review different types of figurative language students may encounter as they read. Make a copy of the figurative language cards and answer key on page 36. Cut the cards apart and stack them facedown in a pile. Then have Player 1 from Team 1 draw a card, read it aloud, and tell which type of figurative language it represents: simile, metaphor, idiom, alliteration, onomatopoeia, personification, or hyperbole. If she is correct, she scores one point for her team. If she also explains its meaning, she scores a bonus point. If she is incorrect, Player 1 on Team 2 tries to answer. Continue in this manner, reshuffling the cards as needed, until everyone has had a turn. Then declare the team with more points the winner. **Figurative language**

Lyrical Readers

Use choral readings to increase fluency. Give each child a copy of the lyrics to the first verse of "The Star-Spangled Banner" on page 37. Have him listen as you read the lyrics aloud. Then have students read the words along with you. Once students have read the selection aloud several more times and increased their awareness of the song's rhythm and cadence, invite them to bring in lyrics of other appropriate songs to practice in the same way! **Fluency**

The Star-Spangled Banner
(first verse)

Oh! Say, can you see, by the dawn's early light,
What so proudly we hailed at the twilight's last gleaming?
Whose broad stripes and bright stars, through the perilous fight,
O'er the ramparts we watched, were so gallantly streaming?
And the rockets' red glare, the bombs bursting in air,
Gave proof through the night that our flag was still there.
Oh! Say, does that star-spangled banner yet wave
O'er the land of the free and the home of the brave?

BRAVO!

Phenomenal Performances

Periodically, make each child a copy of the same poem, selection of classical literature, or high-interest science or social studies passage. Distribute the copies on Monday and help students mark and identify any unknown words. On Tuesday, discuss how the passage's punctuation affects word flow and expression. On Wednesday, allow students to read the selection aloud to a partner. On Thursday, practice as a group. Then, on Friday, perform the choral reading for another class! **Fluency**

There and Back Again

Give each child a copy of a short poem or story. Have students read the selection together several times. Then, after the last word of the final reading has been said, catch the readers by surprise by challenging each child to read the selection to a partner backward to the beginning! Even though there will be lots of laughs, students will discover that they still have to look ahead in their reading in order to phrase the words correctly and read with expression. **Fluency**

If the Shoe Fits

Match each main-idea sentence to one of the five paragraphs below. Write the letter of each matching main-idea sentence in the appropriate horseshoe.

Main-Idea Sentences

A. Lightning Bolt is headstrong and quick to anger.

B. Butterscotch is very loving and like a mother to all the other horses.

C. Suzie is a little lazy and has a sweet tooth.

D. Goober likes to eat and is a little overweight.

E. Midnight is friendly but shy, especially around new people.

1. She likes to sleep late, so she often doesn't come out of her stall until 9:00 AM. She doesn't like to exercise. Oh, and watch out! She'll raid the sugar bag.

2. He likes to stay by himself in the pasture. He's not much for playing with the other horses. If he doesn't know you, it might take a day or two before he'll let you ride him. Be patient, though, and he'll become your friend.

3. He's very stubborn and will only respond if he gets a sugar cube. So keep a good supply on hand. Watch out for his temper! If he doesn't get what he wants, he may whack you with his head or charge at you.

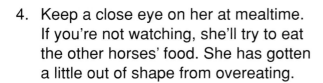

4. Keep a close eye on her at mealtime. If you're not watching, she'll try to eat the other horses' food. She has gotten a little out of shape from overeating.

5. She watches out for all the other horses, especially the little ones. If another horse is sick, she will stick by his side until he feels better. You can often see her helping new mothers take care of their offspring.

©The Mailbox® • Superbook® • TEC61052 • Key p. 309

26 **Note to the teacher:** Use with "Get the Idea?" on page 10.

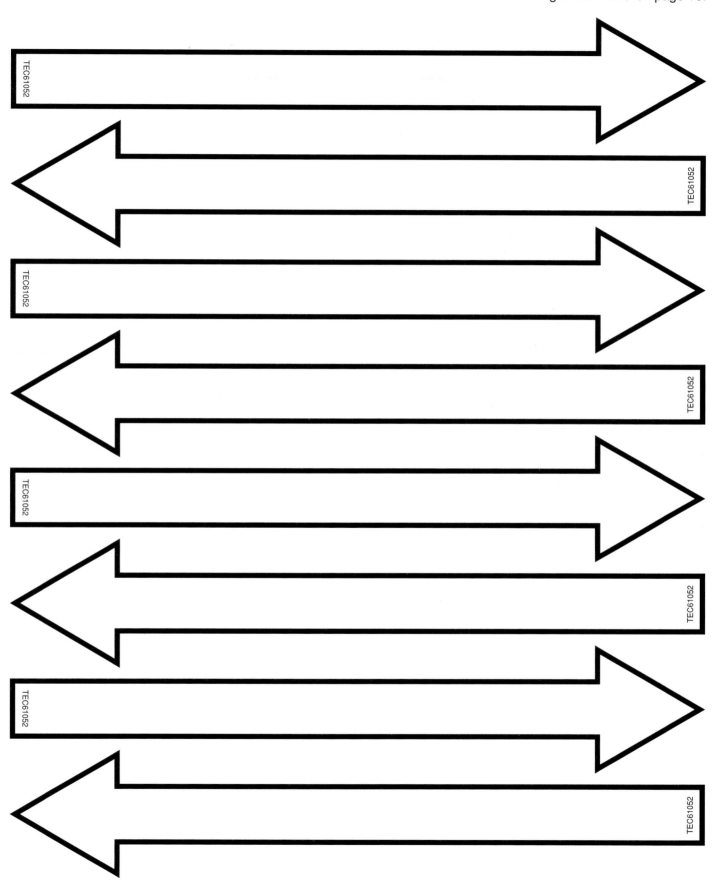

Penelope's Perilous Party!

Read each cause and effect statement. Match each effect to its cause by writing the appropriate letter in the blank next to that number. Then, on the back of this sheet, use the connecting words at the bottom of this page to write sentences with five of your cause-and-effect matches. (You may need to rearrange, change, or add words to create your sentences.)

Example: Because her brother stuck a pin in the balloon, it popped.

Causes

1. Four invitations to Penelope's friends got lost in the mail.

2. When Penelope's mom went shopping, there were hardly any decorations left at The Party Palace.

3. Penelope's Doberman pinscher got loose and jumped on the table that held the cake.

4. Prudence, Penelope's best friend, had a queasy stomach.

5. Peter put a fake snake in a gift box and gave it to Penelope.

6. Paul and Perry insisted that they saw a UFO flying over the backyard.

7. A freak thunderstorm caused the electricity to go out.

8. Penelope's baby brother, Preston, removed the tags from two identically wrapped gifts.

9. The pizza delivery person had a flat tire and was late.

10. Penelope tripped over her new pair of in-line skates.

Effects

A. Everyone was starving by the time the pepperoni pizza arrived.

B. Penelope's guests couldn't listen to the music recordings they had brought.

C. None of the decorations matched.

D. Prudence had to leave the party early.

E. Penelope crashed to the floor and bruised her knee.

F. Penelope screamed and knocked the punch bowl onto the floor.

G. Penelope didn't know which gift was from whom.

H. Paulette, Pamela, Parker, and Patrick didn't attend the party.

I. Chocolate cake flew from one corner of the room to the other!

J. Everyone left in the middle of Penelope's game and ran outside to look at the sky.

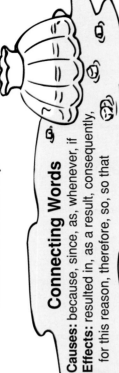

Connecting Words

Causes: because, since, as, whenever, if

Effects: resulted in, as a result, consequently, for this reason, therefore, so, so that

Note to the teacher: Use with "Why Don't You?" on page 15.

What if everything in the world were green?

What if all the teachers in your school were absent on the same day?

What if you suddenly knew everything about math that there is to know?

What if a giant toad hopped up to you and began talking?

What if the school cafeteria served the same food every day all year long?

What if every day were Saturday?

What if there were no clocks in the world?

What if there were no numbers, only letters?

What if people had to walk everywhere they went?

What if everybody looked identical?

Shooting Star Pattern
Use with "Stellar Connections" on page 18.

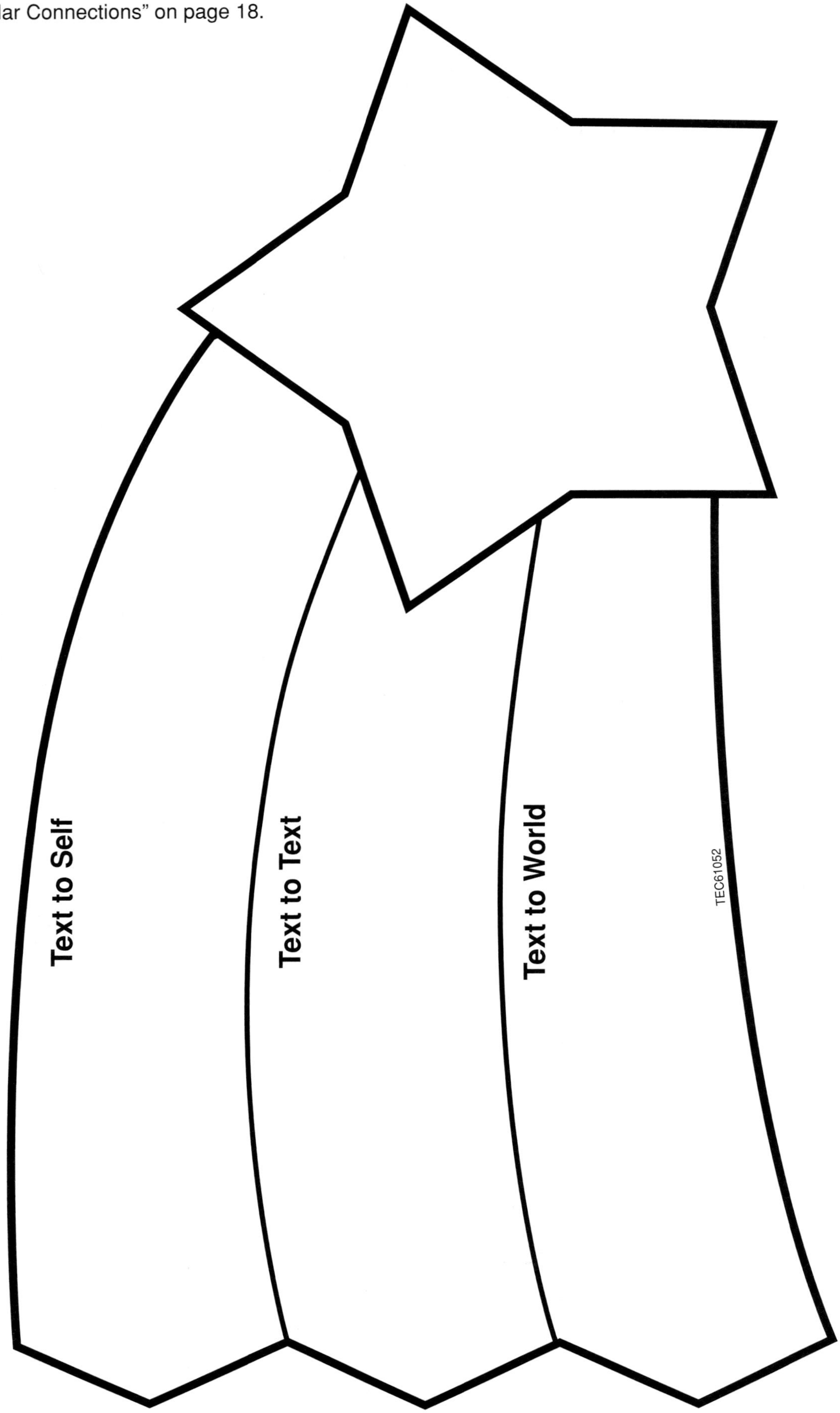

Text to Self

Text to Text

Text to World

TEC61052

Get the Hint?

Read each of the sentences below. Use the clues that describe each situation to help you answer the question that follows it. Underline the clues; then write your answer on the line provided on each file folder.

1. The students in Ms. Adams's class are helping her prepare for the upcoming month's holidays. They've put up red heart cutouts, pictures of Abraham Lincoln and George Washington, and posters of famous African Americans.
Question: For which month are the students decorating?

2. Jason was very excited about his new adventure. He quickly put on his goggles and fins; then he jumped into the crystal-clear water.
Question: In what kind of adventure is Jason participating?

3. With her heart thumping, Leslie stepped up to the podium and arranged the notecards in her hands. The people quietly waited for her to begin.
Question: What is Leslie preparing to do?

4. The only sounds in the quiet room are the opening and closing of books, the shuffling of papers, and at times the cough of an occupant. The rows of shelves are filled with many books, magazines, and reference materials.
Question: What type of room is this?

5. John knew he'd have to hide his mother's present. But where would he hide it? His mother would be able to identify the floral fragrance. He couldn't put it in a drawer—it would get crushed. Besides, he needed to keep it in water so it wouldn't wilt.
Question: What present does John have for his mother?

6. "I can't believe your parents stuck you with that job again!" Chris said to his friend. "Think of all of the things you have to do— feeding, changing diapers, and reading a bedtime story. Yuck!"
Question: What job does Chris's friend have to do?

7. The man in the lab coat adjusted the lens of the microscope so he could clearly see the specimens wriggling on the slide. He told his assistant to hold all his calls so he could finish his work.
Question: What kind of work does this man do?

8. As the young girl rested her head on the cushioned seat, she was offered a drink and a snack. Suddenly there was an abrupt jerking movement, and she noticed a flashing sign that warned her to fasten her seat belt.
Question: Where is the young girl?

Note to the teacher: Use with "Use the Clues" on page 19.

31

Make Your Prediction

Write your prediction in the crystal ball. Underneath "Because…," write up to four reasons for your prediction.

Prediction:

Because…

1. _____

_____

2. _____

_____

3. _____

_____

4. _____

_____

Just the Gist!

To summarize...

- Read the selection.

- Identify the main idea.

- List details (who, what, when, where, why).

- Decide which details are the most important.

- Write one sentence that combines the most important details.

Book Review

I recently read a book titled

_____.

This book had approximately _____ pages, and it took me about _____ days to read it. The main character is a _____ named _____.

The first thing that happens in this book is _____

_____

_____

The next thing that happens is _____

_____

This is followed by _____

_____

You'll have to read the book to find out what happens next. The ending **will/will not** be a surprise. There **is/is not** another book that continues this story.
(circle one)
(circle one)

This book would be enjoyed by someone who _____

_____

One sentence that best sums up the book is _____

_____

I **would/would not** recommend this book to my classmates. I got this book from
(circle one)
the classroom library/the school library/home.
(circle one)

_____
reporter

_____
date

Note to the teacher: Use with "Recap It!" on page 22.

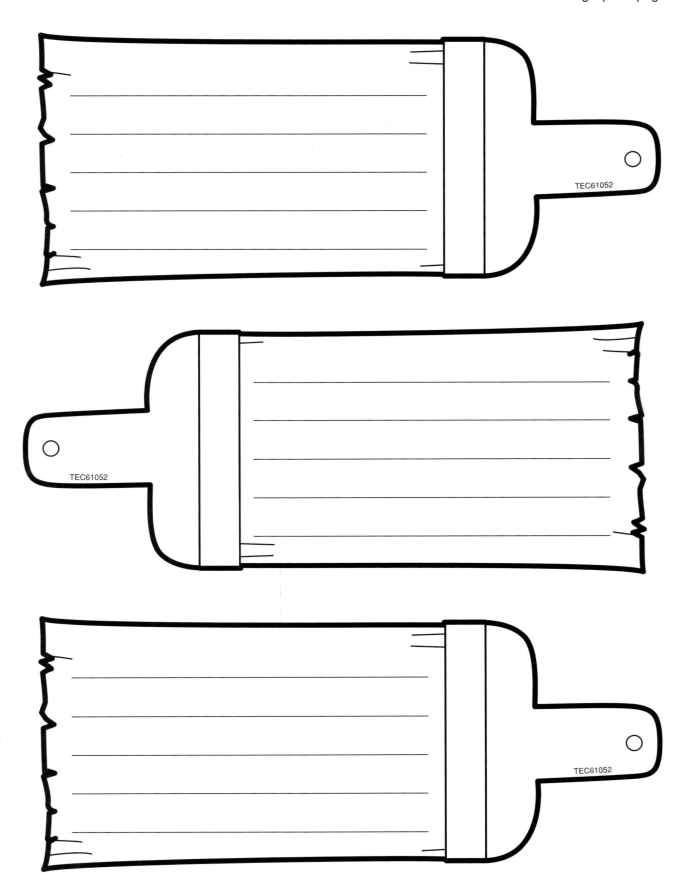

TEC61052

TEC61052

TEC61052

Figurative Language Cards and Answer Key

Use with "Fishing for Meaning" on page 24.

1. The sun peeked over the horizon. TEC61052	2. Today was the lively Lucky Lure fishing tournament. TEC61052	3. The blue water was a shiny mirror. TEC61052	4. As quick as a wink, Andy launched the boat. TEC61052
5. The boat took off like a rocket. TEC61052	6. When the boys saw a boat in their fishing spot, their hearts dropped like rocks. TEC61052	7. They knew they were in a pickle. TEC61052	8. But Andy had a trick up his sleeve. TEC61052
9. Lily pads floated like saucers at the new fishing spot. TEC61052	10. Birds chirped all around them. TEC61052	11. Kerplunk! The lure splashed into the water. TEC61052	12. Andy's line began to zing. TEC61052
13. Andy yelled, "Lend me a hand with the net!" TEC61052	14. The frisky fish fought hard. TEC61052	15. It fought him tooth and nail. TEC61052	16. Andy started sweating bullets. TEC61052
17. Suddenly, he received a stroke of luck and grabbed the fish in the net. TEC61052	18. It was the size of a house! TEC61052	19. He zoomed back to the dock to weigh the fish and claim his prize. TEC61052	20. What a wonderful way to spend a day! TEC61052

Answer Key

1. personification
2. alliteration
3. metaphor
4. simile
5. simile
6. simile
7. idiom
8. idiom
9. simile
10. onomatopoeia
11. onomatopoeia
12. onomatopoeia
13. idiom
14. alliteration
15. idiom
16. idiom
17. idiom
18. hyperbole
19. onomatopoeia
20. alliteration

TEC61052

The Star-Spangled Banner

(first verse)

Oh! Say, can you see, by the dawn's early light,

What so proudly we hailed at the twilight's last gleaming?

Whose broad stripes and bright stars, through the perilous fight,

O'er the ramparts we watched, were so gallantly streaming?

And the rockets' red glare, the bombs bursting in air,

Gave proof through the night that our flag was still there.

Oh! Say, does that star-spangled banner yet wave

O'er the land of the free and the home of the brave?

TEC61052

STORY ELEMENTS

Picture Perfect

Create a portrait gallery of the characters from the novel you are currently reading. Divide your students into small groups—one group for each main character in the novel. Make one copy of page 41 for each group. Instruct each group to complete the page for its assigned character. Tell each group to describe its character's personality traits and physical traits. Then have each group list the other characters who are involved in its character's life, briefly describe its character's involvement in the plot, and illustrate its character in the center square of its reproducible. Direct each group to present its work to the rest of the class; then create a portrait gallery by posting each page on a wall or bulletin board in the classroom. **Character analysis**

Two in One

Pair students and assign each partner the main character from one of two books. Give each student a supply of index cards and have him write a description of his character or an event involving his character on each card. Direct him to underline a key phrase in each description. Next, he shares his ideas with his partner. Then the duo works together to make a T chart showing how the two characters are alike and how they are different, aligning matching cards in the "Alike" column and placing the other cards in the "Different" column as shown. **Comparing and contrasting characters**

Alike			Different	
Ben He moved from Missouri to Oregon.	˜˜˜˜ ˜˜˜˜˜˜	˜˜˜ ˜˜˜ ˜˜˜	Ben He has asthma and does not help much.	
Rachel She moved west from Illinois to California.	˜˜˜˜˜˜˜˜˜˜	˜˜˜ ˜˜˜˜˜	˜˜˜ ˜˜˜˜	
Ben His mom made him keep a journal.	˜˜˜			
	˜˜˜ ˜˜˜˜ ˜˜ ˜˜˜˜			

Bunches of Clues

Make a class supply of page 42 on yellow paper. Give a copy to each student and have her cut out the banana bunch shape. Next, have her write a word on each banana describing a character from a recently read book. The word should give clues to the character's actions, motives, or appearance. Next, have the student write a quote from the book that supports the description. When the bunch is completed, post it and assign it a number. Then have each student visit the display and read the quotes to determine the character described. She records each answer next to its matching number on a sheet of notebook paper. **Character analysis**

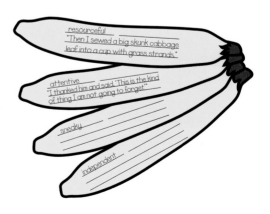

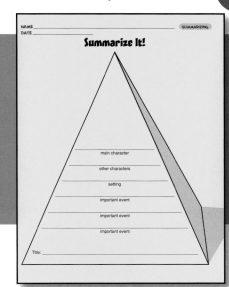

Top to Bottom

Make and distribute a class supply of page 43. Have each student refer to a recent reading to complete the organizer. If desired, have the student use the completed organizer to write a summary of the book or to assist his contributions to a literature circle discussion. **Summarizing**

Funny Findings

Gather enough comic strips so that each student pair has one. Review plot, setting, and character with students and then have each duo choose a comic strip. After they read it, have the pair glue it to a piece of paper and identify the main character, the setting, and the plot. Provide time for student pairs to share their comic strip and their story elements aloud. **Story elements**

Side by Side

To make this simple organizer, fold a piece of 12" x 18" construction paper as shown. Cut five slits on each folded flap as indicated by the dotted line and then label each section as shown. Underneath each matching flap, draw a picture and list the characteristics of the story element named. **Comparing and contrasting two books**

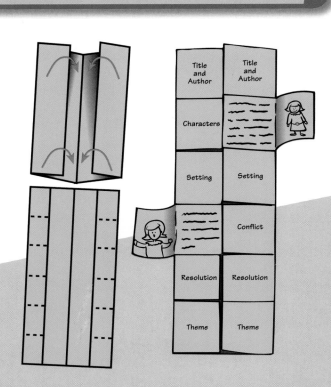

Map It Out

Use a bulletin board display to help students keep track of story events. Cover a bulletin board with paper; then use yellow construction paper to make three cards labeled "Beginning," "Climax," and "Conclusion" as shown. Add illustrations of characters or settings to the board. Post six or more sheets of white construction paper (or one sheet for each major event) and then connect the sheets with yarn or string. For each major event, have a student write a brief summary on the appropriate blank sheet of construction paper. Refer to the story map often while reading the novel to help your students keep track of the time and place. **Story map**

Plots Aplenty

Often a novel will have more than one plot. *Mrs. Frisby and the Rats of NIMH* by Robert C. O'Brien is a perfect example of a novel that contains parallel plots. One plot deals with Mrs. Frisby (a mouse) and her family. The second plot deals with a colony of intelligent rats that have escaped from the National Institute of Mental Health. Each plot has a separate story line, but eventually the two plots become intertwined. Parallel plots make for an interesting read; however, the reader can sometimes confuse one plot with another plot. To help avoid this problem, have your students keep a timeline of events for each plot. Instruct each student to briefly describe the major event for each plot as it occurs in the novel. This exercise will help students clearly visualize the order of events for each plot. **Parallel plots**

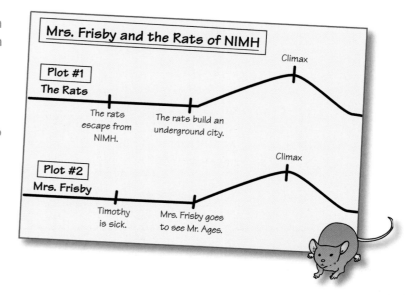

Character Frame

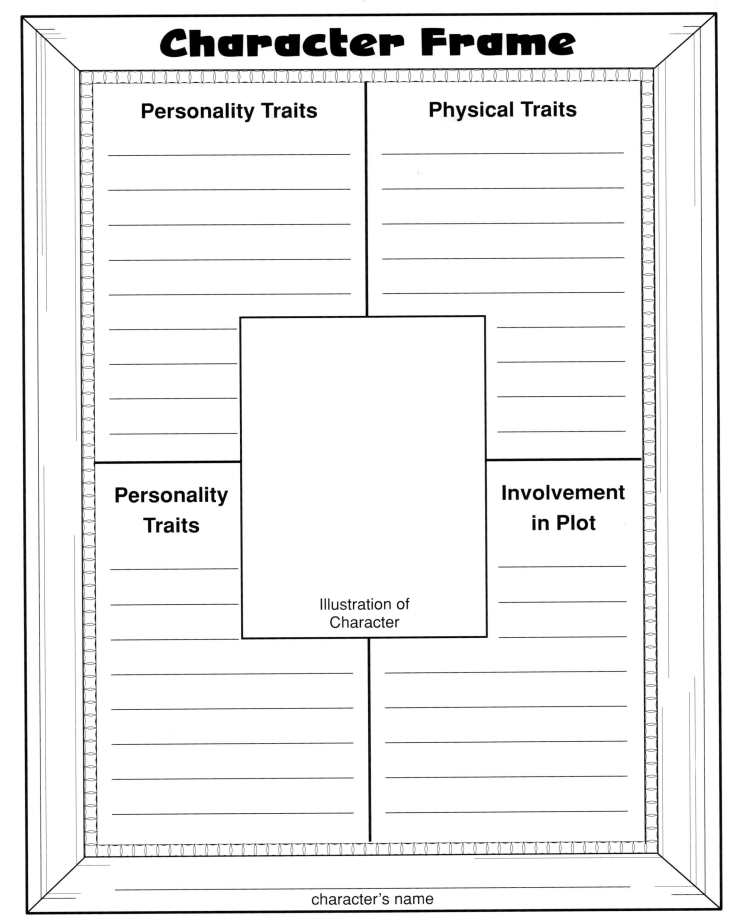

Personality Traits

Physical Traits

Personality Traits

Illustration of Character

Involvement in Plot

character's name

Note to the teacher: Use with "Picture Perfect" on page 38.

Banana Bunch Pattern

Use with "Bunches of Clues" on page 38.

TEC61052

Summarize It!

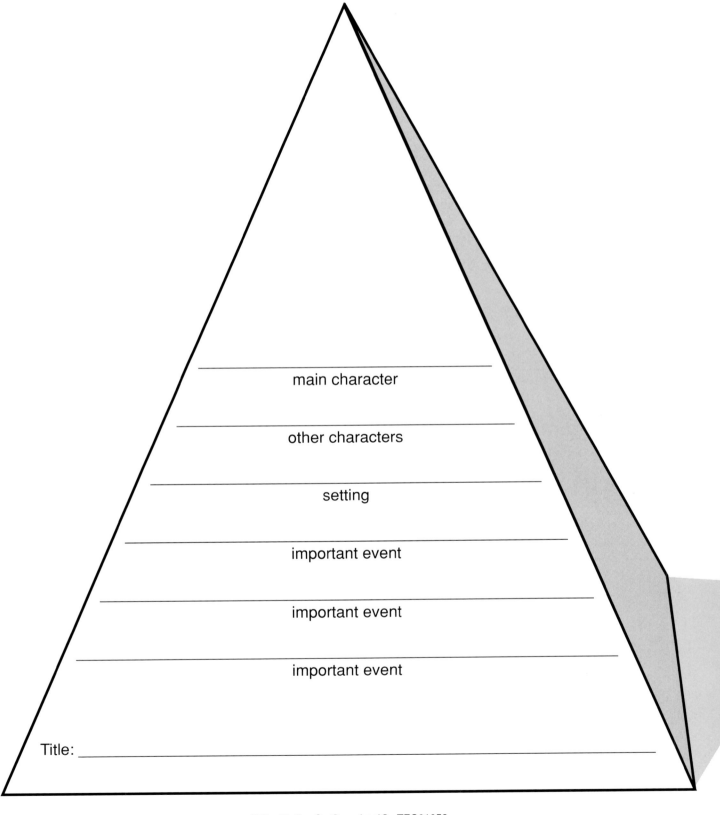

main character

other characters

setting

important event

important event

important event

Title: _____

Note to the teacher: Use with "Top to Bottom" on page 39.

Book Reports & Beyond

Picture Cubes

For an easy art-project book report, have each student construct a picture cube displaying various aspects of his book. Have each student bring in a cubic tissue box. The student covers each side of his cube with a different-colored piece of construction paper. Then he uses five sides of his box to illustrate important characters, the setting, the plot, major events, and the novel's conclusion. On the sixth side, he writes the title and author of his book. Each student presents his cube to the class, describing each side in detail to his classmates. Then display the cubes for others to enjoy.

What's in That Purse or Wallet?

Items in a person's purse or wallet can reveal a lot about that person's personality. Brainstorm with your students a list of items that may be found, such as a driver's license or an ID card, photos of friends and family, cash, shopping or to-do lists, membership cards, car keys, pens, medicine, food, and notes or letters. Instruct each student to collect at least five items that would be found in the purse or wallet of the main character of his novel. Tell the student to put his items in a real purse or wallet or to make one out of construction paper or cloth. Have each student present his character's wallet or purse to the class and explain the significance of each item.

Story Hats

Have students follow the directions below to create story-hat book reports.

Directions:
1. Fold a 14" x 23" sheet of newsprint in half as shown.
2. Place the fold at the top; then fold down the top corners so that they meet in the center as shown.
3. At the lower edge, fold up the top flap twice as shown.
4. Flip the hat and repeat Step 3.
5. Section off the hat's brim into frames for illustrating the sequence of events of your book's plot.
6. Use the two sides at the top of your hat for writing the title and author of the book and a summary of your favorite part.

In the Can!

These book reports are displayed in large recycled cans. To make a project, a student first covers the outside and inside of a large can with light-colored paper. He also cuts a rectangular piece of tagboard so that it fits inside the can and uses it to divide the space in half. Then he thinks of two events from the selected book and illustrates each on the outside of the can. Next, he uses construction paper scraps and other craft materials to create a 3-D action scene in each half of the can's interior. For example, he may show two different settings from the novel—such as day and night or inside and outside scenes. One peek inside the can will reveal a bit about his most recent read!

Picture Pages

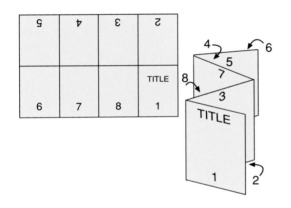

Have students show their understanding of a book with these miniature picture books. Give each student a large sheet of construction paper. To make a book, the student divides the paper into eight equal sections and numbers them as shown. Then she designs a title page in section 1. In each of the following sections, she illustrates a story event and writes a description of it, making sure to sequence the events correctly. Finally, the student folds her paper in half lengthwise and accordion-folds it as shown.

More Than a Book Review

Take book reviews to another level in your classroom by having each student write a review with a special focus, such as suspense, humor, adventure, or math. Direct the student to reveal the review's focus in her first paragraph. Then instruct her to highlight three of her book's suspenseful events, discussing each event in a different paragraph. In the closing paragraph, have her issue a suspense-filled invitation to others to read her book. You're sure to get a book review that tells more than usual. After all the reviews have been completed, classify and file them in subject-organized notebooks in your classroom library. Then allow your students to consult the notebooks to decide which books to read next!

Whet Your Appetite for Adventure

Investigate Good Mysteries

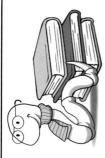

Better Than a Book Report!
Creative Ways to Share About the Book You Just Read

Directions: When you finish reading a novel, choose a project from the list below to complete. When your project is finished, place a check mark on the line next to it.

____ Write a newspaper with articles describing several events. Include articles that describe interesting details about one of the book's main characters and its setting.

____ Create a time capsule for the main characters. In the time capsule, include important items from the story that help tell what happened. Present your time capsule to the class and explain why each item it includes is important.

____ Select a scene to act out. Rewrite the scene in script form. Ask classmates to act out the roles of characters in the scene; then perform it together for your other classmates.

____ Design a travel brochure that advertises the setting as a tourist spot. Fold a sheet of white paper into thirds. Fill the brochure with information on sites and activities of interest, dining and lodging establishments, and any information that would help tourists.

____ Design a poster to advertise your book to other readers. Use lots of colorful adjectives to capture readers' interest. Be sure to include the title, the author's name, the illustrator's name, and a short summary of the book on the poster.

____ Write a short commercial advertising the book. Then record it on an audiocassette tape. At the beginning of the tape, be sure to give your name, the book's title, and the author; then record your commercial.

____ Create a mobile featuring cutouts and pictures that show the major events. Be sure to arrange the hanging shapes in sequential order.

____ Write an acrostic poem about the main character. To do this, write the letters in the character's name vertically on a sheet of paper. Then, after each letter, write an adjective that describes the character and begins with that letter.

____ Design a creative book jacket. Be sure to make your design appealing so that it interests readers. Include the title, the author's name, the illustrator's name, a short summary of the novel, and illustrations on the book jacket.

____ Write a sequel. Use the information you learned about the characters as you read the book.

____ Cover a cube with paper. On one side of the cube, write the title and author of the book you read. Record the five Ws—who, what, when, where, and why—on the other sides.

____ Design a bookmark that advertises the book. Write the title, the author's name, and a summary on the bookmark. Also add an illustration of an important scene from the book.

Name _____

Date due _____

Gotta Have Rules

What student doesn't enjoy hanging up decorative posters? Put this interest to use—and strengthen skills in capitalization—by having your students create posters highlighting capitalization rules. Using their English texts for help, have your students list various capitalization rules on the board. Divide your students into groups of four; then give each group a sheet of poster board and markers or colored pencils. Direct each team to pretend it has been asked by an educational company to design an eye-catching poster about capitalization rules that features examples of each rule. After each team completes and shares its poster, invite other teachers to display one of the posters in their classrooms. **Capitalization**

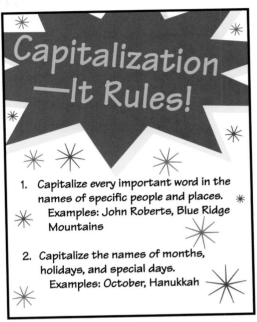

Capitalization —It Rules!

1. Capitalize every important word in the names of specific people and places.
   Examples: John Roberts, Blue Ridge Mountains

2. Capitalize the names of months, holidays, and special days.
   Examples: October, Hanukkah

Reviewing in the Round

To prepare for this game, use only lowercase letters to write sentences from a current class novel or the newspaper on paper circles. (Most of the sentences should contain proper nouns.) Place the sentences facedown in a round basket. In a separate basket, place a class supply of homework passes.

To play, seat students in a circle around the homework-pass basket. Play music and have students pass the sentence basket clockwise around the circle. When the music stops, ask the child holding the basket to take a circle, read the sentence on it aloud, and tell which words need to be capitalized. If he is correct, have him keep the circle. If he is incorrect, have him pass the circle and basket to the player on his left. After a correct answer has been given, restart the music and continue play. Allow the student who gives a correct answer for the last sentence in the basket to distribute homework passes to classmates holding sentence circles! **Capitalization**

the christmas party will be held at the sutton building on monday.

Top-Ten Categories

Give each student three sheets of white paper to fold into a booklet and staple. Have her title the booklet, decorate the cover, and add her name. Instruct her to head the top of each booklet page with a different capitalization rule. Then give her a newspaper section. Challenge her to find and cut out examples of each rule and glue them to the corresponding page. When she's finished, she'll have a handy reference to keep in her writing folder! **Capitalization**

Carly's Capitalization Categories

Capitalize words in titles except articles, prepositions, and coordinating conjunctions.

Man Saves Dog From Burning House

Teed Up for Practice

To prepare for this self-checking center on ending punctuation, write a different sentence on each of a supply of index cards, leaving off the end punctuation marks. Punch a hole along three sides of each card. Write the correct end punctuation mark above one hole and incorrect punctuation marks above the other two holes. Affix a hole reinforcer around each hole on the back of each card and use a permanent yellow marker to color the reinforcer around the hole of the correct punctuation mark. Then place the cards sentence side up at a center along with a golf tee. To use the center, a student puts the tee in the hole he thinks has the correct end punctuation mark for that sentence and turns the card over to check his answer. **Punctuation**

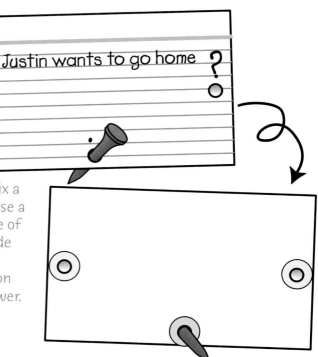

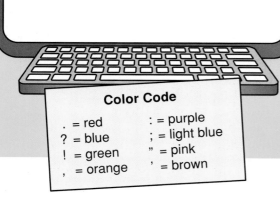

1. "Where's Patches?" Mom asked.

Color Code

. = red   : = purple
? = blue   ; = light blue
! = green " = pink
, = orange ' = brown

Template Punctuation

Your classroom computer is the perfect place for students to practice punctuation skills. Type ten or more sentences into a document, omitting all punctuation marks, and save the document as a template. (Depending on your word-processing program, you may also need to run a grammar check to remove any highlighted errors before saving.) Have each child using the computer punctuate the sentences by adding the missing punctuation marks. To make the activity even more appealing, have each student follow a color code to key in her answers and then print the page! **Punctuation**

Encore Performances

Bring out the ham in your students with this punctuation review! Have students help you brainstorm an acceptable sound or motion for each punctuation mark. For example, the sound of screeching tires could represent a period. Next, choose from a class novel or library book a paragraph or two that contain a good variety of punctuation marks. Then, as a narrator reads the text aloud, invite a group of students to lead the rest of the class in a performance that punctuates the text. Bravo! **Punctuation**

Quotable Quotes

Which topics do people talk or give advice about the most? Have your students brainstorm topics such as money, education, and happiness for you to record on the board. Then write several famous quotes on the board (see the examples at the right) and discuss their meanings with your students. Use the examples to explain the rules for using quotation marks and other punctuation marks in a quoted sentence. Next, give each student a sentence strip and a colorful marker, directing her to choose one of the topics listed on the board. Pair your students; then have each student in the pair make up and dictate her own quote about her topic to her partner. Instruct the partner to record and punctuate the quote on her sentence strip. Afterward, have the students in each pair share each other's quotations with the class. Display the quotes on a wall or bulletin board titled "Our Most Quotable Quotes." **Punctuation**

➤ Benjamin Franklin said, "A penny saved is a penny earned."

➤ "A book," says an old Chinese proverb, "is like a garden carried in the pocket."

➤ "Most folks are about as happy as they make up their minds to be," said Abraham Lincoln.

"Saving money," said Matthew, "is very important."

"A good education is the key to a bright future." said Marsha.

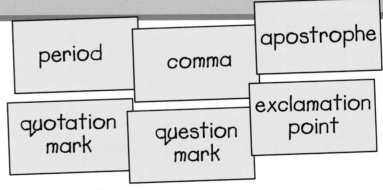

period   comma   apostrophe

quotation mark   question mark   exclamation point

Pasta Punctuation

For this colorful review, select shapes of dry pasta that can represent different punctuation marks. Mix one cup of pasta, at least two teaspoons of rubbing alcohol, and a few drops of food coloring in a large resealable bag. Repeat for each pasta shape and color of food coloring to be used. Spread the pasta on paper towels to dry. Next, write different sentences (omitting the punctuation) on separate sentence strips. Then give each child a sentence strip and a handful of different pasta shapes. Have him place pasta pieces on his strip to punctuate the sentence. Once he places the pieces correctly, allow him to trade strips with a classmate until he has punctuated several sentences! **Punctuation**

Sentence Rx

Play this game throughout the year to sharpen students' punctuation skills! Divide students into teams and give each team member an index card labeled with a different punctuation mark. Then write a sentence on the board, minus all the punctuation marks. Ask the teams whether that sentence needs a particular punctuation mark. For example, ask, "Could this sentence use a comma?" If the answer is yes, the first child to hold up a comma card goes to the board and adds the comma(s) to the sentence. If her placement is correct, her team wins a point for each comma. If not, the first child to hold up a comma card from another team goes up. Continue in this manner until the sentence has all its missing punctuation marks. Repeat with different sentences. When time is up, declare the team with the most points the winner. **Punctuation**

Mark's mom made a banner for the soccer team

Gotta Scramble

To prepare for this game, make a copy of the points chart on page 57 for each team of two to four students. Next, write the parts of speech you want students to practice on a copy of the die pattern on page 57. Then roll the assembled die and announce the part of speech rolled along with any letter of the alphabet. Give the teams two minutes to list words of that part of speech that begin with that letter. Verify the accuracy and spelling of words listed by each team. Then have each team use the chart to tally its score and report it to you to record. To begin another round, roll the die. Declare the team with the most points after ten rounds the winner. **Parts of speech**

noun
adjective verb

H.

Letter	Points
A	1
B	3
C	3
D	2
E	1
F	4
G	2
H	4
I	1
J	8
K	5
L	1
M	3
N	1
O	1
P	3
Q	10
R	1
S	1
T	1
U	1
V	4
W	4
X	8
Y	4
Z	10

Team 1

hand = 4 + 1 + 1 + 2 = 8

hunter = 4 + 1 + 1 + 1 + 1 + 1 = 9

hamburger = 4 + 1 + 3 + 3 + 1 + 1 + 2 + 1 + 1 = 17

8
9
+ 17

34 points for Round 1

Grammar Gridlock

For this nifty activity, make a copy of the grid and cards on page 58 for each pair of students. Have the duo cut its cards apart and sort them on the grid under the correct columns. When students are finished, have each set of partners compare answers with another twosome. Discuss with students that some words may be more than one part of speech depending on how the word is used in a sentence. Have students help you locate examples of words that may be more than one part of speech. To follow up, have each child write a sentence that includes at least one of each part of speech on the grid. To vary the activity, replace the grid's headings with other parts of speech and use different words on the cards, even seasonal ones! **Parts of speech**

Nouns	Verbs	Adjectives	Prepositions	Conjunctions	Pronouns
gerbil	eat	furry	under	or	he
scientist	crash	exciting	over	but	her
computer	write	grumpy	through	yet	she
month	jump	new	behind	and	mine

A-hunting We Will Go

Give each child a copy of a short passage from your current read-aloud or an interesting selection of nonfiction text to read. When he is finished, have him turn his paper over and take out a blue crayon. When everyone has a blue crayon, signal students to turn their papers over and circle every noun they find in the passage. After 30 seconds (or another appropriate time limit), instruct students to put their crayons down. Then check the answers together. Repeat the activity, using a different part of speech and crayon, for each part of speech you want students to review. **Parts of speech**

Parts of Speech Word Wall

If your students often hit a brick wall when it comes to identifying a vocabulary word's part of speech, try this simple activity. On a large sheet of bulletin board paper, draw a bricklike wall pattern with one block for each student. Leave a blank space below the wall for a key. Create the key, designating a different color for each part of speech you are studying (for example, red = noun, blue = adjective, yellow = verb, etc.). Post the paper on a wall or bulletin board and place a container of markers by it. Then, as your class reads a classroom story or novel, have each student write both a vocabulary word and the sentence in which that word is found within one of the blocks. After a lesson on the different parts of speech, have each child choose one word listed on the wall. Direct him to identify the vocabulary word's part of speech (in the context of the recorded sentence) by shading the block the color indicated by the key. Follow up the activity by having each child complete a copy of page 59 as directed. **Parts of speech**

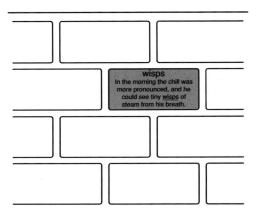

Collector's Collage

Use this hands-on activity to combine reviewing parts of speech with a little bit of artistry! Divide students into teams. Assign each team a different part of speech, such as a noun, an adverb, or an adjective. Also supply each team with a magazine and newspaper, a 12" x 18" sheet of construction paper, scissors, and glue. Direct the team to search its magazine and newspaper for words and pictures that represent its part of speech, cut them out, and glue the cutouts in collage fashion to the sheet of construction paper. If desired, have each team add its own decorative examples to the sheet. **Parts of speech**

Amazing Adjectives

Open your students' eyes to the benefits of using descriptive words with this picturesque activity! Write a sentence on the board that contains several nouns but no adjectives; then follow the steps below.

1 Direct students to close their eyes and visualize the sentences you will read.

2 Read aloud the sentence on the board; then, after a minute, read it again, adding an adjective before each noun.

3 Have students open their eyes; then ask how their visualizations of the two sentences differed.

4 Discuss how the adjectives in the second sentence make it more descriptive and help create a more vivid picture in a reader's mind.

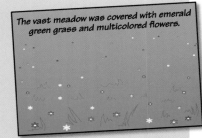

The vast meadow was covered with emerald green grass and multicolored flowers.

5 Have each student write the sample sentence on a sheet of loose-leaf paper, filling in a different adjective before each noun.

6 Collect the papers; then redistribute them, giving a paper to each student along with an 8½" x 11" sheet of drawing paper and crayons or colored pencils.

7 Direct the student to copy the sentence on the paper at the top of her sheet of drawing paper and then draw a picture of what she sees when she reads the sentence.

Have each child share her sentence and drawing with the class. If desired, display students' work on a bulletin board or wall space titled "Amazing Adjectives!" **Parts of speech**

Dynamic Dual Describers

Give each group of students a picture from an old calendar. Allow the groups two minutes to list nouns that they see pictured. Next, challenge the group to add two appropriate adjectives to each noun listed. As each group reports its findings to the class, instruct them to circle any boring adjectives and replace them with stronger descriptors. Then have each child write a short story that includes at least five of her group's phrases. To vary the activity, have groups add adverbs to vivid verbs! **Parts of speech**

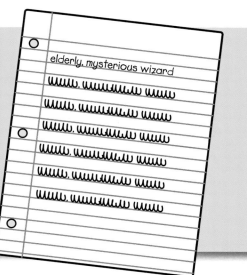

elderly, mysterious wizard

Recipe for a Verb Hunt

Add a little home cooking to your next review of verbs! Have each child bring in a copy of a favorite family recipe. Then have him trade recipes with a classmate and highlight all the verbs he can find. Next, have the partners work together to determine whether the highlighted words are action verbs, linking verbs, or helping verbs and list them in the appropriate columns of a copy of the chart on page 60. Collect the charts and copy students' verbs onto a poster that can be displayed as a classroom reference. To get more examples to add to the poster, repeat the activity, using copies of passages from a current read-aloud, a popular student magazine, or students' own pieces of writing! **Parts of speech**

Picture-Perfect Verbs

Ask students to bring in a photograph of themselves doing one of their favorite activities. Next, have each child pretend to be a reporter assigned to cover the event. Have him write a paragraph explaining the event in the photo. When he is finished, have him trade papers with a classmate and underline all the verbs in his partner's paragraph. After you check his work, have him highlight the underlined words. Then collect the corresponding photos and paragraphs and arrange them on a display titled "Reporting the Action!" **Parts of speech**

Which Way?

Use this self-checking center to help students recognize the differences between a complete sentence, a fragment, a rambling sentence, and a run-on. Make copies of the car pattern on page 60 on colorful paper. Then write on the front of each car an example of either a complete sentence, a rambling sentence, a fragment, or a run-on and its category on the back. Pin the cars to a bulletin board with a road that forks four ways as shown. Have students using the center read what is written on each car and pin it to the matching road. Once all the cars are pinned in place, the cars can be turned over to check students' answers.
Sentences

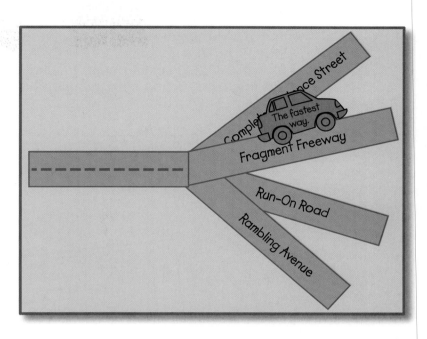

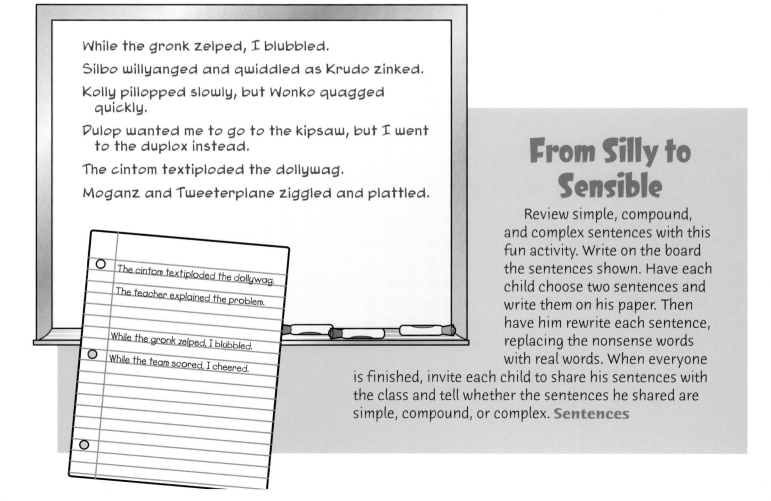

While the gronk zelped, I blubbled.

Silbo willyanged and qwiddled as Krudo zinked.

Kolly pillopped slowly, but Wonko quagged quickly.

Dulop wanted me to go to the kipsaw, but I went to the duplox instead.

The cintom textiploded the dollywag.

Moganz and Tweeterplane ziggled and plattled.

The cintom textiploded the dollywag.
The teacher explained the problem.

While the gronk zelped, I blubbled.
While the team scored, I cheered.

From Silly to Sensible

Review simple, compound, and complex sentences with this fun activity. Write on the board the sentences shown. Have each child choose two sentences and write them on his paper. Then have him rewrite each sentence, replacing the nonsense words with real words. When everyone is finished, invite each child to share his sentences with the class and tell whether the sentences he shared are simple, compound, or complex. **Sentences**

Listen Up!

Give students' ears a workout with this subject-verb agreement activity! In advance, select several poems from a book. Use a pencil to lightly write in a few incorrect verbs to substitute for some correct ones. Slowly read each selection aloud, challenging students to listen for agreement mistakes. When students hear an error, direct them to tug one of their ears. Then ask one child to correct the mistake. **Sentences**

Roll a subject:

1 = your favorite cartoon character

2 = a family member

3 = someone who works at your school

4 = a singer in a famous band

5 = a TV actor

6 = a friend

Ms. Miller make great brownies.
Raven calls her best friend.

Cleanup Crew

Help students spot subject-verb agreement problems with this fun partner activity. Display a chart similar to the one shown and give each pair of students a die. Have one partner roll the die to determine a subject and write a sentence that includes it. Direct his partner to repeat the steps. Then instruct each duo to rewrite one of its two sentences so that the agreement is incorrect. Next, have the partners trade papers with another pair of students, identify the incorrect sentence, and clean it up (rewrite it to correct the agreement problem). **Sentences**

Put It on Paper!

Review subject-verb agreement with this simple activity. Direct each child to fold a sheet of paper in half twice and then unfold it to create four sections. Next, write on the board two singular and two plural nouns related to the season, a current read-aloud, or a science or social studies unit. Direct each student to think of each noun as the subject of a sentence and copy one noun at the top of each paper section. Then give students five minutes to list as many appropriate predicates as they can to go with each subject. After the lists have been shared, invite the child who listed the most predicates to choose the subjects for the next round. **Sentences**

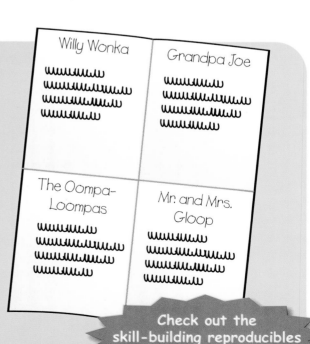

Willy Wonka

Grandpa Joe

The Oompa-Loompas

Mr. and Mrs. Gloop

Check out the skill-building reproducibles on pages 61–63.

Die Pattern and Points Chart

Use with "Gotta Scramble" on page 50.

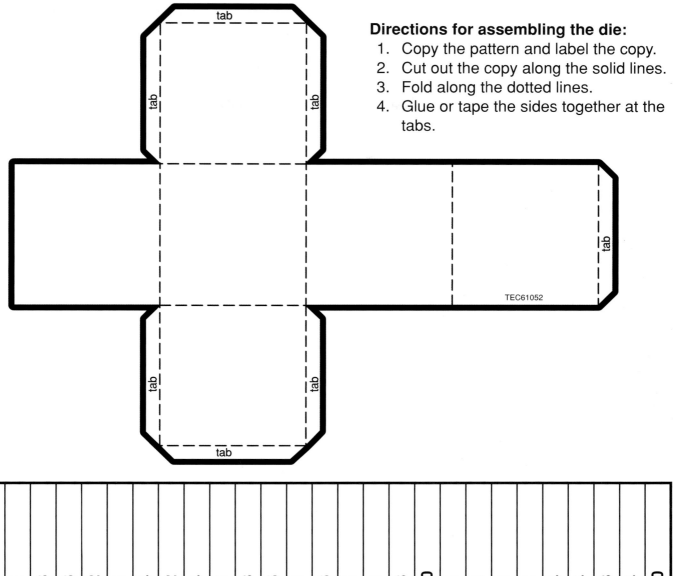

Directions for assembling the die:

1. Copy the pattern and label the copy.
2. Cut out the copy along the solid lines.
3. Fold along the dotted lines.
4. Glue or tape the sides together at the tabs.

TEC61052

Letter	Points
A	1
B	3
C	3
D	2
E	1
F	4
G	2
H	4
I	1
J	8
K	5
L	1
M	3
N	1
O	1
P	3
Q	10
R	1
S	1
T	1
U	1
V	4
W	4
X	8
Y	4
Z	10

TEC61052

Parts of Speech Grid and Cards

Use with "Grammar Gridlock" on page 50.

Nouns	Verbs	Adjectives	Prepositions	Conjunctions	Pronouns
		TEC61052			

under	yet	gerbil	her	grumpy	exciting
TEC61052	TEC61052	TEC61052	TEC61052	TEC61052	TEC61052
scientist	write	new	computer	and	she
TEC61052	TEC61052	TEC61052	TEC61052	TEC61052	TEC61052
mine	through	jump	behind	over	month
TEC61052	TEC61052	TEC61052	TEC61052	TEC61052	TEC61052
furry	he	but	or	crash	eat
TEC61052	TEC61052	TEC61052	TEC61052	TEC61052	TEC61052

NAME _____

DATE _____

Packing Up Parts of Speech

Write each underlined word or phrase below on the correct part of suitcase.

Nouns
(name persons, places, things, or ideas)

Verbs
(show action or being)

Adjectives
(describe nouns or pronouns)

Adverbs
(describe verbs, adjectives, or other adverbs)

Pronouns
(take the place of nouns)

1. The <u>mouse</u> <u>swiftly</u> ran under the <u>staircase</u>.

2. Mr. Simon, the <u>librarian</u>, <u>loudly</u> told the students that <u>they</u> were too noisy.

3. <u>We</u> <u>sang</u> a <u>beautiful</u> song as the <u>bus driver</u> drove us to the zoo.

4. My <u>lazy</u> cat just eats, sleeps, and <u>quietly</u> <u>purrs</u> all day long!

5. Even though Samantha thought the race was <u>easy</u>, <u>she</u> <u>fell</u> just a <u>short</u> distance from the finish line.

6. Wow, <u>you</u> <u>ate</u> that piece of pie <u>quickly</u>!

Note to the teacher: Use with "Parts of Speech Word Wall" on page 51.

59

Verb Chart

Use with "Recipe for a Verb Hunt" on page 52.

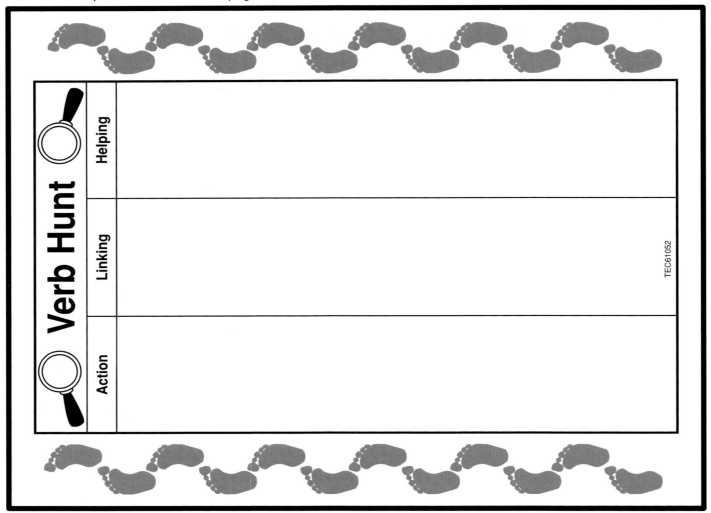

Car Pattern

Use with "Which Way?" on page 55.

NAME _____

DATE _____

Hats Off to Capitalization

Read each sentence.

Draw a hat above the word(s) in each sentence that should have a capital letter.

The first one has been done for you.

1. The bad weather forced disney world to close for the first time in many years.

2. The cookies for the party were bought at The Cookie cutter Bakery.

3. At the soccer game, i cheered each time our team scored a goal.

4. My sister's favorite book is *The view from Saturday.*

5. Dad asked mom, "what time is Carly's piano recital?"

6. In july, our family went to yellowstone national park.

7. Mom has an appointment with dr. fields on friday.

8. when it started raining, she let the cat inside.

9. A french chef won the cooking contest.

10. The wreck occurred on highway 311.

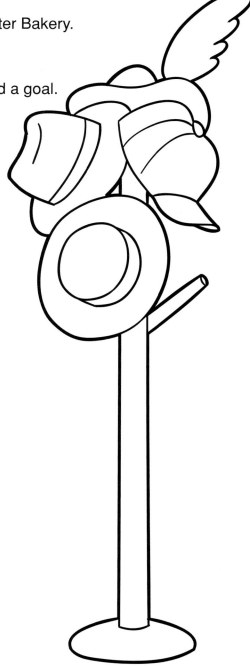

NAME ______________________________

DATE ______________________

WANTED

Name of the Suspect: ______________________________
(the punctuation mark assigned by your teacher)

The suspect is used most often to ______________________________

______________________________.

The suspect might be found ______________________________

______________________________.

The suspect could also be spotted ______________________________

______________________________.

Examples of the suspect in action:

1. ______________________________

____

2. ______________________________

____

3. ______________________________

____

Note to the teacher: Assign a punctuation mark as the "suspect." Direct each student to complete the page by providing information about the assigned punctuation mark.

Ready to Race

Color the car that shows whether the subject and verb of each sentence agree. To find the winner, count the colored cars in each column. Then color the car below that column.

1. The drivers wait for the race to begin.	Yes	No
2. Finally, the drivers can start their engines.	Yes	No
3. The cars has been serviced well.	Yes	No
4. Car 1 speed ahead of Car 2.	Yes	No
5. Car 2 move up quickly.	Yes	No
6. Both cars are the same color.	Yes	No
7. In the first turn, one car almost spin out of control.	Yes	No
8. The other car tries not to crash into it.	Yes	No
9. One car lose a hubcap.	Yes	No
10. The hubcap is removed from the track.	Yes	No
11. The race resumes, and the cars pick up speed.	Yes	No
12. One car zooms ahead of the slower car.	Yes	No
13. Neither driver want to lose.	Yes	No
14. Each driver hopes to be in the winner's circle!	Yes	No

Bonus Box: On the back of this page, rewrite two sentences with colored "No" cars so that their subjects and verbs agree.

Car 1 wins!   Car 2 wins!

WORD SKILLS

SYNONYM CONNECTIONS

Give each student a sheet of graph paper and a thesaurus. Have each child look in the thesaurus for a common word with several synonyms and write it in red ink near the middle of the graph paper. Then have her use black ink to write the synonyms on the grid, connecting the words as shown. If desired, display the completed graphs on a board titled "Synonym Connections." **Synonyms**

```
                        b
                        e
                        h
      t o l e r a n t
                        v
              s         e
            g o o d
              u         p
              n i c e   e
              d         r f e c t
  h i g h - g r a d e
                        c
                        t
```

TWISTED TALES

Have each student write a couple of paragraphs about himself, using at least ten descriptive adjectives. When students are finished, have each child underline those adjectives. Then instruct him to rewrite his passage by replacing each underlined adjective with a circled antonym as shown. Provide time for students to share their twisted tales with the class.

Antonyms

The (before-school) activity I like the most is riding my (used) BMX bike. Every day, I get off the (quiet) bus and head inside my house to grab my (dull) helmet and (hated) bike. My (worst) friend, Matt, meets me at the park, and we ride the (straight) trails. Sometimes, we stay so late that my (pleased) mom has to send my (younger) brother to call me in for a (tasteless) dinner.

The afterschool activity I like the most is riding my brand-new BMX bike. Every day, I get off the noisy bus and head inside my house to grab my shiny helmet and beloved bike. My best friend, Matt, meets me at the park, and we ride the twisting trails. Sometimes, we stay so late that my angry mom has to send my older brother to call me in for a delicious dinner.

DIP INTO SYNONYMS AND ANTONYMS

dangerous
famous
perform
strong
destroy

Get your students to take a dip into synonyms and antonyms while giving them practice with analogies. Draw two large swimming pool shapes on the board. Fill the first pool with vocabulary words that your students are currently studying. Fill the second pool with a synonym or antonym for each vocabulary word. Then use the words from the pools to write incomplete analogies on the board (see the examples shown). Direct each student to complete each analogy using a synonym or antonym from the pools. Afterward, have your students share their answers. Finally, have pairs of students pool their knowledge to create more analogies using different synonyms and antonyms. To provide additional practice with synonyms, have students complete a copy of page 72. **Synonyms and antonyms**

execute
demolish
renowned
perilous
feeble

Dangerous is to *perilous* as *destroy* is to _____.

Famous is to _____ as *perform* is to *execute*.

Take a Spin

For this small-group game, make several copies of the spinner on page 73 and laminate them. Divide the class into groups of three or five students each. Give a spinner to each group. Then list 12 homophones (such as those shown) on the board and have a student from each group use a wipe-off marker to write one word in each section of his group's spinner.

To play, Player 1 in each group spins and uses the homophone in a sentence. Player 2 tells another way to spell the word and uses it in a sentence. A point is given for each correct response. Play continues around the group until time is up. The student with the most points wins. **Homophones**

knows · miner · bored · principal · waist · made · pier · son · cheep · blue · groan · whole

FLYING HIGH

perilous · risky
dangerous
unsafe · hazardous
safe
secure

Pair students and assign each duo a vocabulary word. Have the pair make a construction paper kite with a tail, as shown, and write the vocabulary word on the kite. Using a dictionary, a thesaurus, or both, the duo finds synonyms of the word and writes each one on the kite. Then the students find antonyms and write them on the tail. After students share their kites, display the projects on a board titled "Sky-High Words." Synonyms and antonyms

ONE-MINUTE AFFIXES

For a fast-paced partner game, write a different prefix or suffix on each of ten to 12 milk jug lids. Store the lids and a one-minute egg timer in a container at a center. To play, one player chooses a lid and turns over the timer. Then each player writes as many words as she can using the affix on the lid. When time is up, the players check each other's lists, crossing out any misspelled words or words that are on both lists. The student with the most words left uncrossed on her list wins. **Prefixes and suffixes**

Weave a Word Web

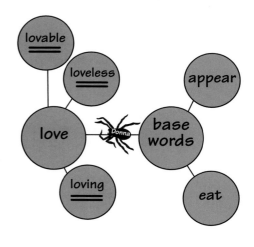

Help your students understand the structure of base words with this web-wise activity. Cut out a large circle from construction paper. Label that circle "base words" and post it on a large wall or bulletin board. Next, cut out ten medium-size circles and a supply of smaller circles—five to ten more than the number of students in your class. Label each medium-size circle with a different base word; then attach each medium-size circle to the larger circle with string or yarn to create a web. Put the smaller circles aside.

Challenge each student to find a different word built from one of the posted base words. Direct her to write that word and its meaning on one of the smaller circles and connect it to the appropriate base-word circle with yarn. Extend this activity by making a class supply of black construction paper spiders. Each time a student identifies ten appropriate words, write her name on the spider with chalk and attach it to the web. Reward each student who achieves spider status on the word web with a special treat. **Base words, prefixes, and suffixes**

MAKE A MATCH

To prepare this fun game, make a copy of the game cards on page 74 for each student pair. Have the duo cut the cards apart and fold each card on its dotted line. Then direct students to randomly place the cards in a grid, as shown, with the labels *prefix*, *suffix*, and *root word* facing up. On each turn, a player turns over three cards—one prefix, one suffix, and one base word. She combines as many of the word parts as possible to make a new word. A player earns two points for using two of the cards and five for using all three. Any unused card is turned back over, and the other player takes a turn. Play continues until all cards have been used or all possible words are made. The player with the higher score is the winner. Base words, prefixes, and suffixes

prefix	suffix	root word	suffix
root word	prefix	suffix	prefix
root word	root word	prefix	suffix
prefix	root word	suffix	root word

pre-	test	-ed

FIVE POINTS!

ROOT-O!

On the board, write a list of words, such as the ones shown, that contain familiar roots. Then have each student program a copy of the gameboard on page 75 with some of the words. To play, call out the definition of a word from the board. If a student finds the correct word on his gameboard, he uses a wipe-off marker to underline each of the word's roots. Have a student call out, "Root-o!" if he underlines the roots of five words in a row, column, or diagonal on his board. Check to be sure the student correctly identified the words you defined and each root. Then have students clear their gameboards and begin again. **Roots**

ROOT-O

<u>auto</u>matic	thermos	photograph	<u>erupt</u>	biography
cyclone	<u>hydra</u>te	television	multicolor	popular
manual	audio	**ROOT~O**	pedal	in<u>spect</u>
tripod	<u>pedi</u>cure	thermostat	portable	tractor
biology	finish	equality	uniform	<u>mini</u>mum

Light Up Your Words

To prepare this center, make a few copies of the beam patterns and several copies of the flashlight pattern on page 75. Program each beam with a different prefix and each flashlight with a base word as shown. Place the pieces at a center. To complete the activity, have each student try to match each flashlight to at least one beam. Then have the student use the words he created to write sentences on his paper. To reuse this center activity, simply program the new beam copies with different prefixes or suffixes. **Prefixes and suffixes**

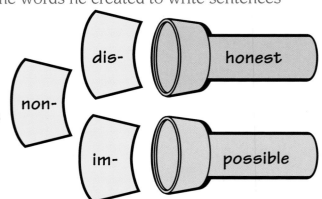

dis-   honest

non-

im-   possible

A GARDEN OF WORDS

Assign each student a prefix or suffix. Then have each child find her affix's meaning and examples of words that use it. Next, have the student create a paper flower, writing the affix and its definition on two separate leaves as shown. Then have her write the examples on the flower's petals. Display the flowers on a board titled "Blooming Words." **Prefixes and suffixes**

discover

disappear   disagree

disbelieve   displaced

disorder   disinterested

not, or away from

dis-

SPELLING HUNT

Supply a center with a copy of the week's spelling list, graph paper, scissors, glue, and construction paper. Have a student program the graph paper with each spelling word as shown. Then have the student fill in the remaining boxes with random letters of the alphabet. The student then cuts out the word search and glues it to a sheet of construction paper. Allow the student to title and decorate his puzzle as desired. At the end of the week, pass out the word searches and challenge students to find all their spelling words. What a great way to review for a test! *Spelling*

One Letter at a Time

Divide students into two teams for this relay spelling game. Read aloud a sentence containing a spelling word. At the signal, the first student from each team goes to the board, writes the first letter of the spelling word, tags the next team member, and goes to the back of the line. The next student goes to the board and writes the next letter or corrects a single letter of a previous mistake. The first team to spell the word correctly earns a point. Then read aloud another sentence and continue play. The team with more points wins. **Spelling**

uni   uniqu

TUNE IN TO SPELLING

Provide each student with a file folder, a ruler, a pencil, scissors, and markers or colored pencils. Direct the student to write her name on the folder's tab and "Tune In to Spelling" at the top. Next, have the student draw a 3" x 3" square in the center of the folder, and a larger square around that square to create a television set as shown. Instruct the student to add details to the TV set; then have her cut along both vertical lines of the inside square.

After introducing the week's spelling words, give each student a sentence strip. Then guide her through the steps below to complete the organizer.

1. Use a marker to divide the sentence strip into three-inch segments (front and back).
2. Write a spelling word in each segment.
3. Weave the sentence strip from the back of the top leaf of the file folder, up through the right slit, and down through the left slit.
4. Pull the strip across the screen to study each spelling word.

For added practice, have each student complete a copy of the contract on page 76. Before duplicating, program the stars on the sheet with the number of activities a student should complete to earn each grade listed on the sheet. Direct her to keep the contract inside her folder along with any completed work. *Spelling*

Catherine Smith
Tune In to Spelling

vacuum   reliable

au to bi o gra phy

THAT'S IT!

SUPER STRATEGY

What does a student do when he needs to write a word he doesn't know how to spell? Use this strategy to give him a tool to use before he resorts to the dictionary. First, have him clap out the syllables and draw a blank line for each syllable on a sheet of paper. Then have him try to spell the smaller word parts and write the letters on the lines. If the word still doesn't look like it is spelled correctly, he checks the word in a dictionary. **Spelling**

More Than a Spelling Game

Divide the class into teams. Have each team write each spelling or vocabulary word on a separate index card. Next, have each team arrange the cards on a desktop word side up. Then call out instructions such as "Hold up a word with a suffix" or "Hold up a word that would be found on a dictionary page with the guide words *baggage* and *bevy*." Have students hold up any card that meet the instruction's criteria. Award two points to the first team and one point to any other team that holds up a correct word within 15 seconds. After several rounds, declare the team with the most points the winner. **Spelling**

Massachusetts

HOLD UP A WORD WITH FOUR SYLLABLES.

synonym—unsure
antonym—sure

un—prefix
certain—base word

I am uncertain about the amount of money in my wallet.

not knowing

uncertain

SPELLING DESERVES A HAND

Give students a hands-on way to study spelling words! Have each child trace her hand and cut out a tracing for each spelling word. Then, on each handprint, she writes a spelling word on the thumb; the word's definition on the index finger; a sentence using the spelling word on the middle finger; any base word, root word, prefix, or suffix on the ring finger; and a synonym and antonym on the pinkie finger. She staples the handprints together for an easy-to-use study booklet. **Spelling**

SPELLING MAGNETISM

For this game, divide students into two groups. Give each group a shoebox of two or more inexpensive sets of plastic magnetic letters stored in a shoebox. To play, the first two members of each team go to the board with instructions to remain silent during their turn. Call out a word. Player 1 on each team searches his team's box for each letter and passes it to Player 2, who arranges the letters on the board in the correct order. When the word is complete, Player 2 calls out the word. The first team to spell the word correctly earns a point. If incorrect, the other team can try to complete the word to earn the point. Continue playing—having different players head to the board for each new round—until all words on your list have been spelled or time runs out. The team with more points is the winner. Spelling

QUESTION OF THE DAY

Each morning, post a question on the board that requires students to use reference materials to locate the answer. Each student writes the answer, its source, and the page number (if appropriate) on a piece of paper. Then he puts the answer in a designated container. At the end of the day, draw answers until a correct one is found. Allow the student that gave the correct answer to submit a future question of the day. Encourage students to suggest questions that require the use of a variety of sources. **Using reference materials**

jē-ˈä-grə—fē

Around the World Spelling

Help students learn to read the pronunciations in the dictionary with this Around the World–inspired game. Using a dictionary, write the phonetic spellings of selected words (one per student) on separate sentence strips. Direct each student to sit at his desk. Have the first two students stand. Then reveal one of the phonetic spellings. The first player to pronounce the word correctly moves to stand beside the desk of the next classmate, while the other player sits down at his desk. Play continues around the room until all words have been identified or time runs out. **Dictionary skills**

What are the native countries of the lesser panda?

China, Nepal, Bhutan, India, Myanma
World Book Online Reference Center

Mad-Dash Indexing

Select ten to 12 sentences from various sections of a class textbook. Then read one of the selected sentences aloud. Challenge each student to use only the index of his book to find the sentence as quickly as he can. Have the first student who finds the sentence read it back to you along with its page number and the word or words he used to find it in the index. Repeat using the remaining sentences. **Using an index**

SYNONYM CIRCLES

Have each student draw four circles on unlined paper and divide each circle into six equal pieces. Give each student four different words and have her write each word in a section of a different circle. Then have her find five synonyms for each word in a thesaurus and write each one in a section of its circle. When students are finished, collect the papers and copy a set for each child. Then have each student cut out the circles and staple them together for a handy reference. **Using a thesaurus**

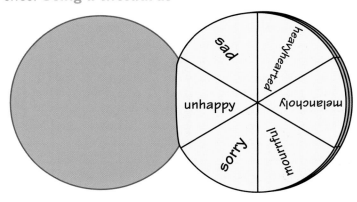

Check out the skill-building reproducible on page 77.

TREASURE HUNT

Cover and label a shoebox so that it looks like a treasure chest. Program several paper coins as shown and place them in an envelope. Place the treasure chest, the envelope, a dictionary, and notebook paper at a center. To complete the activity, each student draws a coin from the envelope. He uses the dictionary to find the information requested on the coin. Then he records his answers on notebook paper, places the paper in the treasure chest, and returns the coin to the envelope. At the end of the week, review as a class the different answers in the chest. **Using a dictionary**

Find aspire.
List the guide words at the top of the page.
What part of speech is this word?
How many definitions are given for this word?
Use this word in a complete sentence.

SPICY SYNONYMS!

Use a thesaurus to help you replace each word in bold print below with three other descriptive synonyms. Write the synonyms for each word in the blanks provided on the spice jars.

1.

We had a **good** day at the zoo.

1. _____
2. _____
3. _____

2.

The weather outside was **nice**.

1. _____
2. _____
3. _____

3.

I often **eat** too much food at a holiday meal.

1. _____
2. _____
3. _____

4.

The **sad** dog slept by the bed.

1. _____
2. _____
3. _____

5.

The circus clown was very **funny**.

1. _____
2. _____
3. _____

6.

The **large** building rose 200 feet into the sky.

1. _____
2. _____
3. _____

7.

The beach was covered with **beautiful** shells.

1. _____
2. _____
3. _____

8.

I **walked** along the path to the park.

1. _____
2. _____
3. _____

Note to the teacher: Use with "Dip Into Synonyms and Antonyms" on page 65.

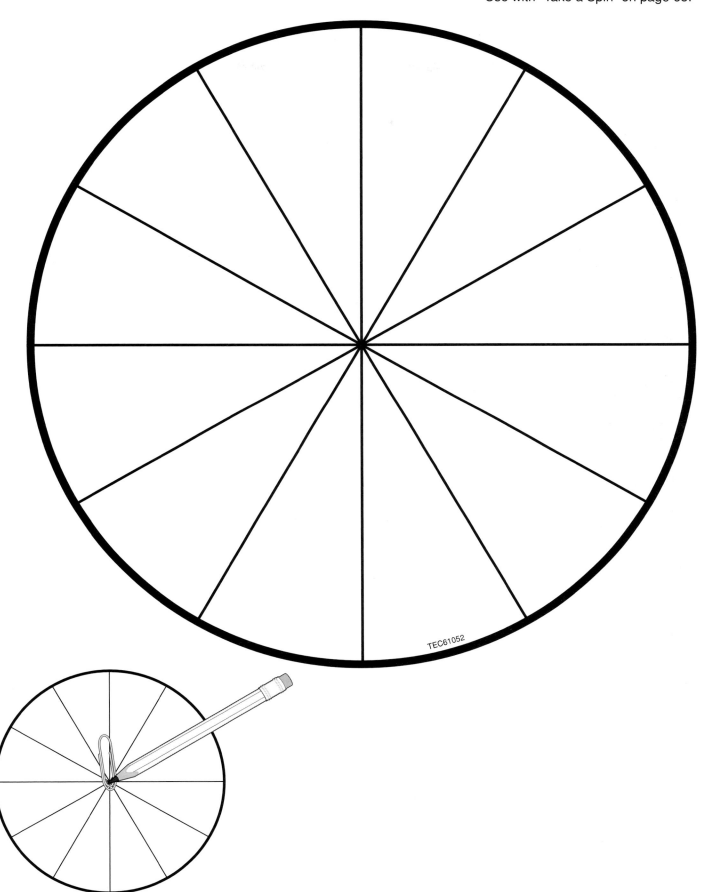

TEC61052

Game Cards

Use with "Make a Match" on page 66.

dis-	mis-	re-	un-
prefix TEC61052	prefix TEC61052	prefix TEC61052	prefix TEC61052
pre-	non-	-able	-ful
prefix TEC61052	prefix TEC61052	suffix TEC61052	suffix TEC61052
-ing	-ed	-ly	-ness
suffix TEC61052	suffix TEC61052	suffix TEC61052	suffix TEC61052
kind	test	respect	color
root word TEC61052	root word TEC61052	root word TEC61052	root word TEC61052
understand	made	stop	do
root word TEC61052	root word TEC61052	root word TEC61052	root word TEC61052

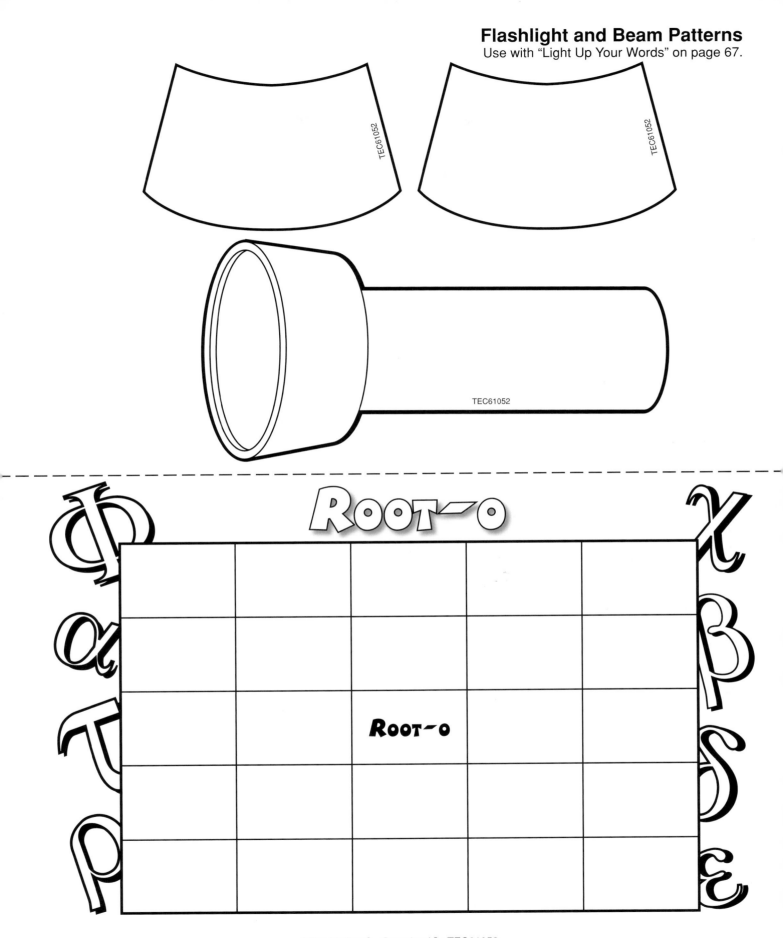

TEC61052

TEC61052

TEC61052

Root-o

Root-o

Note to the teacher: Use with "Root-o" on page 67.

NAME

DATE

76

TUNE IN TO SPELLING

Write your spelling words on the television screen below. Then read each of the following activities you will complete. After completing each activity, color the box next to that task to indicate that you have finished it.

I will complete _____ activities this week.

□ 1. Find and cut out the letters that spell each spelling word in a newspaper or magazine. Arrange the letters to spell each word; then glue the letters onto a sheet of construction paper.

□ 2. Write the letters that spell each word on index cards, a different letter on each card. Shuffle the cards and use them to play a game of Go Fish with a friend.

□ 3. Choose five words. Write a different sentence using the letters of each word. Example: *real—**R**obin **e**agerly **a**te **l**asagna.*

□ 4. Practice spelling your words with your parent.

□ 5. Choose three different spelling words. Write each word in a way that illustrates its meaning.

Example: FRIGID

□ 6. Write one sentence that contains as many of your spelling words as possible.

□ 7. Have a friend write a list of the words, misspelling ten of them. Identify the misspelled words by circling them; then spell each word correctly.

□ 8. Choose five different spelling words. Write each letter of each word on a different strip of construction paper. Glue the strips together to create a word chain for each word.

□ 9. Spell each word on your list, substituting a blank for each vowel. For example, spell *docile* as d _ c _ l _. Then pair up with a classmate and solve each other's puzzles.

□ 10. Choose five different words. For each word, write as many different rhyming words as possible.
Example: *weigh—pray, convey, neigh, obey*

 = A — Star Show!

☆ = B — Great Show!

☆ = C — Good Show!

Note to the teacher: Use with "Tune In to Spelling" on page 68.

Try On Something New

Cross out the overused word in each sentence. Use the old shirt below to help you. Write a similar word above the crossed-out word. Use the words on the new shirt or words from a thesaurus to help you.

like

thing

interesting

take

big

happy

pretty

want

enjoy, adore

object, article

intriguing, curious

choose, seize

heavy, massive

ecstatic, overjoyed

lovely, attractive

require, demand

1. The big bag of goodies was stuffed with cookies, candy, and snacks.

2. We stopped and picked up the ugly thing.

3. They want the kids to help clean the park.

4. I like stopping by the store each weekend.

5. My parents gave me an interesting gift to open.

6. The pretty shirt had many colors and designs.

7. The class was happy about Friday's field trip.

8. Ms. Smith asked me to take a pencil from the can.

Writing

Keeping Up With the Stages

This simple tip helps you keep track of your students' writing process. Cover five small boxes or jars with self-adhesive paper. Label each with a different stage of the writing process. Then have each student write her name on one side of a craft stick with a permanent marker and decorate the back side with wiggle eyes and craft materials. Before each writing session, have each child place her craft stick in the box that matches the stage of her writing. You'll know your students' progress with a quick glance at the boxes. **Writing process**

First Draft

Edit and Proofread

Story Rubric

The story has
- a beginning, middle, and end   1 2 3 4
- good details   1 2 3 4
- complete sentences   1 2 3 4
- correct capitalization and end punctuation marks   1 2 3 4

Writing Binders

To help writers stay organized, have each child keep his work in a three-ring binder with five dividers, each labeled with a different step of the writing process. If the binder's front cover is clear or has a see-through panel, use it to display a copy of the writing rubric that will be used to evaluate the writer's work!
Writing process

STOP IN THE NAME OF WRITING!

This eye-catching visual should definitely get your students' attention when they write! Cut the letters S, T, O, and P from white construction paper. Glue the letters in the center of a red octagon-shaped cutout. Next, glue the stop sign near the top of a sheet of poster board. Then list the questions below the stop sign as shown. **Writing process**

STOP

Does what you've written make sense?
Do you have a topic sentence?
Did you indent each paragraph?
Did you use capital letters where they were needed?
Did you punctuate correctly where needed? Is your paper neatly written?
If you answered yes to all these questions, GO ahead and turn in your writing!

CARE TO SHARE?

To make sure all your budding authors have opportunities to share their work, designate a special chair in your classroom the "Author's Share Chair." List each student's name on a dry-erase board. Attach a dry-erase pen to the board and then place the board near the chair. When a child decides to share her writing with the rest of the class, direct her to circle her name on the board. At the beginning or end of your scheduled writing time, allow several students whose names are circled to sit in the chair and share their writings. After each writer shares, make a check beside her name to show that she has shared. When all the names have been checked, erase the board and begin again. **Writing process**

W.R.I.T.E.

Keep writers focused by displaying a poster such as the one shown. Discuss with the class what each part of the acronym means. Then, before each new writing assignment, have students answer the questions as a prewriting activity! **Writing process**

Writer—Who is telling the story and from what point of view?

Reader—Who will be the audience for the story? How will you direct your writing to them?

Intent—Why are you writing this story, letter, or informational article?

Topic—What is it that you are writing about? Stick to one subject.

Expressive words—What specific words will you use to write about this topic?

Spin a Yarn!

List on the board different topics for writers to choose from; then group students by topic. Give each group a separate paper bag filled with long lengths of yarn. Each child takes a turn selecting a different yarn length from the bag and sharing with his group what he could write about. As he talks, he wraps the yarn around his finger. When the yarn runs out, his time is up, and the next group member takes a turn. When everyone in the group has shared, each child returns to his desk and begins to write! **Writing process**

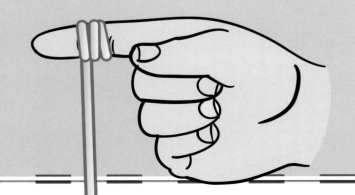

THE ART OF DECIPHERING

Have students scour magazines and newspapers for examples of charts; pictographs; and circle, line, bar, and stem-and-leaf graphs and then cut out and mount each example on a different sheet of construction paper. Give a different graph or chart to each child, directing her to write a paragraph explaining how to read it and understand the information it provides. For example, a student explaining the steps of long division in a flow chart should first state the chart's purpose and then its flow according to the direction of the arrows. Display the completed paragraphs next to the charts and graphs they explain on a bulletin board titled "Clearing the Air About Charts and Graphs." **Expository**

A Rendezvous for Two

Give each pair of students a small-scale city or county map. Each partner chooses a different starting location on the map. Then the pair selects a meeting place on the map. Each partner writes directions that explain how he will get to the meeting place from his starting location. Afterward, the partners read each other's directions, testing them for accuracy. If desired, follow up with the reproducible on page 94. **Expository**

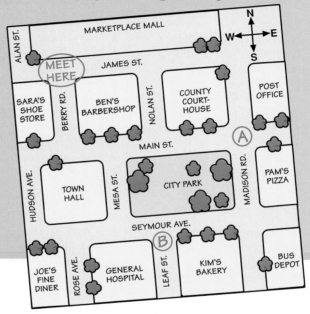

Favorite Fruits of Elementary School Students

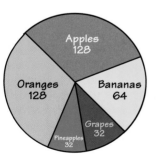

The purpose of this graph is to show ~~~~ Deb

Back-to-Back Directions

Have each child write detailed steps explaining how to do something such as make a paper airplane or draw a clown. Then have him sit back-to-back with a classmate and read his steps aloud to his partner. The partner follows the oral directions and gives the completed project to the writer when he is finished. The writer assesses whether the final product turned out as expected and why or why not. It'll be instantly clear why it's so important to be specific when writing instructions! **Expository**

Oops! That's not how it's supposed to look.

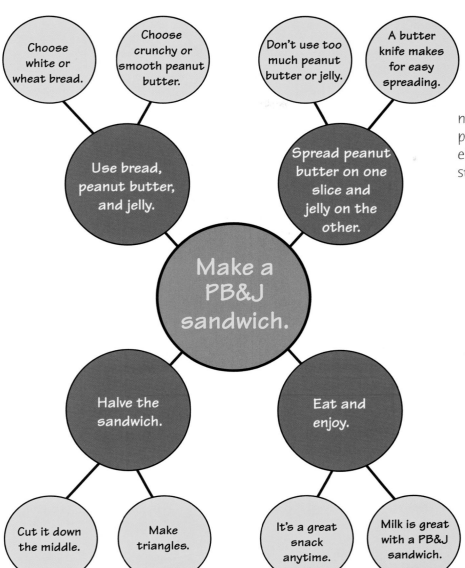

Colorful Clustering

Give each child one sheet of 11" x 14" newsprint and 13 die-cut construction paper circles—one red, four blue, and eight yellow. Then have him follow the steps below. **Expository**

1. Write your writing topic on the red circle and glue it to the center of your newsprint.

2. Write four supporting details about your topic each on a different blue circle.

3. Glue each blue circle to the newsprint around the red circle.

4. Draw a line from the red circle to each blue circle.

5. Elaborate on every supporting detail by writing additional information on each of the yellow circles.

6. Glue each yellow circle around its corresponding blue circle, drawing a line from each yellow circle to the blue circle.

7. Refer to the organizer to write a paragraph.

Circle labels (organizer)

- Choose white or wheat bread.
- Choose crunchy or smooth peanut butter.
- Don't use too much peanut butter or jelly.
- A butter knife makes for easy spreading.
- Use bread, peanut butter, and jelly.
- Spread peanut butter on one slice and jelly on the other.
- **Make a PB&J sandwich.**
- Halve the sandwich.
- Eat and enjoy.
- Cut it down the middle.
- Make triangles.
- It's a great snack anytime.
- Milk is great with a PB&J sandwich.

FROM THREE TO ONE

What do you get when students are challenged to mix a trio of sports? A how-to writing activity that could become a new recess game! Brainstorm with the class a list of different sports. Next, have each child work with a partner to write directions explaining how to play a game that combines some parts of any three of the sports. When the partners are finished, have them share their work with the class and answer questions their classmates might have about how the game is played. The fewer the questions, the better the writing job! **Expository**

Thoroughly Modern Fairy Tales

To practice narrative writing, challenge each of your students to modernize a fairy tale. Give each child a copy of page 92. Next, have her choose a favorite fairy tale on which to base a story written in first or third person. Explain that the student should write a tale similar to its original but in a present-day setting that features current fashions and modern conveniences. For example, a child could have Cinderella arrive at the ball in a limousine and wearing a gown designed by a popular designer. Cinderella could dance until midnight to the sounds of a popular rock band and leave behind a satin evening shoe. As a follow-up, the writer could transform her story into a picture book to share with a younger class or student. **Narrative**

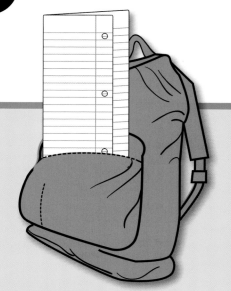

Begin at the End!

Here's a tip for helping a student who rambles and strays from his story's topic. Before he starts to write, suggest that he decide how he wants the story to end. By knowing how the story will conclude, he can plan the events that lead up to it! **Narrative**

Story ending: Alex will find out that his mom sprayed the ants in his room with bug killer because she did not know they were for his science project.

Events leading up to the ending:
-
-
-

I'M OFF TO...

Where would a student head if she could go to any place she wished? Would she go to a friend's sleepover? Or would she go hiking, to gymnastics practice, or to her grandma's house for the weekend? To find out, give each child a copy of the backpack pattern on page 93. Have her color the backpack, cut it out, and then cut a slit along the dotted line. On another sheet of paper, have her write a story that tells where she's going, what she'll put in the backpack, and what she'll do while there. Then have her fold the story and place it in the backpack's opening. Add the backpacks to a display where the stories will be easy for students to grab, unfold, and read. **Narrative**

WHAT A WHOPPER!

Headlines will become tall tales at this narrative-writing center! Place colorful markers and chart paper at a center. Glue interesting newspaper headlines onto separate strips of tagboard; then mount the strips on a wall at the center. To use the center, a child copies a headline on the chart paper with a marker as a story title and then writes the beginning of a tale. The next child to use the center adds on to the tale with a marker of a different color. When a story is finished, a volunteer types it and adds it to a class book titled "Tall Tales From Today's Headlines." **Narrative**

Living in a Colorless World

What would it be like to live in a world without color? To find out, each child creates a scene by gluing cutouts of either his own pencil drawings or black-and-white magazine pictures to a sheet of black, white, or gray construction paper. He studies the completed picture and imagines what it would be like to live in a black-and-white world. Then he writes a personal narrative about what such an experience would be like and shares it with the class. **Narrative**

Tubular Tales

For a time filler that gives students practice with narrative writing, have each child bring in a toilet paper tube decorated with colorful gift wrap. Next, have him write a story starter such as "It was a cold, moonless night" on a sheet of paper, roll up the paper, and put it inside the tube. Collect the tubes and store them in a basket. When you need to fill extra minutes before a lesson, randomly pass out the tubes and have each child add to the existing story until time is up. When a student completes a story, post it on a display for everyone to read. Be sure the child who finishes a story writes a new story starter and puts it in the tube as a replacement! **Narrative**

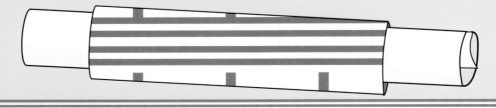

WRITING WARM-UP

Begin your next writing session with this challenging exercise aimed at fine-tuning each student's descriptive-writing skills. Explain that each child will be writing a paragraph about a specific experience. Have the student select a topic from the list shown. After he has selected his topic, explain that he cannot use certain words in his paragraph. For example, if he chooses to write a paragraph about making a banana split, do not allow him to use the words *banana, ice cream,* or *spoon* so that he has to describe those items in a different way. Inform each student of the words he cannot use; then challenge him to write his paragraph. Descriptive

Topic	Words Not to Use
brushing teeth	toothpaste, water, toothbrush, bathroom
making a bowl of cereal	milk, pour, spoon, cereal, bowl
riding a bike	pedal, brake, seat, bike
making a banana split	banana, ice cream, spoon

Descriptive Duos

Descriptive writing requires lots of practice. Take a different approach by having students describe a picture in two different ways for two entirely different purposes. Have students cut out interesting magazine pictures and mount them onto sheets of construction paper. Then have each child choose a different picture, such as a dog curled up asleep, from the collection. Direct him to first write a paragraph describing his subject in a positive way (the dog as a beloved pet) and another paragraph that portrays his subject in a negative way (the same dog as the culprit who just chewed Mom's shoe). Finally, have each student make Wanted posters for his two paragraphs. Direct him to copy his two paragraphs side by side on the bottom half of a 9" x 12" sheet of white construction paper, leaving space at the top to illustrate the subject as it is described in each paragraph. Display the projects on a bulletin board titled "Descriptive Duos." Descriptive

YUMMY DETAILS

To spark students' interest in descriptive writing, just say "ice cream!" Then give each child a copy of page 96 to use as a guide for planning a paragraph that describes his favorite ice-cream sundae. If desired, allow students to share their descriptions during a sundae party while you play the role of a roving reporter for the Food Channel! **Descriptive**

SECRET SNACKS

Ask parents to send in a variety of prepackaged snack foods. Place one snack in a separate paper bag for each student. Give each child a bag and have her secretly look inside the bag, touch and smell the snack, and then eat the snack, listening to the sounds she hears as she chews. Have her also think about what her tongue is feeling and sensing as she enjoys the snack. Then have her write a paragraph with sentences that describe the snack in a creative way without naming it. For example, "It looks like a small bright sun in my hand." As students share their mystery paragraphs aloud, have the class try to guess what each child's snack was! **Descriptive**

"SODA-LICIOUS"

Brainstorm with students a list of tasty soda, juice, or powdered-drink flavors. If desired, bring in samples for students to taste. Each child then chooses two or more flavors that when combined could make an interesting new soda. He writes a paragraph describing what tasting this new drink would be like, including what the drink looks like, smells like, tastes like, sounds like while it's being poured, and feels like while it's inside the mouth. When students share their descriptions, be prepared to hear phrases marketers might use to advertise future products! **Descriptive**

WIN ME OVER

Turn your classroom into a persuasive writers' forum. As a class, brainstorm topics that can be argued from a pro and con standpoint. Write your students' suggestions on the board as sentences. For example, write "Teenagers should have a 10:00 PM curfew on weekdays." Afterward, pair students; then have each pair choose one of the topics from the board and decide which partner will be for the subject and which partner will be against it. Direct each partner to write a persuasive paragraph that gives at least three reasons, facts, or examples that support his view and then share it with the class. After hearing each argument, have the class think about the issues raised by each partner and vote to determine the winning position. **Persuasive**

YOU TALKED ME INTO IT!

Television commercials constantly influence viewers with persuasive tactics. Utilize some of this medium's methods by having students transform persuasive paragraphs into television commercials of their own. Assign each child a topic that can be argued from either a for or against position, such as "A Woman Should Be Elected President." Have each student choose a stance and state it in the topic sentence of his paragraph. Explain that he should then support his position with three detail sentences that give reasons, facts, or examples. After editing, give each student one sheet of 9" x 12" white construction paper. Instruct him to draw a big-screen television on his paper. Copy his paragraph onto the screen and then color and cut out the television. Display the colorful cutouts on a bulletin board titled "Talk Me Into It!" **Persuasive**

CONVINCE A FOURTH GRADER

As an end-of-the-year project, challenge each of your current students to write a picture book that will persuade an upcoming class member to be successful in fifth grade. Direct each child to fill the pages of his book with illustrated advice and examples that an upcoming fifth grader could appreciate. For example, suggest that one page be devoted to giving advice about getting along with the teacher, one be about developing good study habits, and another be about consequences! Suggest that the student title his book "How to Be a Successful Fifth Grader." During the last week of school, have him present his book to a current fourth grader as a gift. **Persuasive**

How to Be a Successful Fifth Grader

PERSUADE ME!

Discover how convincing students can be when they feel strongly about an issue! List different debatable topics such as those shown on the board. Poll the class to find out how students currently stand on each issue. Next, ask each child to choose one of the topics and talk about it with people outside of class to get several different points of view. Then have each student write an essay about his chosen topic, including three or more reasons why someone with a different opinion about the topic should change her mind and think the way he does. When all the persuasive pieces have been presented, poll students again to see whether anyone experienced a change of heart! **Persuasive**

Fifth graders should be in bed by 9 PM.

School should be year-round.

Fifth graders should work for an allowance.

The driving age should be lowered to 13.

Students of any age should be allowed to choose their school.

LETTER TO THE LIBRARIAN

Have each child imagine he has a science or social studies report due at the end of the week. Then have him choose one item from the wish list shown and write a letter to the school librarian asking for permission to check out the book(s) he needs to complete the assignment. Remind students to include several reasons why they should be allowed to check out books. After each writer shares his letter aloud, have the class play the role of the librarian and decide, by voting, whether to honor the student's request. The more convincing the letter, the more positive the vote should be! **Persuasive**

Wish List

- Student wants to renew a book again even though the library's rule is that a book can only be renewed once.

- Student wants to check out a book even though he lost the last library book he borrowed.

- Student wants to check out a book even though he owes a fine on another book.

- Student wants to check out five books even though the limit is three books.

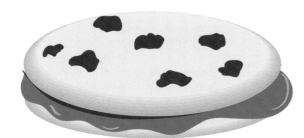

PLEASE PUT IT ON THE MENU

Ask each child to write a letter to your school's cafeteria manager, requesting in a convincing way that a specific item be added to the lunch or breakfast menu. Require that the request include at least three reasons. When the letters have been delivered, ask that the recipient reply to the class with a single letter. Who knows, perhaps some of those items will appear on the menu at a later date! **Persuasive**

QUATRAINS

Write the following quatrain on the board:

> I arrive at school at eight.
> Never once have I been late.
> By seven o'clock I'm at the bus stop
> Or riding to school with my dear pop.

Point out that the first two lines rhyme, as do the second two lines. Explain that it is also acceptable to instead have the first and third lines and the second and fourth lines of a quatrain rhyme. Pair students; then have each pair write its own poem—featuring at least two quatrains—about a typical day at school. After students have finished writing, have each student pair present its poem orally. Then compile all the poems in a binder for your classroom library. **Poetry**

INVENTED POETRY

Introduce invented poetry with an activity that invites giggles. First, share the example of alphabet poetry in the illustration. Next, explain that an alphabet poem uses a section of the alphabet as the outline for a humorous list poem. Then challenge each student to choose any section of the alphabet and create her own list poem. **Poetry**

All
Boys
Consume
Delicious
Eggplant
For
Good
Health!

LIMERICKS

Students could howl over this humorous poetry-writing exercise. Begin by explaining the standard limerick rhyming pattern: lines one, two, and five rhyme and have three stressed syllables, and lines three and four rhyme and have two stressed syllables. Next, share the following limerick:

> There once was a man named Thad
> Who went along with every new fad.
> He got a tattoo,
> Then dyed his hair blue.
> The final result was quite sad.

After sharing the limerick, direct each student to write his name at the top of a sheet of paper. Then have him write the first line of a limerick about any subject. Next, ask each child to pass his paper to the student on his right. Instruct each student to then write a second line for the limerick he receives. Continue in this manner until all five lines of the limerick have been written. Then have the last student return the paper to its original owner. Conclude by having each child share his resulting limerick with the class. **Poetry**

Jake
There once was a girl named Kay
Who went outside to play every day.
But she tripped on a log
And kissed a tree frog.
Now "ribbit" is all she can say!

COLOR POEMS

What color is a good day? To answer this question, challenge students to write couplets that connect colors and emotions. If possible, read aloud *My Many Colored Days* by Dr. Seuss. Then ask students to consider the question, "If emotions had color, what color would each emotion be?" To help students make specific responses, distribute colorful markers, pencils, or crayons that are labeled with unusual names—such as *watermelon* and *marigold*. Next, give each child a copy of the reproducible on page 97 to complete as directed. As he completes the sheet, suggest that he use interesting color names and model his couplet after those in Dr. Seuss's book. If desired, have each student choose one of his couplets to copy onto an appropriately colored, irregular shape of paper. Then display the shapes over black background paper on a bulletin board titled "Our Many Colored Days." **Poetry**

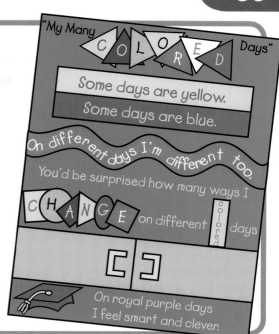

"My Many COLORED Days"
Some days are yellow.
Some days are blue.
On different days I'm different too.
You'd be surprised how many ways I
CHANGE on different colored days
[ ]
On royal purple days I feel smart and clever.

COUPLETS

Provide each student with a magazine, glue, and scissors. Direct her to cut out any ten words from her magazine. Explain that each word will become part of a different couplet—a two-line verse form that expresses one thought and often rhymes. Write the two couplets below on the board and discuss them with your students. Then direct each child to write ten couplets, gluing a cutout word at the end of one line in each couplet as shown. Invite your students to share their couplets with the class; then post them on a bulletin board titled "Crazy About Couplets." **Poetry**

I rode the Ferris wheel at the fair
While the whipping wind blew *my hair.*

The leaves fell slowly from the tree,
Having reached the end of a long journey.

Last week I learned to skate.
I was proud because it really felt **GREAT!**

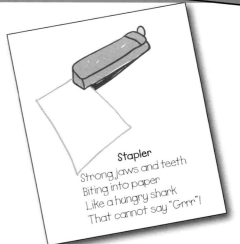

Stapler
Strong jaws and teeth
Biting into paper
Like a hungry shark
That cannot say "Grrr"!

FREE VERSE

Everyday objects are the inspiration for this rhyme-writing activity. If possible, read aloud several poems from Dee Lillegard's *Hello School!: A Classroom Full of Poems* as fun examples of poems that have been written about common classroom items. Next, have each child choose a classroom object and brainstorm a list of sensory words and phrases that describe that object. Then have him write and illustrate a poem about the object, incorporating some of the words and phrases from his list, to share aloud with the class. As they listen to the rhymes, students are bound to agree that poetry is everywhere! **Poetry**

Journal Prompts

September

September is Self-Improvement Month. This month celebrates the importance of lifelong learning and self-improvement. Name something about yourself that you'd like to improve and then list the steps you will take to do it.

Apples abound this month! How many dishes can you think of that are made with apples? List them.

Write a description of a pet you have now, one you have had in the past, or one that you would like to have in the future. Include a sentence that recognizes the pet's best qualities.

The summer has come to an end, and it's time for heading back to school. If you were commissioned to design the ultimate school, what would your school be like?

The planet Neptune was first discovered on September 23, 1846. Pretend that a unique species lives on the planet. Describe the physical characteristics of these creatures and then tell what a day in their lives is like.

October

National Cookie Month is in October. Describe the best cookie imaginable.

Create a new monster for Halloween. Describe what the monster looks like; then tell what it will do on Halloween night.

Peace, Friendship and Good Will Week falls annually the last seven days in October. Its purpose is to establish good human relations throughout the world. Write a letter to the people of the world telling them five ways they can make the world a friendlier place to live.

Think of the most unorganized person you know. Describe what this person can do to get himself or herself organized.

Germany, once a divided country, was reunited on October 3, 1990. How would you feel if the United States were a divided nation? How do you think your life would be different if this happened?

November

National Authors' Day is observed on November 1. Write a letter to your favorite author telling what you like about his or her books. Give the author some suggestions on what he or she could write about in an upcoming book.

November 3 is the birthday of John Montague, the Earl of Sandwich. What did he invent? The sandwich, of course! Write a recipe for a new and unusual sandwich.

Mickey Mouse first appeared in a cartoon on November 18, 1928. Draw a cartoon featuring a new kind of mouse.

Hunting is a very popular sport this time of year. Write a paragraph telling why you are for or against this sport.

Write about your favorite family Thanksgiving tradition.

The Christmas shopping season traditionally begins the day after Thanksgiving. If you could get the perfect gift for everyone in your family, what gift would you get each member and why?

December

Many people celebrate the holiday season by decorating a freshly cut tree. Imagine you are a tree that is just about to be cut down. Write a dialogue between yourself and a tree cutter.

Emily Dickinson is considered to be one of the United States' greatest poets. Most of her poems—published after her death in 1886—were found written on such things as scraps of paper and the backs of envelopes. Write your own poem on an unusual material in honor of her birthday (December 10, 1830).

Underdog Day falls annually on the third Friday in December. Name a book character that you think is an *underdog,* or someone predicted to lose. Tell why you think this character is an underdog.

Winter begins in December with the coming of the *winter solstice,* the shortest day of the year. Curling up in front of a fire with a good book, steam from a cup of hot cocoa—what are some of the things that remind you of winter?

December 31 is New Year's Eve. Before setting goals for the new year, list all the things you have accomplished this past year.

Journal Prompts

January

Begin the New Year with some innovative thinking! Describe an innovative way of doing an ordinary activity or a new invention that you'd like to create.

Z Day on January 1 honors people whose names begin with the letter *Z* and are usually thought of as last. Describe what your day would be like if everything suddenly started going in reverse order.

January 11 is International Thank You Day. Write a letter to yourself expressing thanks for something you did for someone else.

Civil rights leader, minister, and Nobel Peace Prize winner Dr. Martin Luther King Jr. was born on January 15, 1929. Explain what the word *prejudice* means to you.

Need an excuse to just do nothing all day long? Since National Nothing Day is celebrated in January, here's your chance! Describe a day in which you don't have to do anything except what you want.

February

National Pet Dental Health Month is celebrated in February. Write a broadcast for a local radio station reminding pet owners of the importance of good dental care for their pets.

February 4 is the birthday of Charles Lindbergh, the first person to fly solo across the Atlantic Ocean without stopping. Imagine you are flying from New York to Paris. Write about the things you will think about during the flight.

Many animals have a difficult time finding adequate food and shelter during the cold winter months. Write about the kind of animal you'd like to be during the wintertime. What would you do to survive?

February is American Heart Month. Write a heart-to-heart conversation that you'd like to have with a parent about exercising and eating healthier foods.

The Chinese celebrate their New Year during the month of February. If you could go back to the old year and change one thing, what would it be?

March

People magazine was launched on March 4, 1974. Imagine yourself on the cover of the magazine 20 years from now. Why would you be chosen as the magazine's Person of the Year?

Theodor Seuss Geisel, better known as Dr. Seuss, was born on March 2, 1904. Write the title of your favorite Dr. Seuss book and then tell why it is your favorite.

Write about what life would be like if wearing the color green were made illegal.

On March 18, 1995, Michael Jordan announced he was returning to professional basketball after resigning 17 months earlier. Is there something you quit that you later wished you hadn't? Explain.

List the things about spring that make you feel happy.

April

April Fools' Day is observed on April 1. Who in your family has the best sense of humor? Describe something funny this person said or did.

Eggs are a popular food this month. Name a food that you absolutely hate. Describe the taste, texture, appearance, and smell of the food.

Earth Day was first celebrated on April 22, 1970, with the slogan "Give Earth a Chance." Its purpose was to bring attention to why we need to care for the earth. Think of a slogan for this year's Earth Day; then tell how you would promote the day.

National Library Week is celebrated in April. If you could ask anyone in the world to read a book to you, whom would you ask? What book would you read together, and why would you choose that book?

In 1910, President William Howard Taft began a new sports tradition by throwing out the first baseball of the season. If you could be a star at any sport, which one would it be and why?

May

The United States' premier horse race, the Kentucky Derby, first began on May 17, 1875. Describe an animal that you consider to be truly beautiful.

National Teacher Day falls annually on the Tuesday of the first full week in May. List all the duties your teacher has to perform within a year. Then pay tribute to your teacher through a kind word or action.

Limericks, funny five-lined poems, were made popular by a man named Edward Lear. Limericks follow a specific rhyming pattern: the first, second, and fifth lines rhyme, and the third and fourth lines rhyme. In honor of Lear's May 12 birthday, write a limerick of your own.

Memorial Day (the last Monday in May) pays tribute to those who have died, especially those who have died in battle. Do you think the United States should get involved in wars between other countries? Why or why not?

With the end of May approaching, summer is in the forecast! Plan a summer vacation for yourself and your best friend.

I've a Story to Weave

title

What kind of story will you write?
- [ ] A short story
- [ ] A tall tale
- [ ] A fable
- [ ] A humorous tale
- [ ] Other: _____
  _____

When does the story happen?
Name the year, the season, and the time of day.

_____
_____
_____
_____
_____

Where does the story take place?

_____
_____
_____
_____
_____

Who are the characters in your story?

_____
_____
_____
_____

What is the hero or heroine's main goal?
- [ ] Rescue someone
- [ ] Find a treasure
- [ ] Solve a mystery
- [ ] Escape danger
- [ ] Win a race, prize, or contest
- [ ] Return safely from a trip
- [ ] Achieve fame
- [ ] Invent something
- [ ] Other: _____

Who or what gets in the hero's way?

_____
_____
_____
_____
_____

What problems does the hero have to solve to reach his goal?

_____
_____
_____
_____

What happens to the hero and the other main characters at the climax?

_____
_____
_____
_____
_____

What is the theme of your story? (What lesson or moral does it teach?)

_____
_____
_____

Note to the teacher: Use with "Thoroughly Modern Fairy Tales" on page 82.

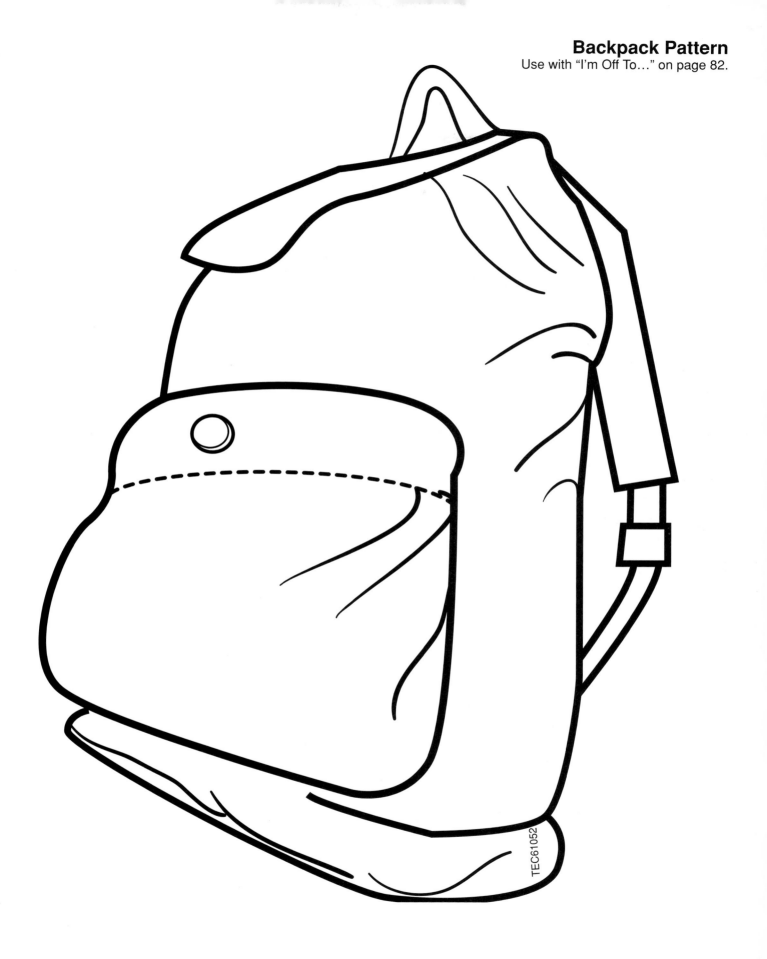

TEC61052

Meet Me!

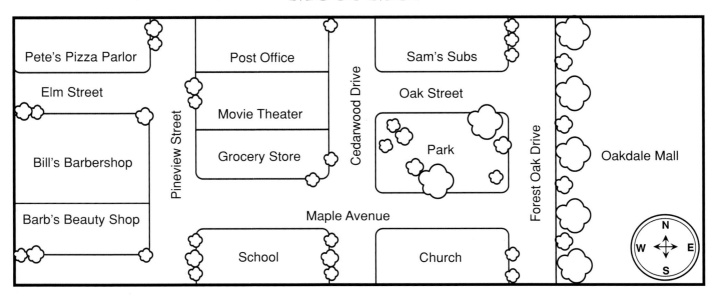

A. Study the map to find out how you could travel from Pete's Pizza Parlor to meet two friends at the mall. With a pencil, trace the path you would take. Then write a paragraph explaining this path on the lines provided. Use time-order words such as *first, next, then,* and *finally* to show the order of your steps.

_____

_____

_____

_____

_____

_____

B. Pretend that you and your friends are going to a movie after leaving the mall. On the lines provided, write numbered steps that tell how to get from the mall to the movie theater.

_____

_____

_____

_____

_____

_____

©The Mailbox® • Superbook® • TEC61052

94   **Note to the teacher:** Use with "A Rendezvous for Two" on page 80.

Piecing It All Together

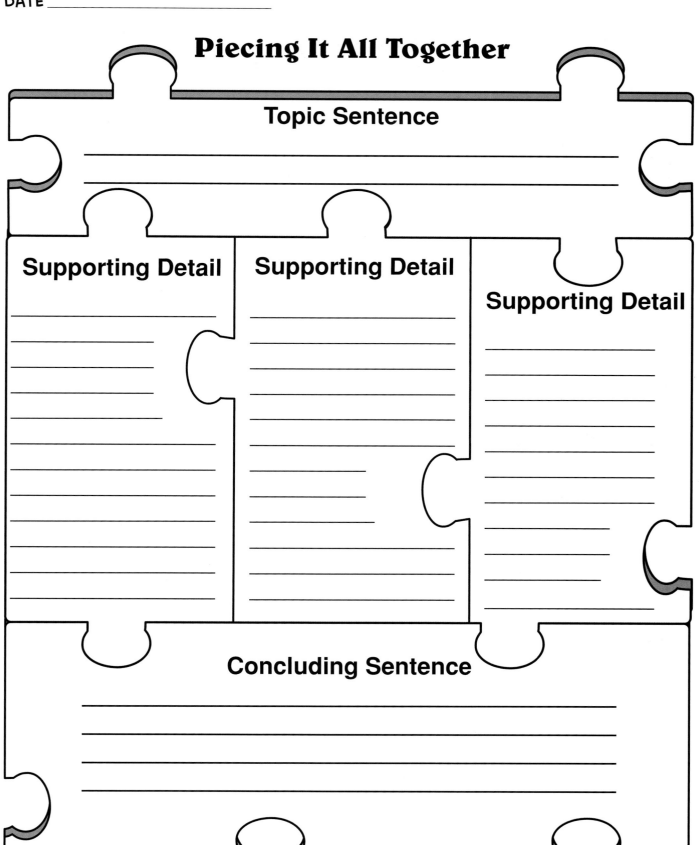

Topic Sentence

Supporting Detail

Supporting Detail

Supporting Detail

Concluding Sentence

Yummy Details!

Describe your favorite ice-cream sundae by writing words
or phrases in each part of the wheel.

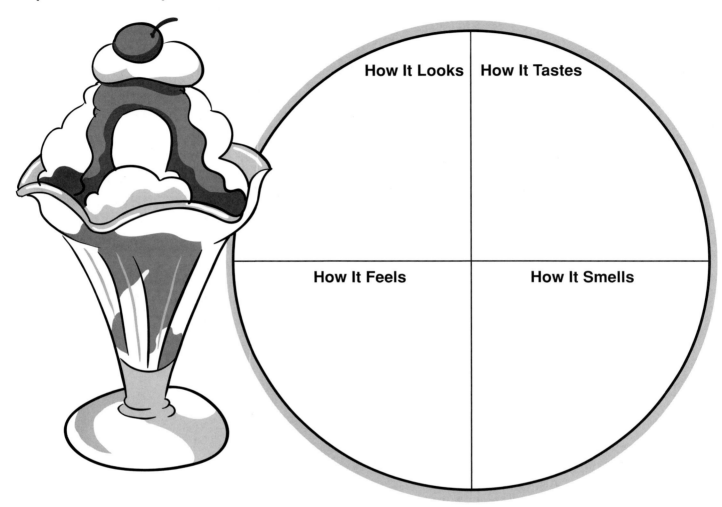

	How It Looks	How It Tastes
	How It Feels	How It Smells

Now follow the steps below to write a detailed paragraph that describes your ice-cream sundae.

1. Begin with a topic sentence.

2. Use the words and phrases on the wheel to help you write four detailed sentences
   about what the sundae looks like, tastes like, feels like, and smells like (one
   sentence for each sense).

3. End with a concluding sentence.

NAME_____

DATE_____

How Many Colors Do You Feel?

Make the ovals below into faces that show the moods you sometimes experience. Label the ovals. Then use markers or crayons to color each face the color you think goes with that feeling. Next to each face, write a rhyming couplet that describes a day of that color for you.

Is a bad day blue for you?
On a bad day, I just cry—boo hoo.

If my day is shockingly pink,
Bright are the thoughts that I think.

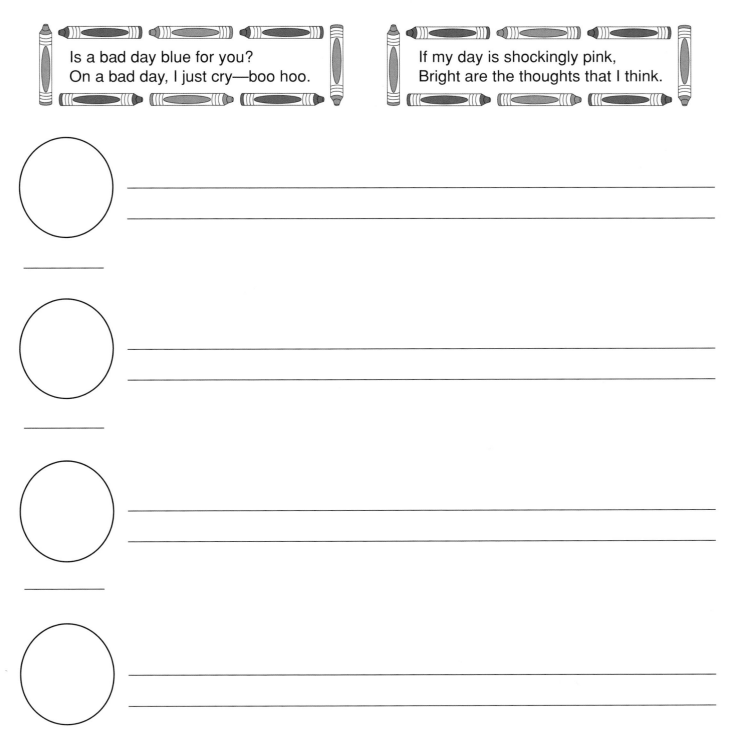

Note to the teacher: Use with "Color Poems" on page 89.

The ABCs of Report Writing

Read the information listed beside each block below. As you complete each part of your report, color that block to show that you've completed that step.

Assemble Resources A

After you've chosen a topic that interests you, gather information about it. Use reference books—such as dictionaries, encyclopedias, almanacs, and atlases—and other nonfiction books on your topic.

Begin Note Taking B

Write down each question you have about your topic on a different index card. Use the resources you gathered to research the answers to your questions. Write your answers, or notes, on each index card using short sentences in your own words.

Construct an Outline C

Plan your report by making an outline. Write the topic of your report as the title. Think of the topic of each question on your notecards as a main idea on your outline. Decide which main idea you will tell about first and write it next to the roman numeral I. Write your second main idea next to the roman numeral II, and so on. Under each main idea, write the answers to your questions as details. Write each detail next to a different capital letter: A, B, C, and so on.

Draft a Rough Copy D

Read the first main idea in your outline. Write it as the topic sentence of your first paragraph. Use the details in your outline to add sentences that give details about that main idea. Start a new paragraph for each new main idea and its supporting details.

Edit and Revise E

Read your report to yourself and think about how you could improve it. Ask yourself questions such as those shown below. Use editing marks to make changes on your paper.

Do I have interesting main-idea sentences, and did I indent each new paragraph?
Do my details tell more about the main-idea sentences?
Did I use my own words, and are my sentences clear and complete?
Did I spell my words correctly?
Did I use punctuation marks correctly?

Finalize Your Paper F

Type or neatly write a final copy of your work. Check the copy one last time for correct spelling, capitalization, and punctuation. Place your report in a cover to keep it neat and organized.

Give Others Credit G

Make a *bibliography,* or list, of the sources you used to write your report. List your sources alphabetically by the author's last name (or by the title if no author is given). Follow the example that shows an entry's correct order, capitalization, and punctuation. Place the bibliography at the end of your report.

For a book: Author (last name, first name). Title. City where the book was published: Name of publisher, copyright date. Example: Kroll, Steven. Pony Express! New York: Scholastic Inc., 1996.
Note: Ask your teacher or media specialist for help writing a bibliography entry for an encyclopedia, a magazine, a film, or a pamphlet.

Hold a Presentation H

Remember your audience! Look at your listeners as you share your report. Speak slowly and clearly. Create a visual aid—such as a poster, graph, or model—to make your presentation more exciting.

Number Concepts and Place Value

160,539

Numbers in a Flash!

This fast-paced activity will have students working at top speed to record numbers to the hundred thousands place. Tell students that you will flash a six-digit number to the class, one place value at a time, by quickly holding up your fingers. Explain that the first number you flash is for the hundred thousands place, the second for the ten thousands place, and so on. Have each student record each number on a sheet of paper as it is flashed. Then call on a student volunteer to read the number aloud. If he reads the number correctly, invite him to flash the next set of numbers for his classmates to record. **Place value**

Spinning and Rounding

Reinforce your students' rounding skills with this whole-class game. Use the pattern on page 101 to create a spinner on a blank overhead transparency as shown in the illustration. Project the spinner on your overhead projector; then select one student to spin the spinner for the entire game. Next, divide your class into groups of two or three students. Direct each group to copy a place-value chart to the hundred millions place onto a sheet of paper and have another sheet handy for recording answers. **Rounding**

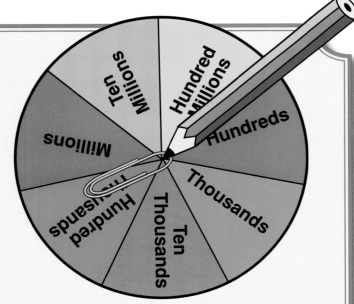

To play the game:
1. Call out a large number, such as 234,670,823.
2. Instruct each group to write that number correctly in its place-value chart.
3. Have the selected student spin the spinner.
4. Give the groups one minute to round the number to the place value shown on the spinner and write an answer on their second sheet of paper. For example, if the spinner pointed to "Hundred Thousands," each group would round 234,670,823 to 234,700,000 and record it on paper.
5. After one minute, call, "Pencils down." Visit each group to check its answer, giving each group one point for a correct answer.
6. Continue calling numbers for a desired number of rounds. Declare the team with the most points at the end of the game the winner.

Cross the Board!

Give each pair of students a copy of page 103 and two game markers. Have the duo cut apart the gameboard and spinner and write a number between 2 and 50 in each gameboard box. Using a pencil, a paper clip, and the spinner, Player 1 spins and places his game marker in a corresponding box on the bottom row. If there is not a box that corresponds to the spin or the only corresponding box is occupied by another game marker, the player's turn is over. Play alternates with players moving, if possible, one step in any direction with each spin. The first player to reach the top of the gameboard wins! **Prime and composite numbers**

CROSS THE BOARD

Finish

25	11	7	13	47
3	49	22	35	40
23	29	2	17	12
10	8	⬤	31	18
⬤	30	15	5	38

Start

Mobile Numbers

Pair students and have each duo cut out a copy of the place-value strips and cards on page 102. Direct each twosome to scramble its cards and stack them facedown. Also have each student place a strip in front of him. To play, each student draws six cards. Then each player simultaneously arranges the cards on his strip, attempting to create the number with the largest value possible. Once the numbers are created, each player reads his number aloud. The player with the larger number receives a point. The twosome then shuffles the cards and plays again. The player with more points after a set amount of time wins the game. **Place value**

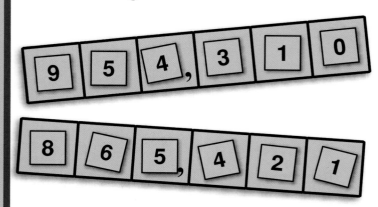

Create a Number

Pair students; then write a decimal point and three different digits—such as 4, 6, and 8—on the board. Challenge each pair to write all 24 possible numbers that can be formed from those three digits and the decimal point. Explain that each digit should be used only once in each number and that no number should be repeated. After writing all 24 possible numbers, challenge each pair to list the numbers in greatest to least order. Vary the activity by changing or adding to the digits that are used or by removing the decimal to compare just whole numbers. **Comparing**

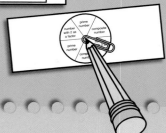

864.	6.84
846.	6.48
684.	4.86
648.	4.68
486.	.864
468.	.846
86.4	.684
84.6	.648
68.4	.486
64.8	.468
48.6	
46.8	
8.64	
8.46	

Check out the skill-building reproducible on page 104.

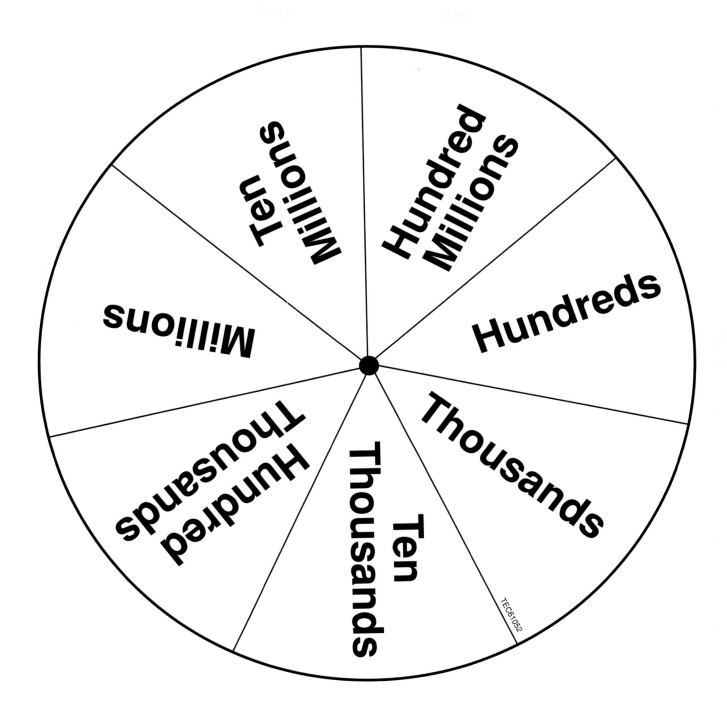

TEC61052

Place-Value Strips and Cards

Use with "Mobile Numbers" on page 100.

0 TEC61052	**0** TEC61052
1 TEC61052	**1** TEC61052
2 TEC61052	**2** TEC61052
3 TEC61052	**3** TEC61052
4 TEC61052	**4** TEC61052
5 TEC61052	**5** TEC61052
6 TEC61052	**6** TEC61052
7 TEC61052	**7** TEC61052
8 TEC61052	**8** TEC61052
9 TEC61052	**9** TEC61052

CROSS THE BOARD

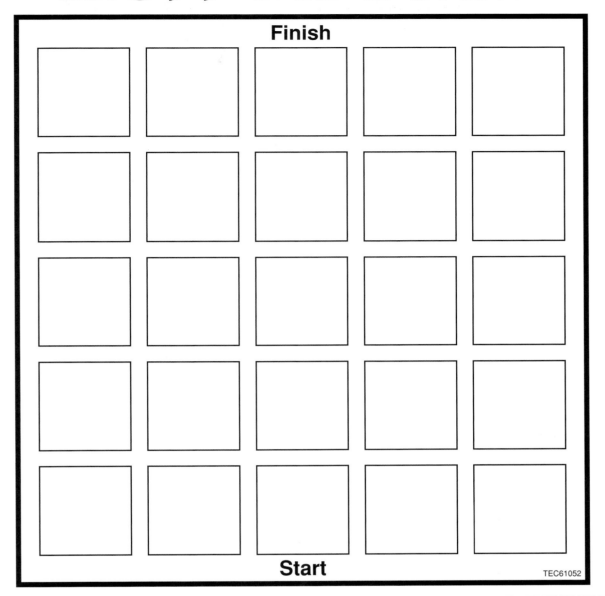

Finish

Start

TEC61052

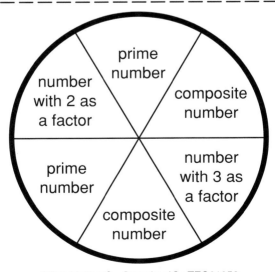

Note to the teacher: Use with "Cross the Board!" on page 100.

ALL AROUND TOWN

Round each number to the given place value.
Color the box with the correct answer.

1. 23,987 (hundreds) _____

2. 45.62 (tenths) _____

3. 0.637 (hundredths) _____

4. 801,699 (ten thousands) _____

5. 302.87 (tens) _____

6. 17.55 (ones) _____

7. 3,478.2 (thousands) _____

8. 44,681 (hundreds) _____

9. 592,302 (hundred thousands) _____

10. 45.097 (ones) _____

11. 15.264 (tens) _____

12. 46,203.4 (thousands) _____

13. 28.398 (tenths) _____

14. 1.298 (hundredths) _____

15. 846 (thousands) _____

16. 67,400 (ten thousands) _____

17. 0.612 (ones) _____

Market MOVIES CITYVILLE DEPARTMENT STORE Shoes Flowers

P	S	T	B	O	Y	S	E
46,999	46,000	0.64	24,000	600,000	1,000	45.6	45,000
T	A	R	T	K	G	E	L
45	44,700	28.4	28.45	1.3	1	3,000	70,000
R	D	S	H	N	O	Y	P
18	300	0	23,900	20	120	800,000	300.5

Where was Sally found at the end of the shopping day?
To find the answer to the question, write the letters from the
noncolored boxes in order on the lines below.

_____ _____ _____   _____ _____ _____ _____ _____

©The Mailbox® • Superbook® • TEC61052 • Key p. 310

Round-the-Room Review

Time is a factor in this whole-class game that reviews addition and subtraction! Choose a specific skill to be the game's focus, such as addition and subtraction to the hundred millions place or subtraction with or without zeros. Then give one index card to each child and have him write one addition or subtraction problem that uses that skill. Collect the cards and sequentially number each one in the upper left-hand corner. Then follow the directions shown to play the game.
Addition and subtraction

To play:
1. Have each student number a sheet of notebook paper from 1 to the number of index cards.
2. Give each child an index card.
3. Tell the student that he has one minute to solve the problem and record his answer next to the corresponding number on his paper.
4. After one minute say, "Pass." Then have him pass his card to the next student.
5. Continue play until each student has solved every card's problem. Check the answers together.

5
$$5,350,032 + 1,237,895$$

6
$$354,678,013 - 212,946,804$$

Check out the skill-building reproducible on page 107.

DOMINO DIFFERENCES

For this partner game, laminate a copy of the cards on page 106. Cut out the cards and place them at a center along with a set of double-six dominoes and wipe-off markers. Partners select markers and identical cards. To play, partners take turns choosing a domino. Each student writes either of the domino's numbers in any box on his card. Students continue selecting dominoes and recording numbers until each box is filled. Then each partner solves the problem on his card. The student whose problem has the smallest difference earns a point. Partners clean their cards and then start another round of the game. Play continues until one student earns a predetermined number of points. **Subtraction**

Decimal Jeopardy

In advance, draw a grid like the one shown on your board. Begin by dividing the class into two teams. Call Team 1 to the board, and have each member select the problem type and point value that he wishes to solve by signing his initials in the corresponding box. Remind students that they cannot put their initials in the same box as a teammate's. Repeat the process with Team 2, so that each box contains initials from a student on each team. (If you have an odd number of students or don't have enough students to fill the grid, allow some students to play twice.) Next, call a student pair to the board and have them turn away from the board and close their eyes. Then use the point value and problem type chosen by those students to write on the board two identical addition or subtraction problems involving decimals. On the count of three, each child turns around and solves her problem. The student who solves the problem correctly first earns the designated number of points for her team. Continue playing in this manner until each problem has been solved. The team with more points at the end of the game wins. **Decimal addition and subtraction**

Decimal Jeopardy

	3 digits	4 digits	5 digits	6 digits
5 points				
10 points				
15 points				
20 points				

Subtraction Cards

Use with "Domino Differences" on page 105.

TEC61052

TEC61052

TEC61052

TEC61052

TEC61052

TEC61052

©The Mailbox® • *Superbook*® • TEC61052

Hang Time

Add. Write the missing numbers in the boxes. Each time you use a number, cross it out on the map.

1. $\boxed{}\,9\,\boxed{}$
    $+\ 3\ \boxed{}\ 8$
    ―――――――
    $8\ \ 2\ \ 2$

2. $5\,\boxed{}\,\boxed{}$
    $+\ 3\ 2\ 8$
    ―――――――
    $\boxed{}\ 0\ \ 0$

3. $1,\boxed{}\,\boxed{}\,9$
    $+\ \ \ \ 8\ 5\ \boxed{}$
    ―――――――
    $\boxed{},\,5\ 9\ 5$

4. $2\,\boxed{}\,\boxed{}$
    $+\ \boxed{}\ 7\ 3$
    ―――――――
    $8\ \ 6\ \ 9$

5. $\boxed{},\boxed{}\,3\,5$
    $+\ 1\ ,\ 3\ 7\ \boxed{}$
    ―――――――
    $4\ ,\ 8\ \boxed{}\ 7$

6. $7\,,\boxed{}\,\boxed{}\,1$
    $+\ 2\ ,\ 1\ 3\ \boxed{}$
    ―――――――
    $\boxed{}\ ,\ 9\ 8\ 7$

7. $5\,,\boxed{}\,3\,\boxed{}$
    $+\ 2\ ,\ 2\ \boxed{}\ 5$
    ―――――――
    $\boxed{}\ ,\ 1\ 4\ 9$

8. $3\,\boxed{}\,3$
    $+\ 3\ 9\ 8$
    ―――――――
    $\boxed{}\ 0\ \ 1$

9. $\boxed{}\,,\,2\ 9\ 6$
    $+\ 3\ ,\boxed{}\,\boxed{}\,4$
    ―――――――
    $4\ ,\ 4\ 0\ 0$

10. $\boxed{}\,4\ 8$
    $+\ 3\ \boxed{}\,\boxed{}$
    ―――――――
    $1\ ,\ 1\ 7\ 1$

11. $\boxed{}\,6\,\boxed{}$
    $+\ 2\ \boxed{}\ 3$
    ―――――――
    $7\ \ 8\ \ 4$

12. $\boxed{}\,,\,1\,\boxed{}\,3$
    $+\ 1\ ,\ 7\ 9\ \boxed{}$
    ―――――――
    $8\ ,\ 9\ 7\ 1$

13. $6\,,\boxed{}\,3\ 7$
    $+\boxed{}\,,\,1\ 9\ 8$
    ―――――――
    $1\ 3\ ,\ 6\ \boxed{}\ 5$

14. $8\,,\boxed{}\,\boxed{}\,\boxed{}$
    $+\boxed{}\,,\,3\ 7\ 4$
    ―――――――
    $1\ 5\ ,\ 3\ 1\ 6$

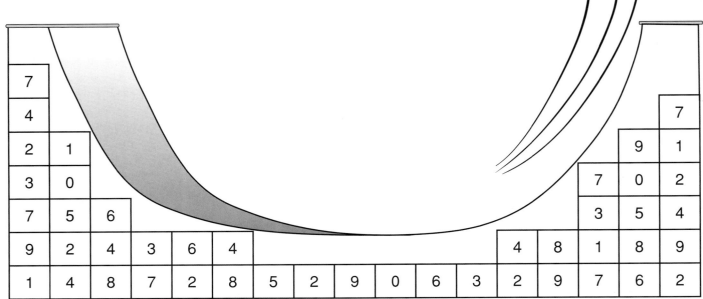

7														7
4													9	1
2	1											7	0	2
3	0											3	5	4
7	5	6									4	8	1	8	9
9	2	4	3	6	4									
1	4	8	7	2	8	5	2	9	0	6	3	2	9	7	6	2

Multiplication and Division

Spinning for Multiples

Put a new spin on reviewing multiples! Invite five students to come to the board and stand facing the class. Write a different digit from 1 to 10 on the board above each child's head. Instruct the remaining students, one at a time, to call out a two-digit number. Direct each student at the board to spin in place one time when a number is called that is a multiple of the number written above her head. If she does not spin when she should or spins at the wrong time, have that child sit down and select another to take her place. Everyone will want in on the action! **Multiples**

Let's start with 60!

Number		Factor to Subtract		Difference
60	–	20	=	40
40	–	10	=	30
30	–	15	=	15
15	–	5	=	10
10	–	2	=	8
8	–	4	=	4
4	–	2	=	2
2	–	1	=	1

Fun Factor

To begin this partner game, Player 1 records an even number from 30 to 100. Player 2 then thinks of a factor of the number Player 1 selected and subtracts it from Player 1's number. (Player 2 cannot choose the number itself as a factor.) Player 1 then records a factor for the remaining number and subtracts it. Play continues in this manner until the difference is 1. The player who reaches 1 first is the winner. **Factors**

Beach Ball Bash

Program an inflatable beach ball with different point values. Divide the class into teams and toss the ball to a student. Have the child who catches the ball announce the point value located under his left thumb. Next, call out a multiplication problem, such as 15 x 5, for all players to solve as quickly as possible, instructing them to raise their hands when they are finished. Allow the first child finished to share his answer. If the answer is correct, award the previously announced number of points to that player's team. If the answer is incorrect, toss the ball to another team and give the ball catcher a chance to solve the problem correctly to earn those points. Continue play until one group reaches a predetermined number of points. **Multiplication**

$5\overline{)555}$	$2\overline{)23}$	$2\overline{)24}$
$3\overline{)393}$	$8\overline{)56}$	$7\overline{)497}$
$4\overline{)848}$	$2\overline{)17}$	$2\overline{)633}$

Tic-Tac-Toe Math

Draw a tic-tac-toe game like the one shown on the board. Have each pair of students copy it on a sheet of paper. To play, Player 1 solves a problem in one square, and Player 2 checks his work using a calculator. If correct, Player 1 places an X in that square. If incorrect, Player 2 places an O in that square. Next, Player 2 takes a turn in the same manner, placing an O in the square if he solves the problem correctly. The first player to get three Xs or Os in a row is the winner. To play again, simply draw a new board with new problems. Division

Tag-Team Division

Divide your class into groups of four students. Each group forms a straight line facing the board. Explain that each group will work the same division problem and that each step of the division problem will be worked by a different member of the group. Give the first group to work the problem correctly two points and all other groups with a correct answer one point. Then call out a new problem and continue in the same manner. After playing several rounds, declare the group with the most points the winner. Division

$$20\overline{)522} = 26\ R2$$

1. Divide.
2. Multiply.
3. Subtract.
4. Bring down.

How Do Your Interests Rate?

Earn top ratings by finding averages! Divide your class into groups of four students. Name one of the topics listed at the right. Instruct each group member to rate that topic on a scale from one to ten with ten being the best. Then have each group compute the average of its four ratings. Continue the activity by naming a new topic and having each group rate it and then compute the average rating. After playing a few rounds, have each group estimate the average rating before actually computing it. *Averages*

Topics to Rate

- books written by Gary Paulsen
- watching a baseball game
- pizza with mushrooms
- chocolate ice cream
- school on Saturday
- Christmas
- math class
- dance music
- chewing gum
- art class
- recess

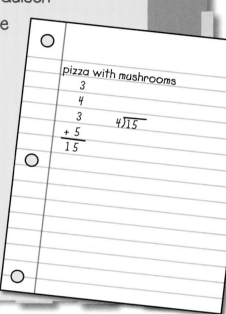

pizza with mushrooms
3
4
3
+ 5
―――
15

4)15

Wheel of Quotients

Take a spin with division skills! Provide each student with a copy of the wheel patterns on page 111. The child programs the sectioned wheel with division problems and answers as shown. He then attaches the labeled wheel with a brad. Once the wheels are complete, students exchange them, solve the problems on the classmate's wheel, and lift the flap to check the answers. *Division*

Hangman: Math Style

Secretly select a math vocabulary word related to multiplication or division. On the board, draw a blank line for each letter of the vocabulary word chosen. Have students take turns guessing letters to spell the word. If they guess correctly, write the letter on the correct blank. If they guess incorrectly, write on the board one digit of a multiplication or division problem, whichever illustrates the use of the particular word. Play continues until either the word is completely spelled or the entire problem is revealed. If the word is spelled out first, the student who provided the last letter must then state the definition of the word. He then chooses the word and sample problem for the next round. If the math problem is revealed before the word is spelled, each student must solve the problem. The first student to solve the problem correctly chooses the word and sample problem for the next round. *Vocabulary*

D I V I _ _ R

5)35

Sorry, there are no *T*s.

Check out the skill-building reproducibles on pages 112–117.

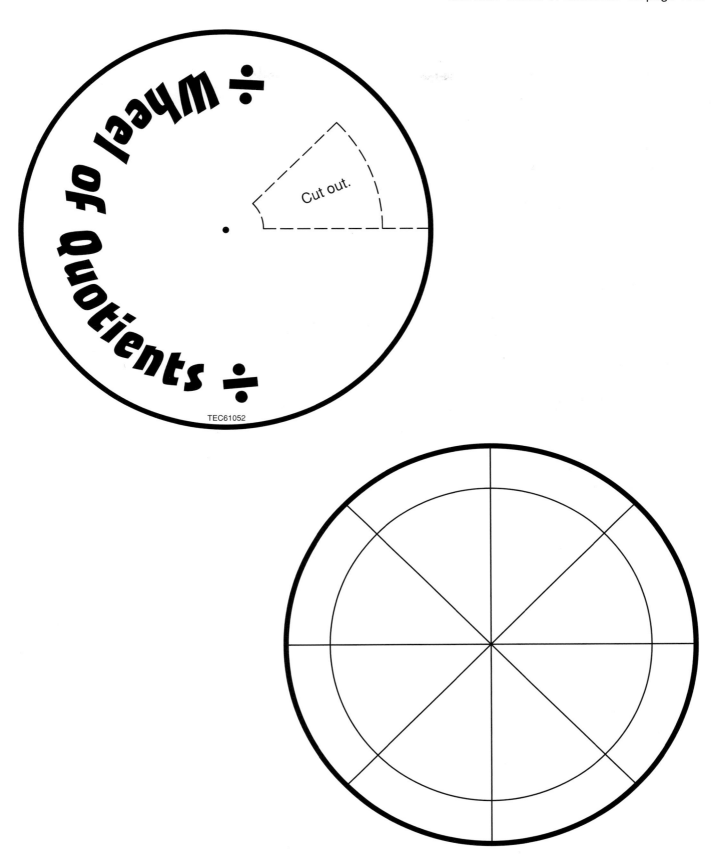

NAME _____

DATE _____

Fish Fun

List several multiples for each number. Then circle the least common multiple for each pair.

1 | multiples of 3: _____

multiples of 4: _____

2 | multiples of 7: _____

multiples of 10: _____

3 | multiples of 2: _____

multiples of 15: _____

4 | multiples of 5: _____

multiples of 6: _____

5 | multiples of 8: _____

multiples of 12: _____

6 | multiples of 9: _____

multiples of 11: _____

7 | multiples of 10: _____

multiples of 5: _____

8 | multiples of 7: _____

multiples of 8: _____

9 | multiples of 3: _____

multiples of 6: _____

10 | multiples of 4: _____

multiples of 9: _____

Win a New Car!

Multiply. Color the key with the matching answer.
The one not colored is the winning car key.

 A 47
         x 32

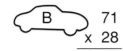 B 71
         x 28

C 77
   x 44

D 92
   x 36

E 23
   x 17

F 68
   x 51

G 84
   x 49

H 76
   x 61

I 90
   x 56

J 41
   x 16

 K 97
         x 76

 L 37
         x 29

 M 89
         x 88

N 83
   x 13

O 55
   x 35

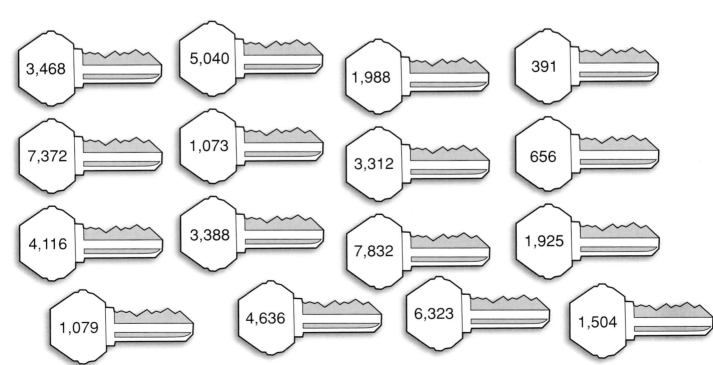

3,468   5,040   1,988   391

7,372   1,073   3,312   656

4,116   3,388   7,832   1,925

1,079   4,636   6,323   1,504

S.O.F. (Save Our Factors)

List the factors for each number. Circle the greatest common factor for each pair.

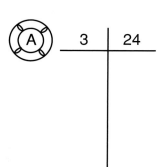 A   3 | 24

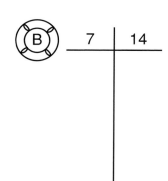 B   7 | 14

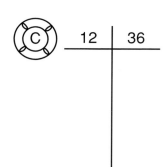 C   12 | 36

D   9 | 15

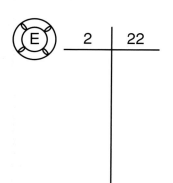 E   2 | 22

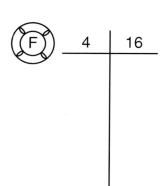 F   4 | 16

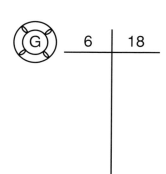 G   6 | 18

H   15 | 33

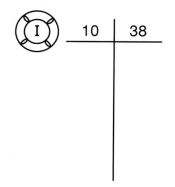 I   10 | 38

J   5 | 30

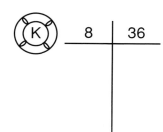 K   8 | 36

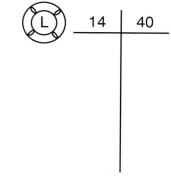 L   14 | 40

NAME _____

DATE _____

THE GREAT DIVIDE

Divide. Then check your answers.

A. 6)$\overline{1,208}$	B. 3)$\overline{709}$	C. 4)$\overline{5,080}$
D. 7)$\overline{2,107}$	E. 8)$\overline{903}$	F. 6)$\overline{6,044}$
G. 2)$\overline{3,066}$	H. 4)$\overline{4,208}$	I. 5)$\overline{8,008}$

A Hairy Situation

Divide. Then color each answer below.

A.	B.	C.	D.	E.
6)‾353‾	4)‾695‾	10)‾176‾	12)‾117‾	9)‾312‾

F.	G.	H.		
3)‾143‾	2)‾105‾	14)‾8,214‾		

9 R9 ○

17 R6 ○

52 R1 ○

586 R10 ○

58 R5 ○

47 R2 ○

34 R6 ○

173 R3 ○

Stay the Course

Solve the first problem. Then use its answer to solve the second problem.
Continue this pattern until you reach the finish line. Show your work.

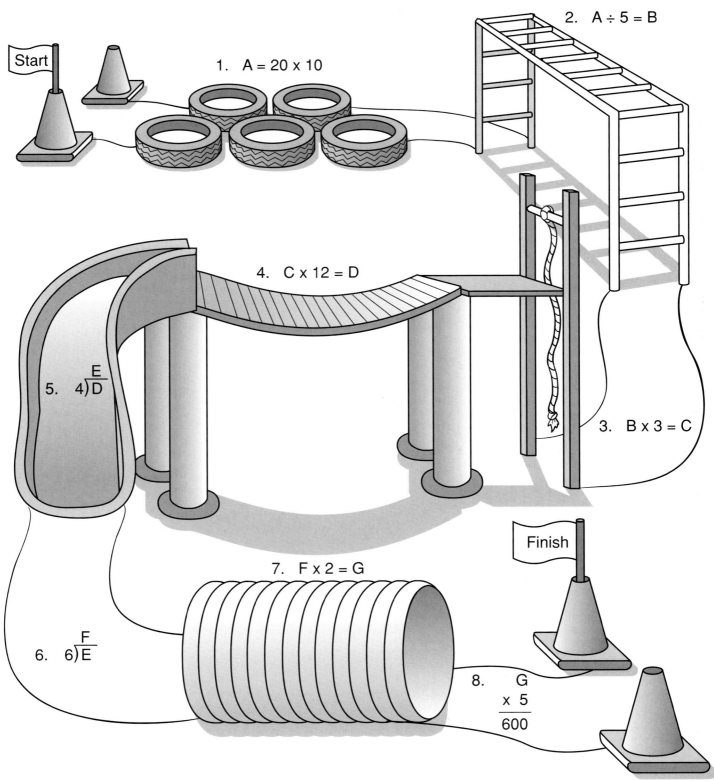

Start

1. A = 20 x 10

2. A ÷ 5 = B

4. C x 12 = D

5. 4)$\overset{E}{\overline{)D}}$

3. B x 3 = C

Finish

7. F x 2 = G

6. 6)$\overset{F}{\overline{)E}}$

8. $\begin{array}{r} G \\ \times\ 5 \\ \hline 600 \end{array}$

Fractions

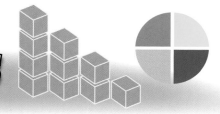

Visions of Fractions

Your students will be seeing fractions with this Geoboard activity! Make and display an overhead transparency of dot paper. Give one Geoboard, several copies of dot paper, and a supply of rubber bands to each student. Instruct each child to divide her Geoboard in half in as many different ways as possible, recording each method on dot paper. Invite a few students to come to the overhead and share one of their designs with the class. Continue the lesson by having each child discover how to divide a Geoboard into fourths and then eighths. Finally, challenge each student to divide her Geoboard so that it simultaneously shows the fractions $\frac{1}{2}$, $\frac{1}{4}$, and $\frac{2}{8}$. Have her list several equivalent fractions or equations that can be shown on a Geoboard, such as $\frac{1}{4} = \frac{2}{8}$ and $\frac{1}{2} = \frac{2}{4} = \frac{4}{8}$ or $\frac{1}{4} + \frac{1}{4} = \frac{1}{2}$ and $\frac{1}{4} + \frac{2}{8} + \frac{1}{2} = 1$. Follow up by having each student complete a copy of page 120 as directed. **Exploration**

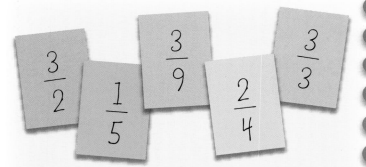

Fraction War

Launch a full-scale attack on comparing fractions with this partner game! Cut 20 index cards in half to make a deck of cards. Label each card with a different fraction. To play, one partner deals the cards facedown in two separate piles. Then each player simultaneously turns over the top card from her pile. The player with the larger fraction takes both cards. If the fractions are equivalent, each player turns over another card. This time, the player with the larger fraction takes all four cards. If players cannot agree which fraction is greater, they refer to a fraction chart. The player with more cards after all the cards have been revealed wins the round! **Comparing**

Fill the Box!

For this team game, label ten index cards from 1 to 10 and place them in a paper bag. Write on the board 20 equivalent fraction equations such as those shown, making sure the answer for each box is a number from 1 to 10. To play, a player from Team 1 draws a number from the bag, announces it to the class, and then puts the number back in the bag. A player from Team 2 writes that number in an equation on the board for his teammates to approve. If his answer is correct, he erases the equation and a player from Team 2 draws a number for a player from Team 1 to write in an equation. If the Team 2 player's answer is incorrect, another player from Team 2 writes an answer. If that answer is also incorrect, a player from Team 1 gets a chance to write an answer. The team that erases the most equations wins! **Equivalence**

$$\frac{3}{10} = \frac{\Box}{20}$$

$$\frac{4}{\Box} = \frac{8}{10}$$

Recipes for Success

To target a specific fraction skill, choose from the recipe activities below.

- **Simplifying fractions:** Change the specified amount of every ingredient in a favorite recipe to an equivalent fraction. For example, change ¼ cup sugar to ⁵⁄₂₀ cup sugar. Give a copy of the revised recipe to each student; then have him rename the fractions in the ingredient list in simplest form.

- **Adding fractions:** Give a copy of any two recipes with similar ingredients to each student. Instruct her to compile a shopping list after calculating how much of each ingredient will be needed to make both recipes. For example, if one recipe calls for ¾ cup sugar and the other calls for ⅓ cup sugar, then a total of 1¹⁄₁₂ cups of sugar would be needed for both recipes.

- **Subtracting fractions:** Give each student a copy of the same recipe. On the board, list the recipe's ingredients. Next to each ingredient, write an amount greater than what the recipe requires. Explain that the quantities on the board represent how much of each ingredient is on hand. Then have each student determine how much of each ingredient on the board would be left after preparing the recipe he was given.

- **Multiplying fractions:** Give a copy of the same recipe to each student. Have her double, triple, or quadruple the recipe by multiplying the quantity of its ingredients by 2, 3, or 4.

- **Dividing fractions:** Revise a recipe's ingredients by multiplying the measurements by any whole number. For example, if a recipe calls for ¾ cup flour, multiply ¾ by 3 to get 2¼ cups flour and so on. Then have each student reduce the measurements on his copy of the revised recipe to reflect the amount needed for ⅓ of the recipe (2¼ ÷ 3 = ¾).

Sort It All Out!

This small-group activity has students mentally calculate whether fractions are closer to 1, ½, or 0. Give each group a copy of the fraction cards on page 121. Instruct group members to sort their cards into three piles: closest to 1, closest to ½, or closest to 0. Then call on each group to explain how it completed the task.
Rounding

Check out the skill-building reproducibles on pages 122–125.

Fraction Quilt

Follow the directions below to design a square for a class fraction quilt.

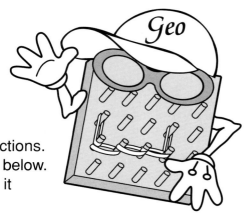

Directions:

1. Use rubber bands to create a design on a Geoboard.
2. Make the design show halves, fourths, eighths, sixteenths, thirty-seconds, sixty-fourths, or any combination of those fractions.
3. Use a ruler to help you draw your design on the blank square below.
4. Label each section of the square with the fractional part that it represents.
5. Color and cut out your square.

Note to the teacher: Use with "Visions of Fractions" on page 118. Give each student or pair of students a Geoboard, rubber bands, a ruler, scissors, and crayons or colored pencils. Arrange the completed designs to create a class quilt on a bulletin board.

$\frac{3}{8}$ TEC61052	$\frac{1}{6}$ TEC61052	$\frac{5}{7}$ TEC61052	$\frac{1}{3}$ TEC61052
$\frac{3}{4}$ TEC61052	$\frac{4}{9}$ TEC61052	$\frac{2}{3}$ TEC61052	$\frac{5}{8}$ TEC61052
$\frac{7}{8}$ TEC61052	$\frac{2}{5}$ TEC61052	$\frac{3}{5}$ TEC61052	$\frac{1}{7}$ TEC61052
$\frac{5}{6}$ TEC61052	$\frac{1}{4}$ TEC61052	$\frac{4}{5}$ TEC61052	$\frac{2}{9}$ TEC61052
$\frac{4}{7}$ TEC61052	$\frac{1}{8}$ TEC61052	$\frac{2}{7}$ TEC61052	$\frac{1}{5}$ TEC61052

NAME _____

DATE _____

Making Bricks

Follow the directions. Then answer the questions.

Directions:

1. Number the papers your teacher gives you in the lower right corner from 1 to 4.
2. Fold Sheet 1 into halves (one fold). Unfold it. Color one section green. Write "$\frac{1}{2}$" on the colored section.
3. Fold Sheet 2 into fourths (two folds). Unfold it. Color two sections red. Write "$\frac{1}{4}$" on each colored section.
4. Fold Sheet 3 into eighths (three folds). Unfold it. Color four sections blue. Write "$\frac{1}{8}$" on each colored section.
5. Fold Sheet 4 into sixteenths (four folds). Unfold it. Color eight sections orange. Write "$\frac{1}{16}$" on each colored section.
6. Cut the colored sections apart to create a supply of colored boxes.

1. What fraction does the green box represent? _____ The two red boxes? _____

   The four blue boxes? _____ The eight orange boxes? _____

2. Cover the green box with the two red boxes. What do you notice? _____

   _____

3. Cover the two red boxes with the four blue boxes. What do you notice? _____

   _____

4. Cover the four blue boxes with the eight orange boxes. What do you notice? _____

   _____

5. Do all the colored sections of your sheets represent the same amount? _____

6. Write the four equivalent fractions that you formed. _____ = _____ = _____ = _____

7. What pattern(s) do you see in these equivalent fractions? _____

   _____

   _____

8. What would have happened if you had colored five boxes blue on Sheet 3 instead of four?

   _____

   _____

Note to the teacher: Each child will need four sheets of unlined paper, scissors, and four crayons (green, red, blue, and orange) to complete this page.

It's Off to Camp We Go!

Use the map to help you solve the problems. Show your work on this sheet; then write the correct answers on the lines provided.

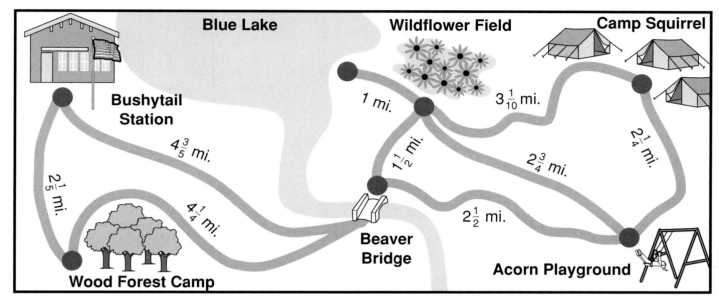

Blue Lake   Wildflower Field   Camp Squirrel

Bushytail
Station

$4\frac{3}{5}$ mi.

1 mi. $3\frac{1}{10}$ mi.

$1\frac{1}{2}$ mi.

$2\frac{1}{4}$ mi.

$2\frac{3}{4}$ mi.

$2\frac{1}{5}$ mi.

$4\frac{1}{4}$ mi.

Beaver
Bridge

$2\frac{1}{2}$ mi.

Wood Forest Camp   Acorn Playground

1. On Monday morning, the campers hiked from Camp Squirrel to Acorn Playground and then to Wildflower Field. How far did the campers hike that morning? _____

2. While at Wildflower Field on Monday afternoon, the campers decided to hike across Beaver Bridge to Bushytail Station. How far was this hike? _____

3. How much farther was the campers' afternoon hike than their morning hike? _____

4. On Monday evening, the campers decided it was too late to hike all the way back to Camp Squirrel, so they decided to hike the $2\frac{1}{5}$ miles to Wood Forest Camp and spend the night. How many total miles did the campers hike on Monday? _____

5. Tuesday morning the campers loaded up their gear and hiked from Wood Forest Camp to Beaver Bridge, then to Wildflower Field, and then to Camp Squirrel. How far did the campers hike that day? _____

6. On Wednesday, camper group A decided to hike from Camp Squirrel to Beaver Bridge. How many miles long is the shortest route that the campers can take? _____

7. Camper group B hiked from Camp Squirrel to Acorn Playground and then to Beaver Bridge. Which group hiked farther on Wednesday? _____

8. How many miles is it to hike from Bushytail Station to Wood Forest Camp, then to Beaver Bridge, and then back to Bushytail Station? _____

9. How many miles is the shortest hike from Camp Squirrel to Beaver Bridge and then to Wood Forest Camp? _____

10. If some campers want to hike about 10 miles, which route should they take? Write your answer on the back of this sheet.

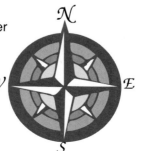

NAME _____

DATE _____

Message in a Bottle

Color if correct.
If incorrect, write the correct symbol on the bottle neck.
The first one has been done for you.

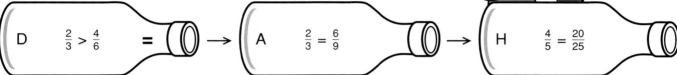

D $\frac{2}{3} > \frac{4}{6}$ = → A $\frac{2}{3} = \frac{6}{9}$ → H $\frac{4}{5} = \frac{20}{25}$

B $\frac{3}{5} < \frac{1}{3}$ → O $\frac{1}{5} < \frac{4}{10}$ → F $\frac{3}{4} < \frac{2}{5}$

Y $\frac{3}{5} > \frac{3}{10}$ → G $\frac{2}{3} > \frac{4}{5}$ → M $\frac{7}{9} > \frac{2}{5}$

A $\frac{3}{8} < \frac{7}{10}$ → F $\frac{3}{4} < \frac{2}{5}$ → W $\frac{6}{7} > \frac{9}{10}$

T $\frac{3}{4} > \frac{3}{5}$ → E $\frac{2}{5} = \frac{8}{20}$ → Y $\frac{2}{3} < \frac{3}{4}$

What did the message in the bottle say?
To find out, write the letters of the colored bottles in order on the lines below.

___ ___ ___ ___ ,   ___ ___ ___ ___ ___ !

SAVVY SHOPPING

Solve each problem two ways.
The first one has been done for you.

1. The normal price for a computer game at Bull's-Eye Toys and Games is $18.00.
    How much is a game if it is on sale for $\frac{2}{3}$ off the regular price? __$6.00__

    Picture it: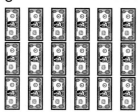

    2 of 3 rows = 6 + 6 = 12
    $\frac{2}{3}$ of 18 = 12
    18 − 12 = 6

    Multiply it: 18 x $\frac{2}{3}$ = $\frac{18}{1}$ x $\frac{2}{3}$ = $\frac{36}{3}$ = 12

2. Z-mart sells skateboards for $21.00 each. If they are on sale for $\frac{2}{3}$
    off this week, how much will a skateboard cost now? _____

    Picture it:

    Multiply it:

3. Mel-mart is selling board games at $\frac{1}{3}$ off the regular price of $15.00
    this week. How much will a board game cost now? _____

    Picture it:

    Multiply it:

4. Roley's is selling computer games at $\frac{3}{4}$ off the regular price of $16.00.
    How much does a computer game cost at Roley's? _____

    Picture it:

    Multiply it:

Bonus Box: Both Roley's and Bull's-Eye Toys and Games have a sale on computer games. Which sale is better? Explain your answer on the back of this page.

DECIMALS

Do-Si-Do Digits

For this easy-to-play game, each student cuts each of four index cards into thirds. She labels one card with a decimal point, ten cards with the numbers 0–9, and discards the 12th card. Call out a number that can be built using any combination of the 11 cards, such as 3,405.78 or 103.56. Each child arranges her cards to form the number called. Circulate to assess students' work; then write the correct standard form on the board. Each player then checks her answer, giving herself one point if it is correct. To vary the game, call out several numerals and a decimal point in a specific order. Have students form the number and then write it in word form. **Reading and writing**

Places, Please!

Each child uses the digits 0–9 to write five different decimal numbers ranging in size from millions to thousandths. He trades lists with a partner and writes his partner's numbers in order from greatest to least. Next, the partners combine their numbers into one list of ten numbers arranged from greatest to least. Finally, they work with another student pair to create another list of numbers in which each sequential number on one list is compared with the corresponding number on the other student pair's list. For more practice, have each child complete a copy of page 129 as directed. **Comparing and ordering**

1. 1,023,456.789
2. 759.842

1. 1,203,875.694
2. 608.325

1. 1,023,456.789 < 1,203,875.694
2. 759.842 > 608.325

Shopper's Express

All you need for this simple game is old grocery receipts! Announce to students which place value to use when rounding the first set of numbers, such as to the nearest dollar, half dollar, quarter, or dime. Then read one item at a time and its cost from a grocery list. Keep track of the items and their rounded prices. After students have estimated the cost of five to ten items, ask for the total estimated cost of those items. Play additional rounds as time permits. If desired, follow up by having each child complete a copy of page 128 as directed. **Rounding**

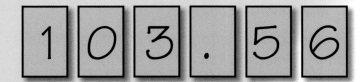

$ 1.58
$ 0.79
$ 1.26
$ 3.99
$ 2.49
$ 4.98

Round each price to the nearest dollar.

Hot off the Press

Give student pairs practice in problem solving as well as ordering and computing decimals with this activity. Collect an assortment of sales flyers and newspapers. Then guide the partners through the directions below.

1. Scour the newspapers and flyers for 15 numbers that have decimals.

2. Cut out the numbers and glue them to construction paper in least to greatest order.

3. Use the numbers to make up five word problems dealing with addition, subtraction, or multiplication. Make a key.

4. Staple the problems and key to a sheet of construction paper and give it to your teacher.

During the next math class, pair students as before. Redistribute the problems, making sure that no pair gets its own problems. Direct each pair to solve the problems and check its answers by the corresponding key. If desired, follow up by having each student complete a copy of page 130 as directed. **Ordering decimals, problem solving**

You have $2,500 to buy new furniture for your home. Select the items you wish to purchase from this catalog. Record each item and its price on another sheet of paper. Then add the prices of the items to get the total. Get as close to $2,500 as possible without going over this amount.

Enjoy Elegant Luxury

Catalog Shopping

Put all the catalogs you receive in the mail to good use at this center. Attach to each catalog a shopping list of ten items featured in that catalog, including the brand name and desired quantity of each product. Or staple to each catalog a scenario such as the one shown. To use the center, a student either finds the correct total for each shopping list or creates a list of items whose total cost does not exceed a set limit. **Adding**

Winners All

Invented sports statistics make this practice activity easy to do! Display a list of ten names, each with a different decimal number written next to it as shown. Each child uses the data to write five subtraction problems to trade with a partner. She solves her partner's problems and then adds to check each answer.
Subtracting

Mandy	12.7
Ricky	19.63
Catrice	14.56
Ned	18.07
Latasha	18.07
Carter	13.0
Katie	19.52
Connor	12.3
Devonna	16.05
David	13.9

Check out the skill-building reproducibles on pages 128–130.

SPARKY'S SPECTACULAR SALE

Use the sign above each item and the attached sales tag to estimate the sale price for that item. Then choose the correct price from the price box and write it on the sales tag below the item.

Save about $20.00!

$61.00

1.

Save about $25.00!

$49.50

2.

Save about $3.00!

$11.65

3.

Save about $5.00!

$43.00

4.

Save about $7.00!

$19.75

5.

Save about $1.00!

$10.85

6.

Save about $9.00!

$38.98

7.

Save about $12.00!

$32.00

8.

Save about $15.00!

$49.50

9.

Price Box
$12.99 $39.99 $8.99 $19.50 $34.99 $9.99 $37.99 $24.99 $29.99

NAME

DATE

Build Numbers!

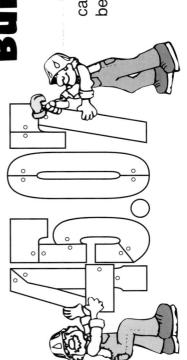

Cut out the five cards at the bottom of this sheet. Use all five cards, using each card only once, to form a four-digit decimal number that matches each description below. Write your answers in the blanks provided.

1. Greater than 750 _ _ _ _ _ _ _ _

2. Between 540 and 570 _ _ _ _ _ _ _ _

3. Less than 5 _ _ _ _ _ _ _ _

4. Between 70 and 70.5 _ _ _ _ _ _ _ _

5. Between 0 and 0.5 _ _ _ _ _ _ _ _

6. Between 5 and 5.1 _ _ _ _ _ _ _ _

7. Less than 5.7 and greater than 4.5 _ _ _ _ _ _ _ _

8. As close to 40 as possible _ _ _ _ _ _ _ _

9. Between 0 and 0.47 _ _ _ _ _ _ _ _

10. As close to 0 as possible _ _ _ _ _ _ _ _

Bonus Box: Use the digits on your cards to write three more descriptions on the back of this sheet. Then give your sheet to a friend and have him or her build a number that matches each description.

| 0 | 4 | 5 | 7 | • |

129

Costly Conversations

Use the rates in the chart below to figure the cost of the phone calls. Show your work on the back of this sheet; then write your answers on the lines provided.

Country Called	Cost of First Minute	Cost of Each Additional Minute
Spain	$1.13	$0.62
Belgium	$1.56	$0.69
Denmark	$1.75	$0.98
Ireland	$0.98	$0.60
Sweden	$1.15	$0.65
France	$1.47	$0.66

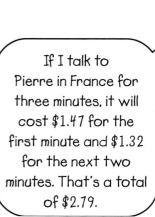

If I talk to Pierre in France for three minutes, it will cost $1.47 for the first minute and $1.32 for the next two minutes. That's a total of $2.79.

1. France for 8 minutes

   Cost = _____

2. Spain for 4 minutes

   Cost = _____

3. Ireland for 11 minutes

   Cost = _____

4. Belgium for 6 minutes

   Cost = _____

5. Denmark for 14 minutes

   Cost = _____

6. Sweden for 7 minutes

   Cost = _____

7. Spain for 22 minutes

   Cost = _____

8. France for 9 minutes

   Cost = _____

9. What is the total cost of the phone bill this month?

   Total cost = _____

10. Which country is the cheapest for a five-minute call? _____

    The most expensive? _____

MEASUREMENT

AT HOME AND ABOUT

To get down to the nitty-gritty of hands-on measurement, list tasks such as those below for students to complete at home with their parents. During the next class, compare students' answers and make class graphs displaying the information where appropriate. **Real-life measurement**

At-Home Measurements

1. List ten things in your house that are about one centimeter long.
2. List ten things in your house that are about one meter long.
3. Use three different units to measure your mom's or dad's height.
4. Calculate the areas of the biggest and smallest rooms in your house.
5. Name five places that you and your family would like to visit; then calculate the distance of each place from your town.

Make a Match!

Each student pair cuts apart a copy of the cards on page 133 and lays out the cards facedown. Player 1 turns over two cards. If the measurements on the cards match, she keeps the cards and turns over two more cards. If the measurements do not match, she returns the cards facedown to their original positions and Player 2 takes a turn. The player with more matches when all the matches have been made wins. **Equivalent measurements**

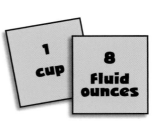

FOLLOW MY RULES

This partner activity will show how adept students are at using rulers and following directions. Have each child use a ruler and two sheets of drawing paper to create a design consisting of ten line segments. Explain that each successive line segment drawn must be perpendicular to the previous one (see the illustration). When the design is complete, he places his second sheet of paper atop his design and traces the exact starting point with a pencil. Then the partners follow the steps below.

1. One student passes the sheet labeled with the starting point of his design to his partner and then gives her step-by-step oral directions on how to duplicate his design. For example, he might say, "Start at the labeled point and draw a four-inch line segment heading east. From that point, draw a 5¼-inch line segment heading north."
2. The student continues giving directions in this manner until the design is complete.
3. The pair places one design atop the other. If the designs do not match, the partners determine how to make the attempt more accurate.
4. The pair repeats the process using the other partner's design.

To create a design using a metric ruler, give each student a smaller sheet of drawing paper. **Linear measurement**

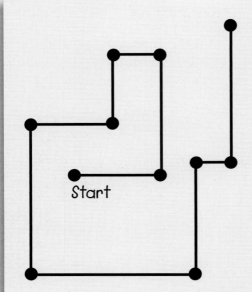

Start

"COLOR-IFIC" CALCULATIONS

For an easy way to reinforce area and perimeter, give each student a pile of color tiles. Call out a letter of the alphabet and instruct each child to create that letter with his tiles. Require that each part of the letter be two tiles wide as shown. Have the student calculate both the perimeter and the area of that letter. Continue calling letters—L, T, H, F, E, and P are the easiest—until students feel comfortable with the activity. Then challenge each child to use the manipulatives to find the perimeter and area of each letter in his first name. **Perimeter and area**

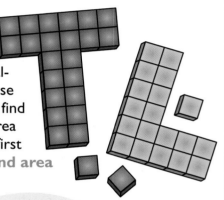

Fruity Flakes

Each child thinks of names and flavors for two cereals. He draws, measures, and decorates two different-sized cereal boxes on separate sheets of paper. He also calculates the volume of each box and writes it on the back. Once his calculations are checked, he trades with a partner and finds the volume of his partner's boxes. For fun, students can display all the boxes, choose the three they think hold the most cereal, and then use the volumes written on the back to check! **Volume of rectangular prisms**

That's Not a Rectangle!

To make finding the area of irregular figures perfectly clear, display an overhead transparency of centimeter graph paper and follow the steps below.

1. Select a student to use an overhead marker to draw a 5 x 7 rectangle on the transparency.
2. Review how to find the area of a rectangle (l × w = area). Calculate the area of the drawn rectangle; then check the answer by counting each square unit inside the rectangle.
3. Select another student to draw a 2 x 2 square on the transparency. Compute the area of the square; then check by counting the squares.
4. Cut out the figures drawn on the transparency; then arrange them on the overhead so that they form an irregular figure (see the illustration).
5. Challenge each student to determine the area of this new figure. Guide students to conclude that the area of this new figure can be found by adding the area of the original rectangle to the area of the original square.
6. Trace the new figure on a blank transparency, dividing the figure to show its two original figures.
7. Demonstrate how to find the area of the two different figures; then add their areas together to determine the total area of the new figure.

If desired, have each child complete a copy of page 136 as directed to follow up. **Area of irregular figures**

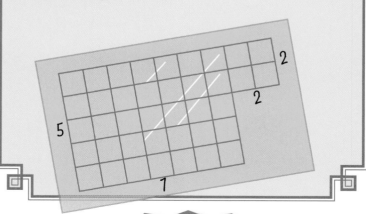

Check out the skill-building reproducibles on pages 134–136.

1 gallon TEC61052	**4 quarts** TEC61052	**16 ounces** TEC61052	**1 pound** TEC61052	**4 cups** TEC61052
1 quart TEC61052	**2,000 pounds** TEC61052	**1 ton** TEC61052	**1 pint** TEC61052	**2 cups** TEC61052
60 seconds TEC61052	**1 minute** TEC61052	**1 cup** TEC61052	**8 fluid ounces** TEC61052	**60 minutes** TEC61052
1 hour TEC61052	**1 yard** TEC61052	**3 feet** TEC61052	**24 hours** TEC61052	**1 day** TEC61052
1 foot TEC61052	**12 inches** TEC61052	**365 days** TEC61052	**1 year** TEC61052	**1 mile** TEC61052
5,280 feet TEC61052	**2 pints** TEC61052	**1 quart** TEC61052	**1 yard** TEC61052	**36 inches** TEC61052

A "Gram-tastic" Race

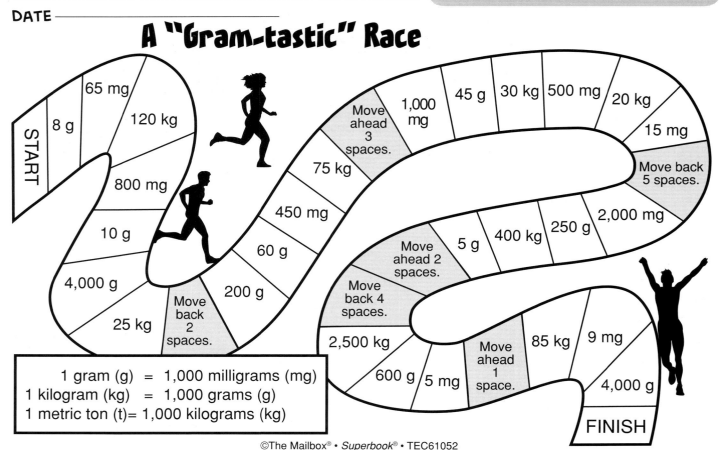

START

65 mg

8 g

120 kg

800 mg

10 g

4,000 g

25 kg

Move back 2 spaces.

200 g

60 g

450 mg

75 kg

Move ahead 3 spaces.

1,000 mg

45 g

30 kg

500 mg

20 kg

15 mg

Move back 5 spaces.

2,000 mg

250 g

400 kg

5 g

Move ahead 2 spaces.

Move back 4 spaces.

2,500 kg

600 g

5 mg

Move ahead 1 space.

85 kg

9 mg

4,000 g

FINISH

1 gram (g) = 1,000 milligrams (mg)
1 kilogram (kg) = 1,000 grams (g)
1 metric ton (t)= 1,000 kilograms (kg)

©The Mailbox® • Superbook® • TEC61052

1 g	500 mg	20 kg
225 g	2,000 kg	1 t
8 mg	5,000 g	6 kg
89 g	12 kg	70 mg

Directions:
Cut out the spinner below; then cut apart the cards on the left and place them facedown in a pile. Spin (see the illustration) to determine who goes first and how many spaces to move your game piece ahead. Draw a card. Compare the weight on the card to the weight on the space with your game piece. Tell which weight is larger (see the table). If you are correct, spin again. If you are incorrect or if the weights are equivalent, do not move your game piece. The first player to arrive at Finish wins.

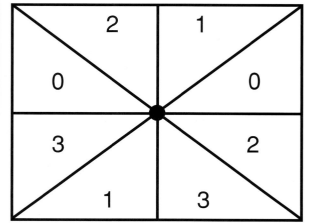

2 1
0   0
3   2
1 3

Note to the teacher: Provide one copy of this page, a paper clip, scissors, a pencil, and two game pieces for each pair of students.

BLACKOUT!

Use the times listed to help figure out how long each city was without power. Write your answers on the lines provided.

1. Jobville had no power from 1:12 AM to 3:12 AM.   _____

2. Salt River was affected from 1:33 AM to 4:43 AM.   _____

3. Twoburg lost power from 10:00 PM to 1:20 AM.   _____

4. Parks City was without power from 2:00 AM to 3:15 AM.   _____

5. Eynon had no power from 11:30 PM to 5:08 AM.   _____

6. Bloomsburg was affected from 12:45 AM to 3:00 AM.   _____

7. Lillington lost power from 1:50 AM to 2:45 AM.   _____

8. Apex had no power from 4:35 AM to 6:15 AM.   _____

Use the information below to set the clock with the correct time. Write your answers on the lines provided.

Reset Clock To

9. The power went off at 3:00 PM and stayed off for 2$\frac{1}{2}$ hours.   _____

10. The power went off at 5:15 AM and stayed off for 1 hour and 45 minutes.   _____

11. The power went off at 10:40 PM and stayed off for 45 minutes.   _____

12. The power went off at 8:25 AM and stayed off for 4 hours and 15 minutes.   _____

13. The power went off at 7:30 PM and stayed off for 3 hours and 10 minutes.   _____

Bonus Box: On the back of this page, write a paragraph telling about a time when the power went off at your house. Tell how it affected you and your family.

NAME _____
DATE _____

136

ONE STEP AT A TIME!

Divide each polygon into two rectangles and then label each rectangle "A" or "B."
Find the area of each rectangle. Then add the measurements of the two rectangles.
The first one has been started for you.

①

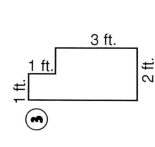

4 cm
3 cm
2 cm
2 cm

A

B

12

Area of A = _____ sq. cm
Area of B = _____ sq. cm
Total area = _____ sq. cm

②

2 cm
1 cm
5 cm
2 cm

Area of A = _____ sq. cm
Area of B = _____ sq. cm
Total area = _____ sq. cm

③

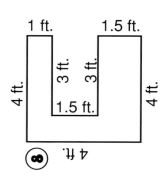

1 ft.
3 ft.
1 ft.
2 ft.

Area of A = _____ sq. ft.
Area of B = _____ sq. ft.
Total area = _____ sq. ft.

④

2 yd.
2.5 yd.
1 yd.
4 yd.

Area of A = _____ sq. yd.
Area of B = _____ sq. yd.
Total area = _____ sq. yd.

⑤

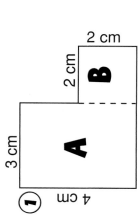

15 mm
25 mm
20 mm
30 mm

Area of A = _____ sq. mm
Area of B = _____ sq. mm
Total area = _____ sq. mm

⑥

1 cm
1.5 cm
5 cm
1.5 cm

Area of A = _____ sq. cm
Area of B = _____ sq. cm
Total area = _____ sq. cm

⑦

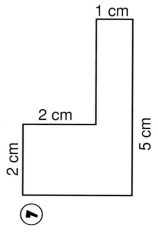

1 cm
2 cm
2 cm
5 cm

Area of A = _____ sq. cm
Area of B = _____ sq. cm
Total area = _____ sq. cm

⑧

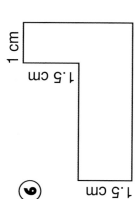

1 ft.
1.5 ft.
4 ft.
3 ft.
3 ft.
1.5 ft.
4 ft.
4 ft.

Find the area of the polygon above. Explain how you got your answer on the back of this page.

©The Mailbox® • Superbook® • TEC61052 • Key p. 312

Protractor Pictures

For this nifty symmetrical activity, each student needs a sheet of white drawing paper, a ruler, and a protractor. He folds his paper, dividing it in half vertically, and uses his ruler to trace the fold line. Next, he uses his protractor to create on the left half a design with up to ten line segments. Each line segment must start on the dividing line but can extend through an existing line segment, resulting in multiple line segments as shown. After making the design, he trades papers with a partner and pretends that the dividing line on the paper is a mirror. Then he uses his protractor to duplicate the design he sees on the left half of the paper onto the right half, measuring each line segment's length and each angle's degrees so that what he draws becomes an exact mirror image of the original. When he's finished, he returns the vertically symmetric design to its original owner, who uses colored pencils or crayons to decorate the design for display on a board titled "It's Symmetrical!"
Symmetry

Three-Pile Sort

To reinforce recognition of similar and congruent shapes, give each small group of students a copy of the cards and answer key on page 139. Instruct group members to cut the cards apart, shuffle the cards, and then sort them into three different categories: both similar and congruent, similar but not congruent, and not similar or congruent. Then have students use the key to check their answers.
Similar and congruent

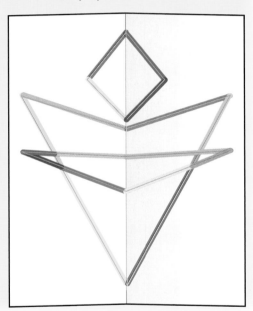

Moldable Figures

This cool center gives learners a hands-on review of the attributes and properties of solid figures. Place a class supply of page 141 at a center along with paper, pencils, and modeling clay. To use the center, a child completes a copy of page 141 and then uses the clay to build all six figures described on the page. To assess her understanding, have her fill in a chart like the one shown. **Solid figures**

Solid Figure	Number of		
	Flat Faces	Straight Edges	Vertices
cube	6	12	8
rectangular prism	6	12	8
square pyramid	5	8	5
cylinder	2	0	0
cone	1	0	1
sphere	0	0	0

Paper Plate Angles

This angle-reviewing activity becomes a partner game. Each child gets two different-colored plates that have been interlocked by cutting a radius in each plate and fitting the plates together as shown. Directions are called out, such as "Show an acute angle greater than 45 degrees" or "Show an obtuse angle less than 100 degrees." Students manipulate their plates to show angles that approximate those measurements. Any child who misrepresents an angle uses a protractor to correct it. Then student pairs play Angle Match according to the directions shown. Identifying angles

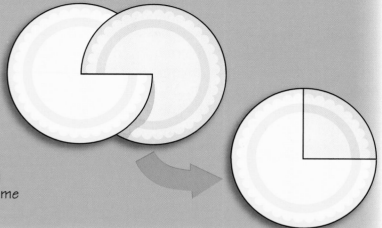

Directions:

1. Player 1 gives Player 2 any measurement between 1 and 360 degrees.
2. Player 2 shows that angle on his plate.
3. Player 1 checks the angle's measurement with a protractor.
4. If the angle is within five degrees of the correct measurement, Player 2 gets one point. If it is not, Player 1 gets the point.
5. Players continue taking turns representing angles and checking measurements until time is called. The player with more points wins.

Puzzling Tessellations

Slides, flips, and turns are what this activity's all about! Each student needs a jigsaw puzzle piece, tape, a tagboard square about the same size as the puzzle piece, a sheet of white paper, scissors, and crayons or markers. To make a tile, he traces half the puzzle piece on the tagboard square and then cuts along the traced line. He slides and turns the cutouts—without flipping them—to align their straight edges and tapes the pieces together. Then he slides, flips, and turns the tile, tracing it in a repeating pattern with no gaps or overlaps, until his paper is completely covered. To finish his design, he colors the tracings in a unique way. **Transformations**

Two-Color Designs

Each child creates an abstract or a realistic drawing consisting of nothing but parallel and perpendicular line segments. To distinguish the line segments, he includes a color key somewhere on the page and then traces parallel segments in one color and perpendicular segments in another. The completed pieces are arranged on a display titled "What's Our Line?" **Parallel and perpendicular**

Check out the skill-building reproducibles on pages 140–141.

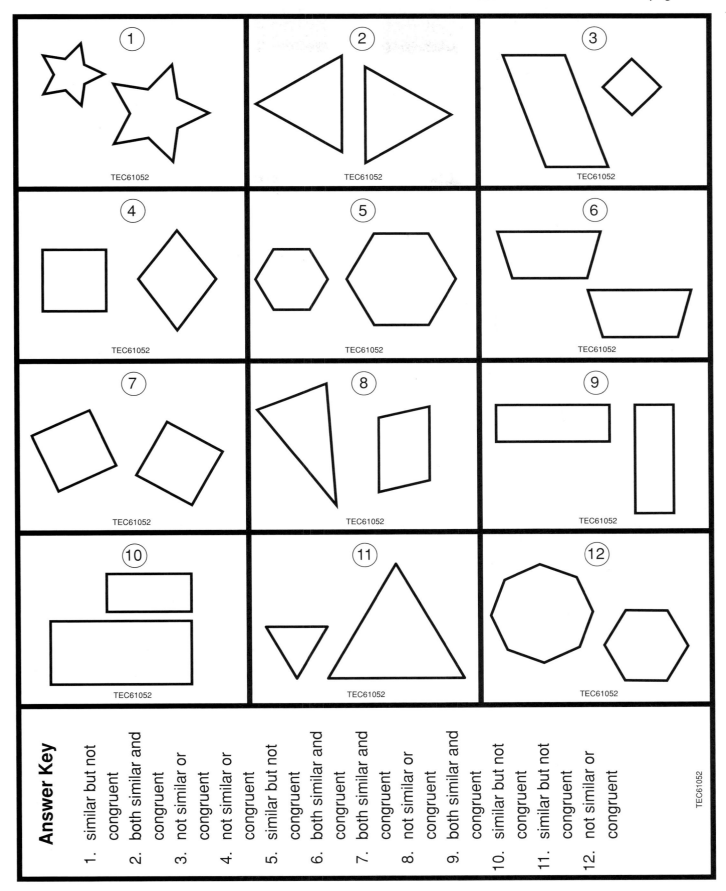

Answer Key

1. similar but not congruent
2. both similar and congruent
3. not similar or congruent
4. not similar or congruent
5. similar but not congruent
6. both similar and congruent
7. both similar and congruent
8. not similar or congruent
9. both similar and congruent
10. similar but not congruent
11. similar but not congruent
12. not similar or congruent

Puzzling Polygons

1. Label each polygon in the puzzle with the letter listed in front of its name below. (The number in parentheses tells how many polygons of that type are in the puzzle.)
2. Cut the puzzle pieces apart along the bold lines.
3. Arrange the polygon pieces on the sheet of construction paper your teacher gives you to create a design. Paste each piece in place.
4. Color and title your design.

A square
B rectangle
C parallelogram (2)
D rhombus
E trapezoid

F pentagon (2)
G quadrilateral (2)
H hexagon
I octagon
J decagon

K equilateral triangle
L right triangle (3)
M isosceles triangle
N scalene triangle

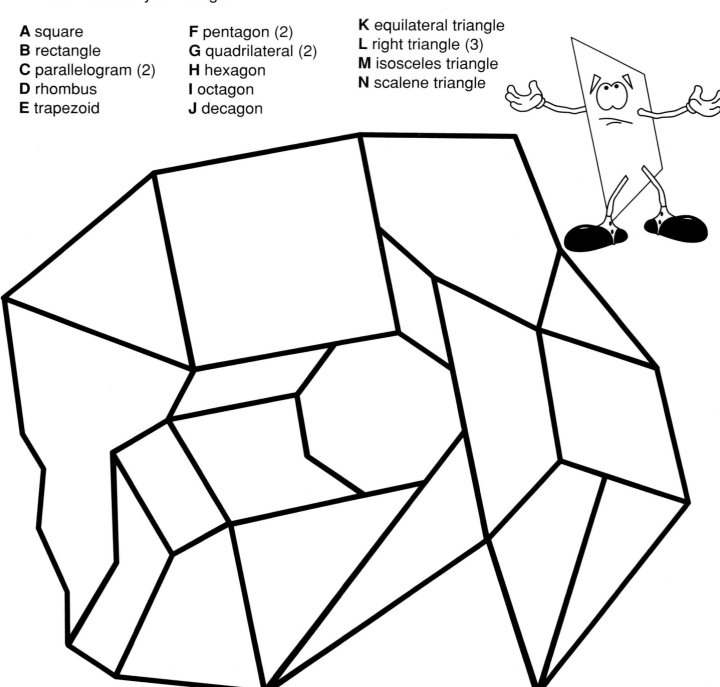

NAME _____

DATE _____

WHO'S THE THIEF?

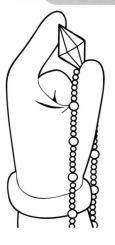

Read the clues.
Write the name of each solid figure being described.

1. a figure with six faces that are all equal in shape and size

   ___ ___ ___ ___
   1 2 3 4

2. a figure that is shaped like a ball

   ___ ___ ___ ___ ___ ___
   5 6 7 8 9 10

3. a figure similar to a shoebox, with square ends and rectangular sides

   rectangular ___ ___ ___ ___ ___
   11 12 13 14 15

4. a figure shaped like a can

   ___ ___ ___ ___ ___ ___ ___ ___
   16 17 18 19 20 21 22 23

5. a figure that has a circular base and a pointed top

   ___ ___ ___ ___
   24 25 26 27

6. a figure that has a square base and triangular sides

   ___ ___ ___ ___ ___ ___ ___
   28 29 30 31 32 33 34

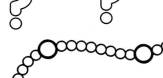

Who took the necklace?
To find out the thief's name, write each letter above in its matching numbered blank below.

___ ___ ___ - ___ ___ ___ ___ ___ ___   ___ ___ ___ ___
23 4 34   7 31 26 34 27 21   12 2 3 29

Graphing & Probability

Coordinate Codes

Transform your students into expert decoding sleuths with this point-plotting activity for partners. Give each student one copy of the grid on page 143. Have the student plot all the letters of the alphabet on his grid. Then instruct the child to write a message to his partner using the coordinates he plotted. Direct his partner to use the coordinates to decipher the coded message. As a variation, allow students to use the grids for practicing their spelling and vocabulary words. **Coordinates**

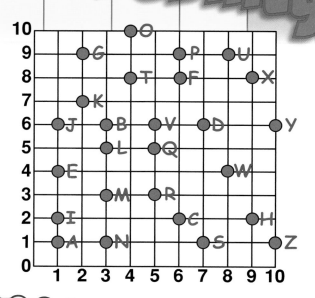

Graphing Grades

Make graphs come alive by having each child keep track of her own grades. Select one subject area, such as spelling, and have the student record her test grades in her notebook for one grading period. At the end of that period, instruct her to design a line, stem-and-leaf, or bar graph displaying her test results. Then have her determine the mean, median, and mode of her test scores. Students will be practicing data collection, and you'll have a great work sample to show at parent conferences. Mean, median, and mode

TIMELY CIRCLE GRAPHS

Data collection comes to life with this activity. Have each student select a family member to be the subject of his study. Explain that he should chart the time his subject spends each day for five consecutive days on activities such as sleeping, eating, working, and doing homework or housework. After all the data has been collected, instruct him to find the average daily time spent on each activity. Explain that each average should be rounded to the nearest hour and that the times may have to be adjusted to equal 24 hours. Next, direct the student to display his data as a colored circle graph. Then have him analyze the graph to answer questions such as "Which activity occupies most of the subject's time? The least?" Circle graph

Check out the skill-building reproducibles on pages 144-146.

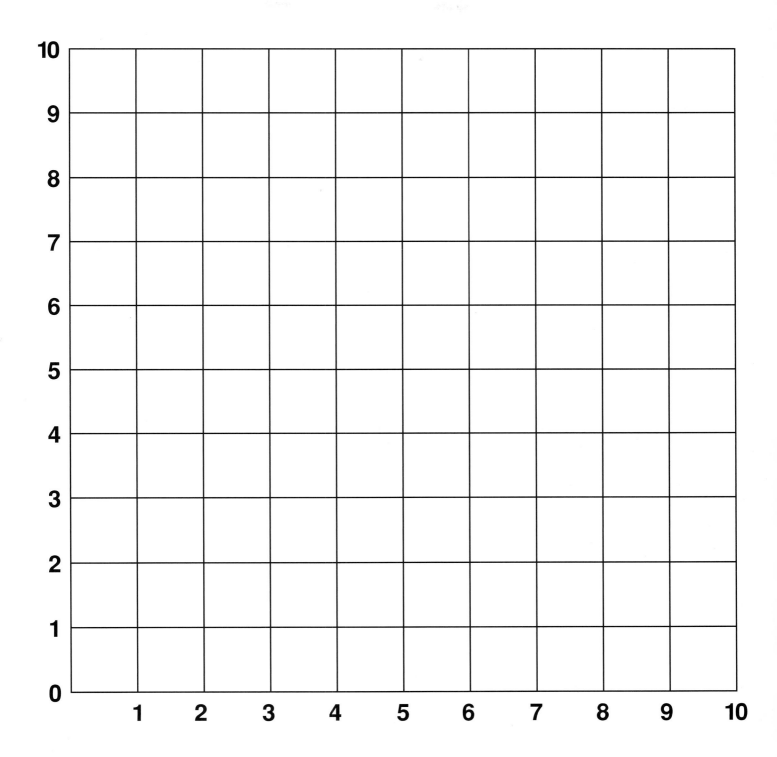

NAME
DATE

144

Sweet Stuff

Complete each graph.

1. Color the bar graph to show the pieces of candy sold.

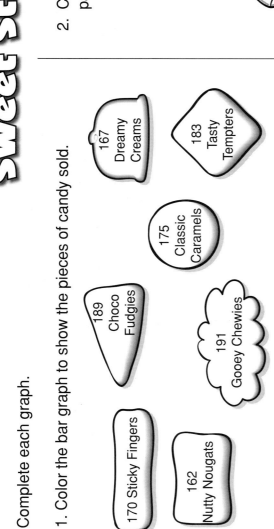

167 Dreamy Creams

183 Tasty Tempters

175 Classic Caramels

189 Choco Fudgies

191 Gooey Chewies

170 Sticky Fingers

162 Nutty Nougats

Dandy Candies

Number of Candies Sold

200
195
190
185
180
175
170
165
160
155
150
145

Sticky Fingers | Choco Fudgies | Nutty Nougats | Classic Caramels | Tasty Tempters | Dreamy Creams | Gooey Chewies

Types of Candies

2. Color and label the circle graph to show the number of pastries sold.

5 blueberry

10 cherry

10 lemon

25 apple

50 cream cheese

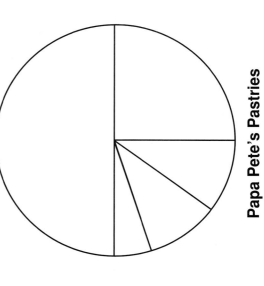

Papa Pete's Pastries

©The Mailbox® • Superbook® • TEC61052 • Key p. 313

DATE _____

WHAT ARE THE ODDS?

Read about each game. Then answer the questions.

1. To play Mouse in the House, pick the door you think a mouse will enter to get a piece of cheese. What are your chances of winning this game? _____
Do you think this is a fair game? _____
Explain. _____
_____

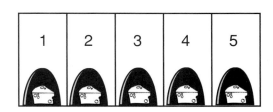

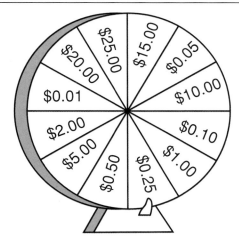

2. To play Wheel and Deal, you pay $0.50 to spin the wheel. You win the amount on which the wheel stops. What are your chances of winning at least the amount you spend to play?_____
Do you think this is a fair game? _____
Explain. _____
_____
_____

3. To play Headquarters, you flip a coin. If the coin lands on heads, you win $0.25. If the coin lands on tails, you lose $0.25. What are your chances of winning?_____
Do you think this is a fair game?_____
Explain. _____
_____

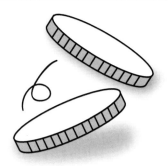

4. In Player's Choice, you pay $0.10 to choose a category and secretly record an answer for that category. If the game host guesses your answer, you win nothing. If the game host does not guess your answer, you win $0.20. What are your chances of winning in each category?

　　Days of the week _____
　　Dates in January _____
　　Month of a year _____
Which category should you choose? _____

Do you think this is a fair game? _____
Explain. _____
_____

TAKE A CHANCE!

Write the sum of each roll.

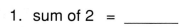

Find the probability of rolling two dice to equal each sum. Write each answer as a fraction in its simplest form.

1. sum of 2 = _____
2. sum of 3 = _____
3. sum of 4 = _____
4. sum of 5 = _____
5. sum of 6 = _____
6. sum of 7 = _____
7. sum of 8 = _____
8. sum of 9 = _____
9. sum of 10 = _____
10. sum of 11 = _____
11. sum of 12 = _____

Shade a box below for each answer. The letters of the unshaded boxes will spell the name of one of two men who worked together to form a theory about probability.

M	U	P	D	A	T	E	H	I	S	C	O	B	A	F	N	L
$\frac{1}{12}$	$\frac{1}{9}$	$\frac{5}{6}$	$\frac{1}{18}$	$\frac{3}{8}$	$\frac{1}{36}$	$\frac{5}{36}$	$\frac{1}{18}$	$\frac{1}{6}$	$\frac{1}{2}$	$\frac{1}{3}$	$\frac{1}{12}$	$\frac{1}{36}$	$\frac{1}{4}$	$\frac{5}{36}$	$\frac{1}{9}$	$\frac{1}{5}$

__ __ __ __ __ __ and Fermat

ALGEBRA

MATH MAGIC

Use this whole-group activity to review algebraic properties! Cut out a black construction paper top hat and glue it upside down to the side of a box as shown. Then program several large strips of paper each with a sample of a different property. On the back of the strip, write the name of the property. Place the strips in the box. With a lot of gusto and fanfare, pull one equation from the hat and display it for the class to see. Call on volunteers to identify the property shown. Once all equations have been identified, challenge each student to program four new strips of paper with original examples of each property. Add the strips to the box and place it at a center for small groups of students to practice identifying properties. If desired, have students complete the reproducible on page 149 for additional practice. **Properties**

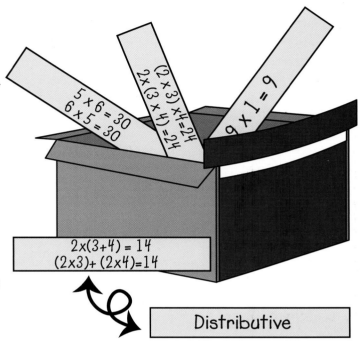

Distributive

Valuable Variables

Use Mr. or Ms. N. E. Number to introduce variables! Attach a large paper *N* to your shirt. Write a sentence on the board with your name in it, only write an *N* in place of your name. Brainstorm with students who *N* stands for. Explain that it can stand for anyone as long as the sentence makes sense when the *N* is replaced. Next, write an algebraic equation on the board using *N* as a variable. Challenge students to solve for *N*. Then discuss what *N* stands for. Repeat this process using different equations. If desired, have each student complete a copy of the reproducible on page 150 for additional practice. **Variables**

N went to the store to buy milk.

$N + 8 = 15$

Hundred Chart Patterns

Help your students see that patterns are all around! Give each pair of students a hundred chart and a handful of beans or markers. Instruct each pair to cover the 9 and all numbers whose digits add together to equal 9. For example, a student could cover the digits 1 and 8 in the number 18 because they add together to make 9. Then ask each pair if they can find anything else that the covered numbers have in common. Guide students to recognize that they are all multiples of nine. Next, direct the pair to cover, in turn, the multiples of 3, 4, 5, 6, 7, 8, and 10. Have the pairs discuss the patterns each set of multiples makes before clearing their boards. **Patterns**

HUNDRED CHART

1	2	3	4	5	6	7	8		10
11	12	13	14	15	16	17		19	20
21	22	23	24	25	26		28	29	30
31	32	33	34	35		37	38	39	40
41	42	43	44		46	47	48	49	50
51	52	53		55	56	57	58	59	60
61	62		64	65	66	67	68	69	70
71		73	74	75	76	77	78	79	80
	82	83	84	85	86	87	88	89	
91	92	93	94	95	96	97	98	99	100

> 77, 79, 72, 74, 67.

THIS RULES!

Have students use this quick idea to start class out on the right foot! Challenge each student to create an algebraic pattern on a scrap piece of paper. Then have the student read aloud the numbers in order and have his classmates try to guess the rule he followed. The student who correctly guesses the rule then reads his numbers aloud. Before long, students will not only have this skill mastered, but they will also work to create harder and harder patterns. If desired, extend the activity to include shapes and objects as well. **Finding patterns**

THE DE-EQUALIZER

For this fun activity, shuffle two decks of cards and then place them in a box labeled as shown. Assign the following values to the face cards: jack = 11, queen = 12, and king = 13. Tell students that aces equal 1. Have each student draw four cards from the box. Then challenge student pairs to work together to form a balanced equation using as many of their cards as possible. If desired, allow the duo to show its work on a piece of paper. Then have the pair share its problem with the class as well as how they reached their solution. **Balancing equations**

The Awe-Inspiring De-Equalizer

$9 + 9 + 11 + 12 = 13 + 13 + 13 + 2$

Check out the skill-building reproducibles on pages 149 and 150.

NAME _____

DATE _____

Math Magic

Cut out each equation below. Glue it in the correct box.

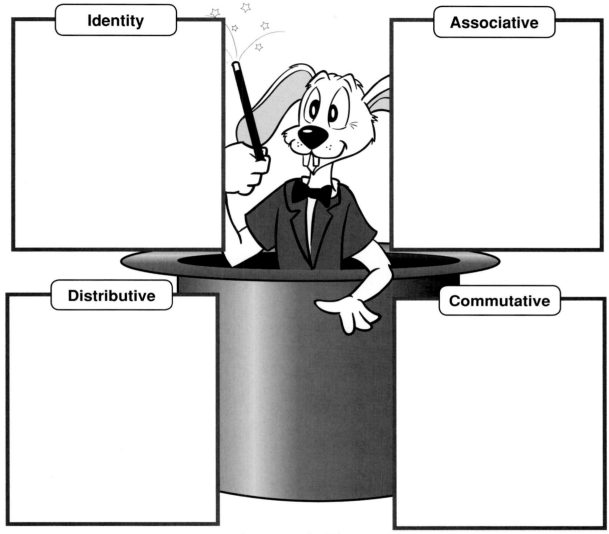

Identity

Associative

Distributive

Commutative

©The Mailbox® • Superbook® • TEC61052 • Key p. 313

21,345 + 0 = 21,345	987 x 1 = 987	879 x (3 + 7) = (879 x 3) + (879 x 7)	137 x (2 + 4) = (137 x 2) + (137 x 4)
6 x 7 = 7 x 6	10 x 45 = 45 x 10	135 x 456 = 456 x 135	12 + (6 + 6) = (12 + 6) + 6
918,273,645 x 1 = 918,273,645	58 x (2 x 3) = (58 x 2) x 3	555 x (5 + 5) = (555 x 5) + (555 x 5)	(100 x 5) x 2 = 100 x (5 x 2)

NAME ______________________________

DATE ______________

VARIABLES

SLV4N

Solve for N.

A. 6 + N = 18

B. 56 – 14 = N

C. 100 x N = 1,000

D. N ÷ 8 = 13

E. N + 12 = 100

F. 146 ÷ 2 = N

G. 12 x N = 108

H. N ÷ 10 = 7

I. 108 – N = 99

J. 15 + N = 23

K. 99 – 76 = N

L. N x 10 = 150

M. 156 + N = 334

N. N ÷ 5 = 55

O. N – 1,657 = 900

P. 76 x N = 228

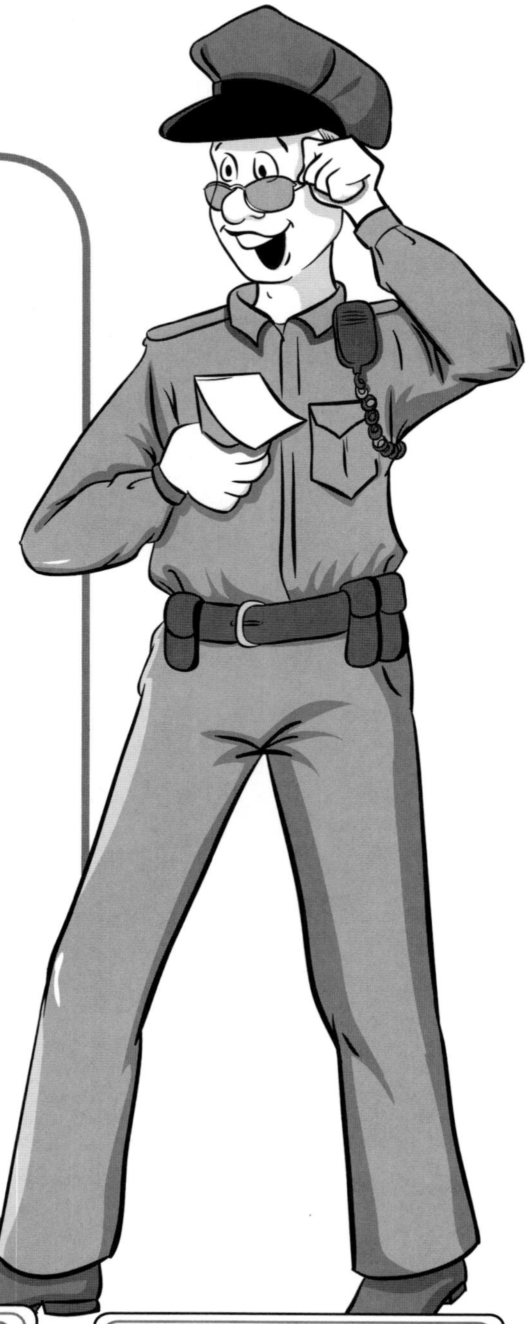

NAHRTBT

NOBRKS

NVRLKBK

ND4SPED

NRG

Problem Solving

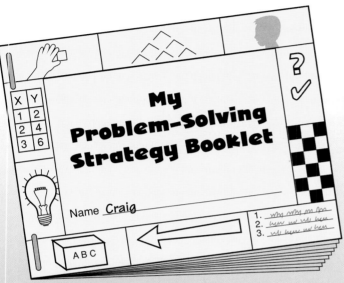

STRATEGY BOOKLET

Strengthen problem-solving skills by having students assemble this handy booklet. Make a copy of pages 152–154 for each child. Instruct him to cut the 12 booklet pages apart and stack them in order. Then have him staple the pages together along the left side to create a booklet he can color and store in his desk as a ready reference.

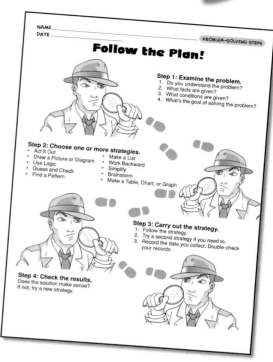

Step-by-Step

Help students organize their thinking when solving problems. Give each problem solver a copy of page 155 and discuss the steps together. Then have her attach the page to the inside cover of her math folder. Remind her to refer to it when solving any kind of problem.

More Than One Way

To help students discover that there is more than one way to solve a problem, write on the board a problem such as the one shown. Give each group of three or four students a sheet of chart paper and markers (or a transparency and overhead markers). Without any direction from you, have group members work together to solve the problem, showing their work on the paper or transparency. When all the groups have finished working, invite a volunteer from each group to present its work and solution to the class and then explain the problem-solving strategy that was used.

Ned's soccer team washed cars to raise money for uniforms. The forwards washed half of the cars. The midfielders washed one-third of the remaining cars. The defenders washed half of the cars that were left. The goalkeeper washed the last five cars. How many cars did the players wash altogether?

We guessed and checked.

We worked backward.

Booklet Cover and Pages 2–4

Use with "Strategy Booklet" on page 151.

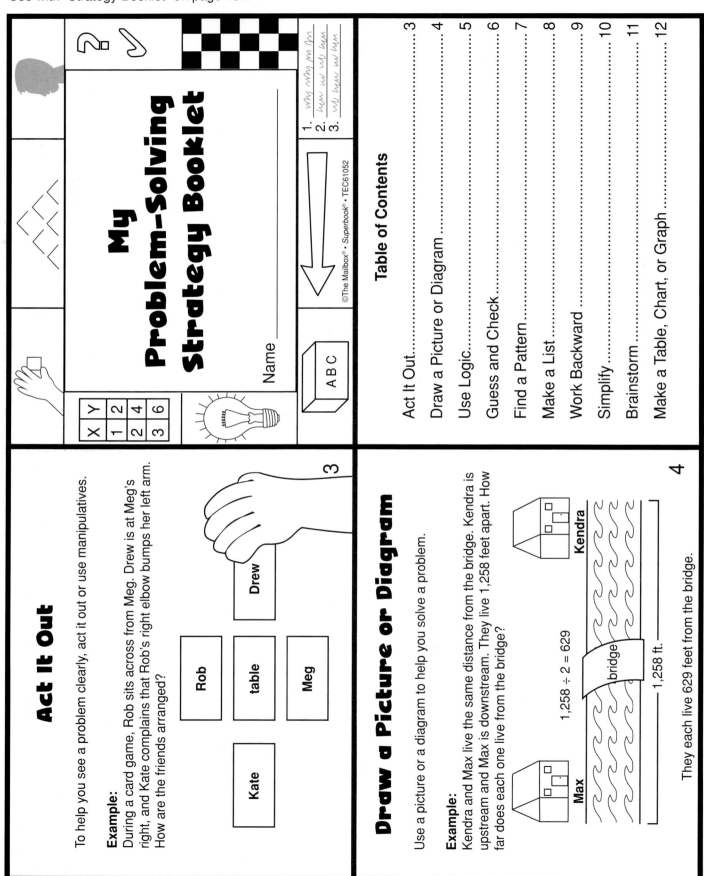

My Problem-Solving Strategy Booklet

Name _____

©The Mailbox® • Superbook® • TEC61052

X	Y
1	2
2	4
3	6

A B C

1. _____
2. _____
3. _____

Table of Contents

Act It Out

To help you see a problem clearly, act it out or use manipulatives.

Example:
During a card game, Rob sits across from Meg. Drew is at Meg's right, and Kate complains that Rob's right elbow bumps her left arm. How are the friends arranged?

Kate   Rob

table

Drew

Meg

3

Draw a Picture or Diagram

Use a picture or a diagram to help you solve a problem.

Example:
Kendra and Max live the same distance from the bridge. Kendra is upstream and Max is downstream. They live 1,258 feet apart. How far does each one live from the bridge?

Max

Kendra

bridge

1,258 ÷ 2 = 629

1,258 ft.

They each live 629 feet from the bridge.

4

Use Logic

5

When given a series of clues, use logical reasoning to help find a solution. Displaying the data in a chart can help you work through the problem.

Example:
John, Dennis, Eric, Alex, and Bill met for dinner. Their waiter mixed up all the orders! Use the clues to help sort out the orders. Put a ✔ in each box that is true and an X in each box that is not true.

Clues:
1. Bill doesn't eat beef or pork.
2. Dennis did not order sausage.
3. Eric prefers his meat sliced.
4. Alex did not order sausage or chopped beef.

	Chopped Beef	Chicken	Sliced Beef	Sausage	Ribs
John	X	X	X	✔	X
Dennis	✔	X	X	X	X
Eric	X	X	✔	X	X
Alex	X	X	X	X	✔
Bill	X	✔	X	X	X

John, sausage; Dennis, chopped beef; Eric, sliced beef; Alex, ribs; Bill, chicken

Guess and Check

6

Take a guess at a problem's answer and check it. If you're not correct, adjust your guess and try again.

Example:
The product of two numbers is 115. What are the two numbers? Since 115 has a 5 in the ones place, you know it is a multiple of 5.

Guess: 5 x 20 = 100 (The answer is too small.)

Guess again: 5 x 23 = 115 (Yes!)
The numbers are 5 and 23.

Find a Pattern

7

Think of one way to get from one number to the next number in a pattern. Then see if this rule works for the rest of the pattern.

Example:
Degas is making a picture. He places one tile in the first row, four tiles in the second row, and seven tiles in the third row. How many tiles will be in the sixth row?

The rule is add three.
The sixth row will have 16 tiles.

Make a List

8

Make an organized list when you need to show all the possible solutions.

Example:
How many different outfits could you make if you bought one red shirt, one blue tank top, one pair of tan pants, and one pair of gray shorts?

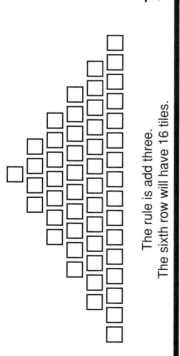

red shirt, tan pants
red shirt, gray shorts
blue tank top, tan pants
blue tank top, gray shorts

You could make four different outfits!

Work Backward

9

Read the problem. Identify the operations used. Then use inverse operations to work backward to the problem's beginning.

Example:
Bill returned from shopping with $3.00. He had spent $9.25 for snacks and $12.75 for comic books. How much money did he have before he went shopping?

Amount Bill had left: $3.00 + Amount spent on snacks: $9.25 + Amount spent on comic books: $12.75 = He started with $25.00!

$3.00 + $9.25 + $12.75 = $25.00

Simplify

10

To help you understand a problem, decide on a way to make the numbers simpler.

Example:
At 7:00 AM on Friday, Carinda finds this note from her mom: "Your aunt will be here in exactly 1,500 minutes." On what day and at what time will Carinda's aunt arrive?

60 minutes = 1 hour
1,500 minutes ÷ 60 minutes = 25 hours
24 hours = 1 day
25 hours = 1 day and 1 hour.
Carinda's aunt will arrive at 8:00 AM on Saturday.

Brainstorm

11

Think of a new, creative way to look at a problem.

Example:
How do five and nine more make two?
If it's 5 o'clock and you move the hour hand ahead 9 hours, it will become 2 o'clock.

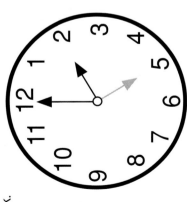

Make a Table, Chart, or Graph

12

Use a table, chart, or graph when you need to keep track of data and see how it changes.

Example:
Bruce is 4 years old and Matt is 13 years old. When will Matt be twice as old as Bruce?

Bruce	4	5	6	7	8	9
Matt	13	14	15	16	17	18

age

Matt will be twice as old as Bruce in 5 years!

Follow the P...

Step 1: Examine ...
1. Do you understand ...oblem.
2. What facts are given? ...blem?
3. What conditions are given...
4. What's the goal of solving the ...oblem?

Step 2: Choose one or more strategies.
- Act It Out
- Draw a Picture or Diagram
- Use Logic
- Guess and Check
- Find a Pattern
- Make a List
- Work Backward
- Simplify
- Brainstorm
- Make a Table, Chart, or Graph

Step 3: Carry out the strategy.
1. Follow the strategy.
2. Try a second strategy if you need to.
3. Record the data you collect. Double-check your records.

Step 4: Check the results.
Does the solution make sense?
If not, try a new strategy.

the States of Matter

Get students moving and familiarize them with the states of matter at the same time. Take your class outside to a basketball court or the blacktop. Instruct students to stand on the basketball court together. Explain that each student represents an atom and the court represents a cooking pot. Then read the descriptions below as each student moves accordingly.

- You are a liquid. You are moving slowly inside the pot. (Students slowly walk around the court.)

- It's getting cold. (Students walk slower.)

- Now you are frozen. (Students stand close together at one end of the court, representing ice at the bottom of the pot.)

- It's getting warmer. (Students slowly walk around.)

- It's getting hot. (Students walk very fast around the court.)

- You're boiling! (Students leave the court, one at a time.)

- You're now a gas!

Bring students back together and discuss the different states of matter that were demonstrated.

Solid or Liquid?

Investigate solids and liquids with this perplexing experiment. Show students a cup of water and ask them to identify it as a solid or liquid. Ask the class which characteristics make water a liquid. Next, show students a mound of cornstarch. Ask students which characteristics make it a solid.

Next, divide students into small groups. Give each group 200 mL of water in a mixing bowl, 350 mL of cornstarch, a craft stick, and the following directions:

1. Using the craft stick, stir the cornstarch into the water, a little at a time. (You may not need all the cornstarch.)
2. Stop stirring the mixture when it becomes difficult to do.
3. Explore the mixture by hand.
4. Determine whether the mixture is a solid or a liquid. Explain your answer.

Tell students that the mixture has properties of both a solid and a liquid. *(When the mixture is squeezed, it feels like a solid. When the mixture is not being squeezed, it returns to a liquid.)* Explain that the molecules in this mixture don't flow easily under pressure (squeezing). During cleanup, put the mixture in the trash to avoid clogging a drain.

Check out the skill-building reproducible on page 157.

An Invisible Firefighter

Demonstrate the presence of an invisible gas with this quick experiment. Place a votive candle inside a beaker. Pour a small amount of baking soda mixed with water into the beaker. Light the candle. Tell students to observe the candle as you add a mystery liquid (vinegar). Being careful not to pour any directly on the candle, add a small amount of vinegar to the beaker *(the flame will go out)*. Ask students what made the flame go out. Then allow a student to try to identify the mystery liquid by smell. Explain that when vinegar is poured into the dissolved baking soda, carbon dioxide is released. The gas fills the beaker, pushing out the oxygen; without any oxygen, the flame cannot burn. Help your students conclude that even though gas cannot be seen, it is still present.

Changes in State

Match each word to its meaning. Write the letter on the matching numbered line below.
Use the Word Bank.

Word Bank				
G. matter	L. physical properties	U. solid	M. liquid	R. gas
Z. evaporation	E. condensation	F. melting	K. freezing	T. boiling

____ 1. state in which matter has no definite shape or volume

____ 2. anything that takes up space and has mass

____ 3. when a substance changes state from a liquid to a gas

____ 4. when a substance changes from a gas to a liquid

____ 5. state in which matter has a definite shape and volume

____ 6. when a substance changes state from a liquid to a solid

____ 7. characteristics of a substance that can be seen or measured without changing the

substance into something different

____ 8. when a substance changes state from a solid to a liquid

____ 9. state in which matter has a definite volume but no definite shape

____ 10. when particles escape from a nonboiling liquid and become a gas

What are two things that occur at the same temperature?
To answer the question, match letters from above to the blanks below.

____ ____ ____ ____ ING and ____ ____ ____ ____ ____ ING
 9   4   7   3   8   1   4   4   10

BODY SYSTEMS

Food on the Move

Introduce the concept of peristalsis with this small-group activity. In advance, cut pairs of old stockings into long tubes. Divide your class into small groups; then give each group one tube. Next, provide each group with a tennis ball. Explain that the ball represents the bolus, the ball of food formed in the mouth by chewing and saliva. To demonstrate peristalsis—the process by which food is pushed through the esophagus and intestinal tubes—instruct one student from each group to place the ball inside the stocking and hold it as shown. Then have the student squeeze the stocking behind the ball so that it moves through the stocking. Direct the students in each group to take turns, allowing each group member to try his hand at this simulation.

IT'S DIGESTION TIME!

Give students a better understanding of the digestive process with this activity. Copy the chart below onto the board. Use a diagram of the digestive system and the information in the chart to explain each step of the digestive process to your students. Then give one copy of page 160, scissors, colored pencils, and a glue stick to each student. Instruct the student to complete the page as directed to make his own model of the digestive system.

SIZING UP THE INTESTINES

Just how long are the small and large intestines? To find out, give each pair of students a 28-foot length of yarn or string. Instruct each partner to hold one end of the yarn, extending it as far as possible. Explain that the length of the yarn represents the approximate length of an adult's intestines. Next, challenge each pair to neatly fold the yarn so that it fits on a sheet of notebook paper. Explain that this represents how the intestines fit inside the body. Finally, display a diagram of the digestive system, pointing out both the large and small intestines. Students will be amazed at the way their bodies utilize space!

DIGESTIVE TIMETABLE

Number of Hours	Action
0	You start eating.
$\frac{1}{2}$	Your stomach is full.
2	Partly digested food called chyme enters the duodenum.
6	Your stomach is almost empty.
12	Your small intestine absorbs nutrients.
18	Wastes begin to form in the large intestine.
24	Solid wastes called feces are ready to leave the body.

Cruising the Circulatory System

Provide each group of students with a six-foot length of white bulletin board paper; red and yellow construction paper; and red, blue, and white yarn. Have the group trace an outline of one student onto the paper. Next, have the students cut out and glue yellow paper lungs and a red paper heart in the appropriate locations on the outline. Then have the group use the color code shown to glue the yarn onto the outline and label the vessels to represent the circulatory system. Finally, provide each student with a copy of page 161. Instruct him to use his group's completed model of the circulatory system to describe what it would be like to journey through the circulatory system, starting in the heart.

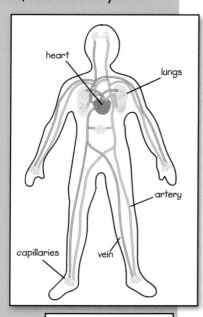

heart
lungs
artery
capillaries
vein

Color Code	
red	= arteries
blue	= veins
white	= capillaries

QUIET AS A MOUSE?

Before introducing the muscular system, challenge students to this simple game. Ask students how long they can sit still without moving a muscle. Set a timer for two minutes and then tell students that if any of their muscles move they are out. As you walk throughout the room, slowly eliminate each student from the game by having her put her head on her desk. Once two minutes are up and every student is out, explain to students that while they may have controlled their voluntary muscles (arms, legs, mouth, etc.), they could not control their involuntary muscles (heart, eyelids, diaphragm, and some stomach muscles). Wrap up the activity by discussing the various muscles in the human body and whether they are classified as voluntary or involuntary. If desired, have each student illustrate voluntary and involuntary muscles on unlined paper.

Put your left femur in. Take your left femur out.
Put your left femur in, and shake it all about.
You do the Hokey-Pokey, and you turn yourself around.
That's what it's all about!

SCIENTIFIC HOKEY-POKEY

Here's a great way to review the major bones of the human skeleton! Have small groups of students stand in circles. When singing and dancing to "The Hokey-Pokey," use the scientific name for the major bones of the body instead of the usual body parts. If desired, allow students to point to bones that are hard to single out. A student must sit down if he identifies an incorrect bone. With each verse of the song, sing faster and faster until all major bones have been reviewed or until only one student remains standing.

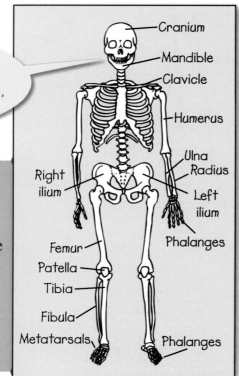

Cranium
Mandible
Clavicle
Humerus
Ulna
Radius
Right ilium
Left ilium
Phalanges
Femur
Patella
Tibia
Fibula
Metatarsals
Phalanges

Tracking Digestion

Color each body part to the right a different color. Cut out each part and glue it in the correct place on the body outline. Label each part with a word from the word bank.

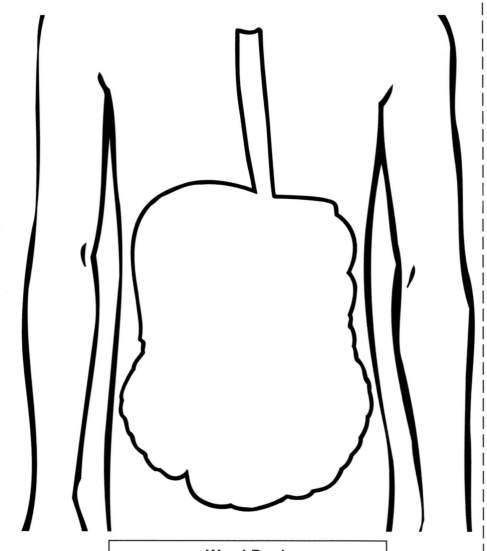

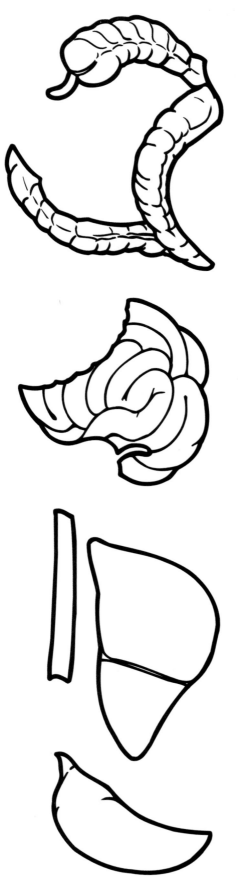

Word Bank

esophagus	stomach
liver	small intestine
large intestine	

Note to the teacher: Use with "It's Digestion Time!" on page 158.

NAME _____

DATE _____

ALL ABOARD!

Imagine you are traveling through the circulatory system.
Starting at the heart, describe what you see along the way.

Beginning

_____
_____
_____
_____
_____
_____

Middle

_____
_____
_____
_____
_____
_____

End

_____
_____
_____
_____
_____
_____

Drawing of the voyage

Note to the teacher: Use with "Cruising the Circulatory System" on page 159.

CELLS

Excellent Mosaics

This hands-on activity will motivate students to take a closer look at the parts of a plant or animal cell. Give each student pair a piece of poster board, some liquid glue, and an assortment of beans, seeds, rice, and pasta. Have them draw an outline of a cell on the poster board and then glue the beans, seeds, and pasta to the outline to illustrate the parts of a cell. Direct the duo to also provide a key.

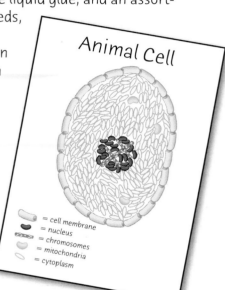

Animal Cell

- = cell membrane
- = nucleus
- = chromosomes
- = mitochondria
- = cytoplasm

CELL TALK

For this class game, divide the class into pairs. Have each pair cut out the gameboard and cards from a copy of page 163 and place the cards facedown. To play, Player 1 chooses a card. He reads it aloud, matches it to the correct term on the gameboard, and initials the card. Then Player 2 takes a turn. If a player thinks that a card has been incorrectly placed on the board, he can place another card on the same board space. At the end of the game, the pair uses a copy of the answer key from page 314 to verify each answer. Each player gets one point for each correct answer and loses one point for each incorrect answer. The player with more points is the winner.

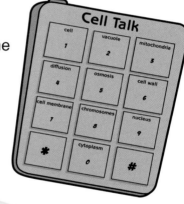

Cell Talk

cell 1	vacuole 2	mitochondria 3
diffusion 4	osmosis 5	cell wall 6
cell membrane 7	chromosomes 8	nucleus 9
*	cytoplasm 0	#

MITOSIS RETELL

Give each child a 3" x 18" strip of paper and have her fold it in half three times, open it, and fold it into an accordion-style booklet with eight pages. After she labels the booklet's front page, have her write about and illustrate each cell division stage in the correct order on a separate booklet page. Then cut the last page from the booklet. Have students use the booklet as a reference throughout your cell studies.

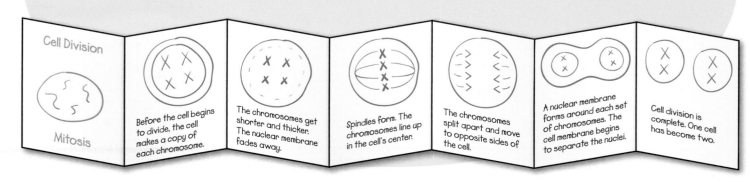

Cell Division

Mitosis

Before the cell begins to divide, the cell makes a copy of each chromosome.

The chromosomes get shorter and thicker. The nuclear membrane fades away.

Spindles form. The chromosomes line up in the cell's center.

The chromosomes split apart and move to opposite sides of the cell.

A nuclear membrane forms around each set of chromosomes. The cell membrane begins to separate the nuclei.

Cell division is complete. One cell has become two.

Cell Talk

cell 1	vacuole 2	mitochondria 3
diffusion 4	osmosis 5	cell wall 6
cell membrane 7	chromosomes 8	nucleus 9
✱	cytoplasm 0	#

©The Mailbox® • *Superbook*® • TEC61052 • Key p. 314

most materials move in and out of cells through this process TEC61052	jellylike substance between a cell membrane and a nucleus TEC61052	the basic unit of living things TEC61052	threadlike structures inside a cell that hold genes TEC61052	in a cell, energy is released from these TEC61052
a tough layer that supports a plant cell TEC61052	a food or waste storage space in a cell TEC61052	this part of a cell controls the cell's actions TEC61052	holds all the parts of a cell together TEC61052	cells get most of their water through this process TEC61052

Survival and Adaptation

All Covered Up

This creative-thinking activity is perfect for helping students review what they've learned about animals' body coverings. Give each student a new pencil and assign her a unique school habitat such as those shown. Ask students to pretend that their pencils are newly discovered animals living in these habitats. Then instruct each student to use construction paper, scissors, and crayons to create an appropriate body covering for the creature. After the student tapes the body covering to the pencil, have her write a short paragraph naming the new animal and describing how its body covering will help it survive. Conclude by having students share their creations with the class.

Habitats
watery pond of the classroom sink
rainy jungle of the class plant
desert sands of the playground
icy chill of the cafeteria refrigerator

My fridgimal lives in the deepest corner of the cafeteria's refrigerator. The refrigerator's temperature stays at 35°F all the time. Not only will the fridgimal's thick, white coat protect it from the cold, but also it will help it hide from Ms. Yummy, the cafeteria manager.

A BODY OF WORK

Further students' study of animals' physical adaptations with this partner activity. Have each twosome choose an animal and research its special adaptations and their importance. Then have the duo make a lift-the-flap project to showcase the information. To make one, the twosome draws on a sheet of construction paper a picture of its animal in its environment. Next, the students cut a flap at each place on the animal's body that represents an adaptation. They cover the back of the picture with glue (except for the flaps) and attach it to a second sheet of construction paper. Under each flap, the partners record information about the corresponding adaptation. After sharing the project with the class, the duo attaches it to a display titled "Amazing Adaptations."

A giraffe has very good eyesight to watch for danger.

Long legs help the giraffe reach leaves on high branches.

MOVING ON

This small-group activity helps students understand the connection between an animal's movements and its ability to move efficiently. Divide students into groups of three and assign each group a different animal. After the group researches the animal, have one student draw an outline of the animal's footprint on a sheet of construction paper and cut it out. Then have the students use the footprint as a template to cut out two additional footprints. Next, direct the group to write the animal's name on one footprint, how it moves on the second footprint, and any adaptation that enables movement on the third. Place each group's footprints at a center or on a display for classmates to read as time allows.

Mexican Gray Wolf

Long, strong legs help it run for long distances.

It runs.

Check out the skill-building reproducible on page 165.

NAME _____

DATE _____

Amazing Adaptations

Read each statement.
Cut out the strips at the bottom.
Glue the correct strip with the matching animal.

1. In the Arctic, the ptarmigan changes from brown to white in the winter.

2. Anglerfish look like the rocks on the floor of the ocean.

3. Some cobras can spit venom into an attacker's eyes.

4. A porcupine has long, sharp quills.

5. The glass lizard detaches its tail when it's attacked.

6. Hard plates cover the body of an armadillo.

7. Gills are found on a tadpole.

8. A bat has a keen sense of hearing.

©The Mailbox® • Superbook® • TEC61052 • Key p. 314

The foe becomes blinded.		An enemy is not able to attack this animal effectively due to its hard shell.
Sounds echo back and allow the animal to fly safely.	The sharp objects pierce the foe's flesh and cause great pain.	It blends in with the snow and is able to hide.
These fish hide themselves to avoid enemies.	This small animal can get oxygen out of the water it lives in.	The attacker becomes side-tracked by the detached tail and allows the animal to escape.

Solar System

By the Light of the Moon

Demonstrate what makes the moon shine with this easy activity. Show the class a bicycle reflector. Point out that the reflector is not a light source. Ask your students what makes a reflector visible in the dark. Turn out the lights and shine a flashlight on the reflector. Explain that the reflector reflects the light of the flashlight. Apply this concept to the sun and moon. Help your students conclude that the moon reflects the light of the sun, and without the sun there would be no moonlight.

Solar Solutions

During a study of the solar system, challenge students to write and solve problems that involve numerical facts. To jump-start students' thinking, post the following problem on the board for them to solve: Light travels at 186,282 miles per second. Earth is approximately 93,000,000 miles from the sun. How long does it take sunlight to reach Earth? Round your answer to the nearest whole number. (93,000,000 ÷ 186,282 ≈ 499 seconds or 8 minutes)

Make a Moon

After discussing how some craters are formed by meteoroids landing on the moon's surface, guide small groups of students in the following experiment.

Materials for one moon:
copy of the recording sheet on page 168
bag of modeling dough (see the recipe)
aluminum pie pan
¼ cup flour
marble
golf ball
meterstick

> **Modeling Dough**
> 1 c. flour
> ½ c. salt
> ½ c. water
> Mix the ingredients together. Store the dough in a resealable plastic bag.

Steps:
1. Spread the dough evenly on the bottom of the pan. Sprinkle the flour atop the dough to represent moondust.
2. From a height of 100 cm, drop the marble onto the dough. Remove the marble and then write the width and depth of the resulting "crater" in the corresponding section of the recording sheet.
3. Repeat Step 2, first dropping the marble from a height of 75 cm and then from 50 cm. Record the resulting measurements.
4. Repeat Steps 2 and 3 using the golf ball.
5. Record on the back of the recording sheet your conclusions about the results.

Planetary Weather Reports

Spotlight the wacky weather patterns of other planets with this role-playing activity. Divide the class into groups, assigning each group a different planet. Challenge each group to research weather facts for its assigned planet and then prepare a weather report. Have each group share its report by using props such as seasonal clothing, painted backdrops, or weather gear. After each group has presented its report, lead students to discuss the similarities and differences among the planets' weather.

> This is today's weather report for Venus. Today will be cloudy with temperatures near 900°F. You may see some lightning. And watch out! There's a chance of sulfuric acid precipitation!

Create an Alien

Are there other life-forms in outer space? There will be after your students complete this research project! Show your class a picture of a giraffe or other animal. Ask your students which features or characteristics help that animal survive in its habitat. For example, the colors of a giraffe's coat allow it to blend with trees, and its nostrils can close completely to keep out dust and sand.

Next, assign each student a different planet, excluding Earth. Give each student a copy of page 169 and a variety of reference materials. Instruct him to follow the directions on the reproducible to describe the characteristics of his assigned planet and to create an alien that could inhabit that planet. Have each student share with the class his findings about his planet and the picture of the alien he created. Then direct each student to cut out his alien picture from the bottom half of the reproducible for a display titled "Life on Other Planets."

Sky Patterns

What do Leo, Pisces, and Orion have in common? They're constellations, of course! Pair students; then assign each pair a different constellation (see the list). Instruct partners to use reference materials to find out what their assigned constellation looks like, the story behind its name, and an interesting fact about it. When the research has been completed, guide each pair through the steps at the right for creating a star can. After the constellation cans have been constructed, darken the room. Have each pair, in turn, share information about its constellation while displaying it.

Extend this activity by giving one copy of the constellations project on page 168 and the materials listed to each student. Instruct each student to complete the project as directed.

Materials: empty tin can, pencil, drawing paper, hammer, 2 or 3 different-size nails, flashlight

Steps:
1. Trace one end of the can on the drawing paper.
2. Draw your assigned constellation within the circle on your paper. Mark the location of the stars heavily so that you can see them from the back of the paper.
3. Turn the paper over and place it on the bottom of the can.
4. Use the hammer and nails to punch holes in the bottom of the can to represent each star. Use different-size nails to show the varying brightness of the stars.
5. Remove the paper and place the flashlight inside the can. Darken the room; then point the flashlight toward the ceiling to project your constellation.

Constellations

Andromeda	Capricornus	Pisces
Aquarius	Cassiopeia	Sagittarius
Aries	Cygnus	Scorpius
Auriga	Gemini	Taurus
Boötes	Hercules	Ursa major
Cancer	Leo	Ursa minor
Canes venatici	Libra	Virgo
	Pegasus	

Make a Moon

	Drop From 100 cm		Drop From 75 cm		Drop From 50 cm	
Marble	___ width	___ depth	___ width	___ depth	___ width	___ depth
Golf ball	___ width	___ depth	___ width	___ depth	___ width	___ depth

Note to the teacher: Use with "Make a Moon" on page 166.

Cool Constellations

Ancient Greeks and Romans observed and named constellations, and now it's your turn! Follow the steps below to create your own constellation. Then name your star group and write a story about the object, person, or animal that it names. Be prepared to share your constellation and story with the class.

Materials: 10 gold star stickers, white crayon or piece of chalk, 12" x 18" sheet of black construction paper

The Dolphin

Steps:

1. Place the construction paper on your desk.
2. Pick up all ten star stickers in one hand and hold them about two feet above your desk. Gently drop the stars a few at a time onto your construction paper.
3. Affix each star to the paper exactly where it fell.
4. Using a white crayon or piece of chalk, create a constellation by connecting the lines between the stars.

Note to the teacher: Use with "Sky Patterns" on page 167.

DATE _____

My Alien Can Survive That!

You have been chosen to create an alien that can live in space. Use reference materials to respond to each of the five items below about the planet you were assigned. Then follow the next set of directions to create a picture of your alien.

1. What is the name of your planet? _____

2. Describe your planet's appearance. _____

_____

_____

3. What is the surface of your planet like?

_____

_____

4. What is the average temperature on your planet?

_____

5. Name some other characteristics or facts about your planet.

_____

_____

Based on the information written above, create an alien that can survive on your assigned planet. On your drawing, label the special parts that enable your alien to live in a habitat on that planet. Be sure to include all of the following: how the alien eats, what he eats, how he adapts to the extreme temperatures on this planet, how he moves around, and how he avoids being captured or eaten by predators. Be creative!

Note to the teacher: Use with "Create an Alien" on page 167.

Motion and Force

Forces All Around

This writing activity gets students to focus on everyday forces. Give each child a copy of page 171 to complete as directed. To extend, have students write responses to the following prompt: "Suppose that the force of gravity will be turned off between 7 AM and 8 AM. Explain how this will affect your morning routine." Post the completed explanations on a board titled "An Hour Without Gravity."

NAME Mark
DATE 12-14-2006

Everyday Forces
FORCES

Draw a picture to illustrate each force. On the lines below each picture, explain what is happening.

A PUSH
People are pushing a car to make it move.

GRAVITY
A leaf falling from a tree is being pulled to the ground.

A PULL
A person is pulling on the rope to move the tree limb.

FRICTION
A person is rubbing her hands together to create heat.

	Distance Traveled by Cannon	Distance Traveled by Cannonball
empty cannonball		
cannonball with one penny		
cannonball with two pennies		
cannonball with three pennies		

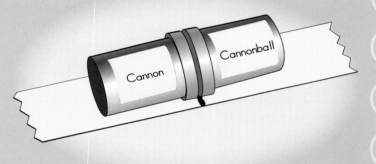

An Exploding Cannon

Demonstrate for students what happens when two forces act upon each other. Gather the materials listed below. Next, place a strip of masking tape on the floor with a starting line marked as shown. Using masking tape and a marker, label one film canister "Cannon" and the other "Cannonball." Fill the cannon with five milliliters of water. Drop one tablet piece in the cannon, quickly snap on the lid, and then position the canisters (with lids touching) on the starting line as shown. In a few seconds, the cannon will explode, moving the cannonball down the tape. Have students record in a chart the distance traveled by both canisters. Repeat the demonstration three more times, each time adding a penny to the cannonball canister. Then discuss the observed relationship between the strength of the force and the mass of the object.

Materials: two 35-mm Fuji film canisters with lids, marker, masking tape, water, seltzer tablet broken into fourths, 3 pennies, graduated cylinder, measuring tape

Check out the skill-building reproducible on page 172.

NAME _____

DATE _____

Everyday Forces

Draw a picture to illustrate each force.
On the lines below each picture, explain what
   is happening.

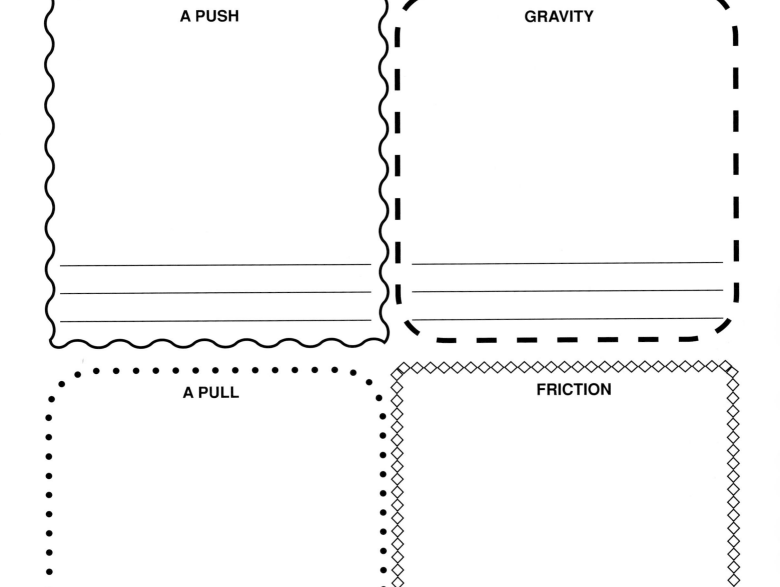

A PUSH

_____

_____

_____

GRAVITY

_____

_____

_____

A PULL

_____

_____

_____

FRICTION

_____

_____

_____

Note to the teacher: Use with "Forces All Around" on page 170.

Racing in Reverse

Follow the steps, using the materials your teacher gives you.

Steps:
1. Thread the string through the straw.
2. Tie each end of the string to the back of a different chair. Slide the chairs apart until the string is taut.
3. Inflate the balloon and close it with the binder clip. Draw a racecar on the balloon.
4. Tape the balloon horizontally to the straw. Slide the straw along the string until the balloon's clipped end almost touches a chair. Release the binder clip.
5. Measure how far your car traveled.

Distance traveled: _____

Newton's Laws of Motion
Law 1: An object at rest will remain at rest and an object moving in a straight line will continue moving in a straight line unless acted upon by an outside force.
Law 2: The change in motion of an object depends on its mass and the force acting upon it.
Law 3: For every action, there is an equal and opposite reaction.

Which one of Newton's laws does this experiment test?

_____

_____

_____

Note to the teacher: Give each student pair a balloon, binder clip, straw, 12-foot length of string, tape, black permanent marker, two chairs, and a ruler.

Earth's Surface

Around-the-House Models

Review the earth's structure by having each child complete a copy of page 175 as directed. Then give each child a few days to look at home for a round object, such as a peach, that when cut in half represents the earth's main layers. Do not allow students to construct the objects. Invite each child to present his object to the class and explain why it is a good model. Expect to see avocados, baseballs, kiwis, hard-boiled eggs, apples, dinner plates with concentric circles, or pictures of these items brought in!

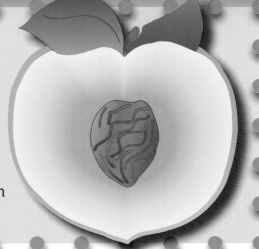

A State of Balance

Demonstrate for students the theory that the continents, ocean basins, mountains, and plains are all in a state of balance. Fill one pan of a pan balance with water to represent the oceans. Add enough sand (the mountains) to the other pan to balance the scale. To model how mountain rock is worn away and carried to the ocean, remove a few spoonfuls of sand at a time and add them to the water. Students will observe that the mountains now become lighter and rise slightly while the oceans become heavier and sink. Discuss how this helps to explain why the erosion of mountains and the buildup of the ocean floors have not leveled the earth's surface.

Earthquake!

Model the action of the earth's plates just before an earthquake. Measure and cut two strips of cloth three inches longer than a cake pan. Place the strips in the bottom of the pan side by side to each other, allowing the excess cloth to extend over either side of the pan. Cover the strips with damp soil; then pack the soil down firmly. Place model houses, cars, and trees on top of the soil to make a neighborhood, being sure to place some models over the area where the two pieces of cloth meet. Gather students around the model. Grasp the edges of both pieces of excess cloth; then simultaneously pull them away from the pan. Have your students observe the effect that the shifting cloth has on the soil and the objects on top of the soil. Challenge the observers to compare the results of this experiment to what might really happen during an earthquake.

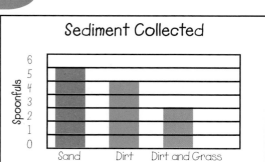

Sediment Collected

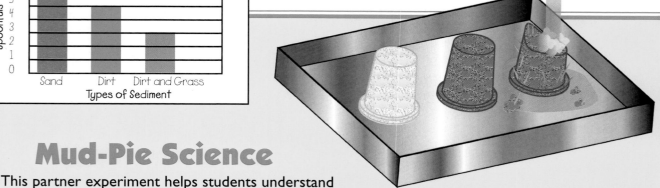

Mud-Pie Science

This partner experiment helps students understand the effect that running water has on soil erosion. Gather enough sand, dirt, and grass clippings for each pair of students to have a cup of sand, 1½ cups of dirt, and one-half cup of grass clippings. In a large plastic tub, mix water with the sand until it is thick enough to build a sand castle. Then give each twosome a plastic cup, a rectangular foil baking pan, and a plastic spoon. Have each pair fill its cup with the sand mixture and deposit it as a mold in one section of the pan. Repeat the process using one cup of the dirt and water and again with one-half cup of dirt, one half-cup of grass, and water so that students have three molds in their pans. Put the pans in a sunny place. When the molds are dry, have the partners slowly pour water over the first mold, use the spoon to collect and measure any sediment that erodes, and record the total in a chart. After students repeat the steps with the two remaining molds, they can graph the data and discuss possible reasons for variations.

Comical Rocks

Assess your students' knowledge of the rock cycle with this fun, creative activity. Give each student a sheet of drawing paper, scissors, and colored pencils or crayons. Have her fold and cut the paper in half lengthwise, making two strips. Direct her to use the first strip to make a rough draft and the second strip for the final copy of a comic strip that explains the rock cycle. Suggest that the student make up names—such as Molly Magma, Inga Igneous, Sally Sedimentary, and Metamorphic Matt—for her rock during its different stages. Make sure that each section of the comic strip includes a picture and caption. Collect the comic strips and display them on a bulletin board titled "Comical Rocks."

I'm Molly Magma. I used to live deep inside the earth.

Then I was pushed out through a volcano. Now my friends call me Lava.

That cold surface air made me harden.

Now I'm a whole new rock with a brand new name— Inga Igneous!

Check out the skill-building reproducible on page 176.

From Crust to Core

Read the passage. Use the boldfaced words to label the diagram.

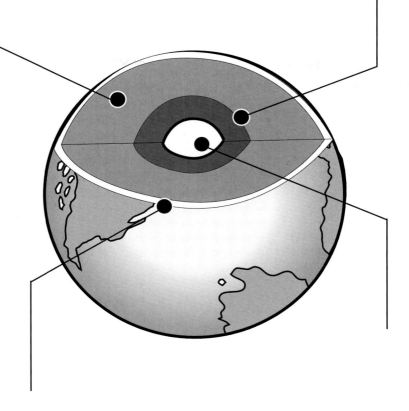

The Layers of the Earth

Scientists have learned that the earth is made of three main layers. The outer layer is the **crust**. It ranges in thickness from five to 25 miles and is made up of solid rocks, soil, and minerals. It has temperatures reaching 1,600°F, which is hot enough to melt rocks.

Under the crust is the **mantle**. It contains a layer of very hot, sometimes molten rock. It supports the crust and is about 1,800 miles thick with temperatures reaching 8,000°F.

Beneath the mantle is the **core**. The **outer core** is about 1,400 miles thick and is made up mostly of melted iron. Its temperatures reach up to 11,000°F. Inside the outer core is the **inner core**, whose center is 4,000 miles below the surface of the earth. It is a ball made up mostly of solid iron. Its temperatures may reach as high as 13,000°F.

To learn the name of the upper rocky layer of the earth that includes the crust and the top part of the mantle, unscramble the boxed letters from the passage and then write them on the lines below.

___ ___ h ___ ___ p h ___ ___ ___

©The Mailbox® • Superbook® • TEC61052 • Key p. 314

Note to the teacher: Use with "Around-the-House Models" on page 173.

175

Aggressive Agents

Read each clue. Color a magnifying glass to tell whether the clue describes water, wind, or ice.

1. It can make fine pieces of rock airborne, causing them to rub away solid rock.

2. As this flows, it can cut into a riverbank to make the river wider.

3. When a large mass of this begins to melt, it leaves behind small rocks, soil, and water.

4. Worn away lake and ocean shores are a good example of this type of erosion.

5. A large moving mass of this can change the shape of a valley from a V to a U.

6. A large mass of this can become heavy enough to move slowly and carry along broken pieces of rock.

7. When it runs, it carries weathered materials into lakes and oceans.

8. It can cause sand to build up into mounds called dunes.

9. It causes erosion on and below the earth's surface.

10. It has the greatest affect in deserts.

Note to the teacher: Before having students complete this activity, discuss the three main agents of erosion—water, wind, and ice—and
176 how they change the earth's surface.

GEOGRAPHY & MAP SKILLS

Picture-Perfect Map Terms

For this team game, divide your students into teams of four. Number the members of each team; then follow the steps below.

To play:

▶ Call Player 1 on each team to a designated spot at the board.

▶ Select one map term (see the list) and whisper that same term to each player at the board. The players illustrate the map term on the board without using words.

▶ When the members of a player's team know the term, have Player 2 run to the board and write the word underneath the drawing.

▶ Give one point to the first team that correctly identifies the term.

▶ Play Round 2 in the same manner, this time having Player 2 illustrate the new term while Player 3 runs to the board to do the writing, and so on.

▶ End the game when all the terms have been reviewed. Declare the team with the most points the winner.

Suggested Map Terms
gulf, bay, sound, strait, peninsula, cape, lake, river, tributary, ocean, country, continent, state, island, delta, scale, capital, international border, highway, city, airport

River

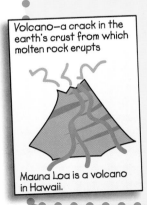

Volcano—a crack in the earth's crust from which molten rock erupts

Mauna Loa is a volcano in Hawaii.

Landforms in Booklet Form

For this booklet project, each student cuts seven sheets of drawing paper in half. Then he uses his social studies textbook and other references to create a booklet page for each of the landforms listed. Each page should include the name of the landform, its definition, an illustration, and an example of where the landform can be found in the United States. He staples the finished pages in alphabetical order between a construction paper cover decorated as desired. Students can use this handy reference throughout the year.

Landforms
coast
island
isthmus
canyon
mountain
basin
cape
plateau
valley
volcano
mesa
peninsula
plain

STATE THE LOCATION

Review U.S. geography and relative location with this whole-class game. Program each of a set of index cards with a different state. Divide students into small groups; then give each child a U.S. map. Have one group at a time draw a card. Without looking at a map, the group writes on the board five statements that tell the location of its chosen place. Give the group two points for each correct statement. If the group cannot write five statements, allow its members to use maps and give them one point each for any additional statements. The remaining groups use their maps to check each statement's accuracy. Play for as long as desired. The team with the most points wins.

Vary the game by programming cards with major U.S. cities, bodies of water, or famous landmarks.

> Colorado is in the United States.
>
> Colorado is in the Rocky Mountain region.
>
> Colorado is east of Utah.
>
> Colorado is south of Wyoming.
>
> Colorado is north of New Mexico.

Imagination "State-tion"

Put each student's mapmaking skills to practice by having her create a map of a new state! Share typical symbols found on a state map. Discuss the information each symbol conveys; then give each student a short length of bulletin board paper, a copy of the bottom half of this page, and colored pencils or crayons.

Instruct each student to follow the directions on the reproducible to design her map. Display the completed maps around the classroom.

NAME _____

DATE _____

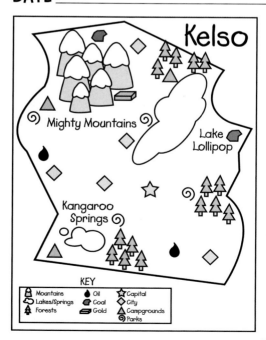

Imagination "State-tion"

Directions: Follow the steps below to create a map of a brand-new state.

1. Draw the shape of your new state.
2. Write the name of your state on the map.
3. Decide which landforms and bodies of water you want your new state to have. Give each landform or body of water a creative name, such as Echo Valley or Flaky Desert.
4. Design at least ten different symbols to use in a key for your map. Have three of these symbols each represent a different natural resource. The other symbols could represent the capital of your state and its cities, landforms, and bodies of water.
5. Position the symbols on your map throughout the state to show their locations.
6. Make a key for your map in the lower left or lower right corner of your map.

Note to the teacher: Use with "Imagination 'State-tion'" on this page.

Map of the United States

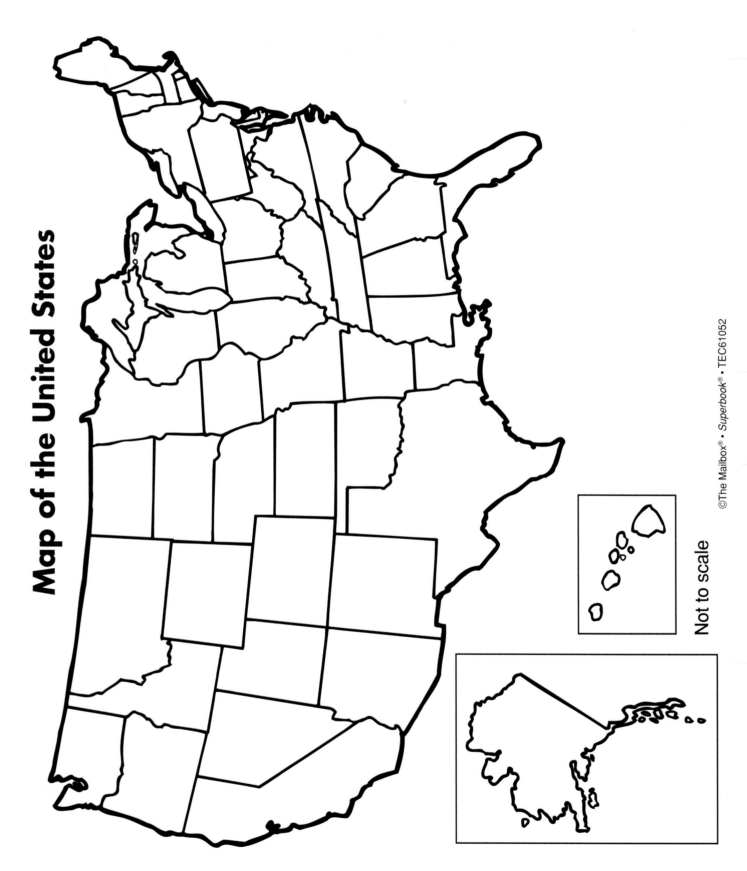

Not to scale

U.S. Government

Branches of Government

Introduce the three branches of the U.S. government with this activity. Begin by drawing a large triangle on the board. Label each angle with the name of a different branch of government as shown. Explain that the U.S. Constitution provides the framework for the federal government and the system of checks and balances that keeps any one branch of the federal government from becoming too powerful. Point out that this triangular organization allows each branch to interact with the other two branches. Visually demonstrate this concept by having three student volunteers come to the front of the room and stand with joined hands in a triangular formation. Strengthen students' understanding of how the three branches of government are related by having each student complete a copy of page 181.

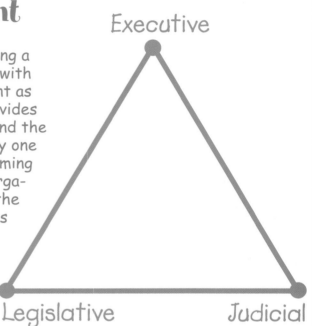

Which Is Which?

Help students learn more about the U.S. Constitution with this partner activity! Copy the amendment cards on page 182 and cut them apart. Place the cards facedown at a center along with a copy of the Constitution (in most social studies textbooks). Students take turns turning over two cards at a time. If a child thinks he has a match, he asks his partner to verify this by checking the amendment number on the copy of the Constitution. If the cards are a match, he keeps them and takes another turn. If the cards are not a match, he returns them facedown to the playing surface and his partner takes a turn in the same manner. Play continues until all cards are matched. The player with more cards wins.

Check out the skill-building reproducible on page 183.

NAME _____

DATE _____

A Balancing Act

The U.S. Constitution is the framework for the U.S. government. It provides for three branches of government—executive, legislative, and judicial. The Constitution also outlines a system of checks and balances to help ensure that no single branch of government becomes too powerful.

Directions: Research and record in the correct boxes the duties of each of the three branches. Then find out how each branch checks—or limits the power of—the other two branches. Write your findings inside the arrows on the diagram.

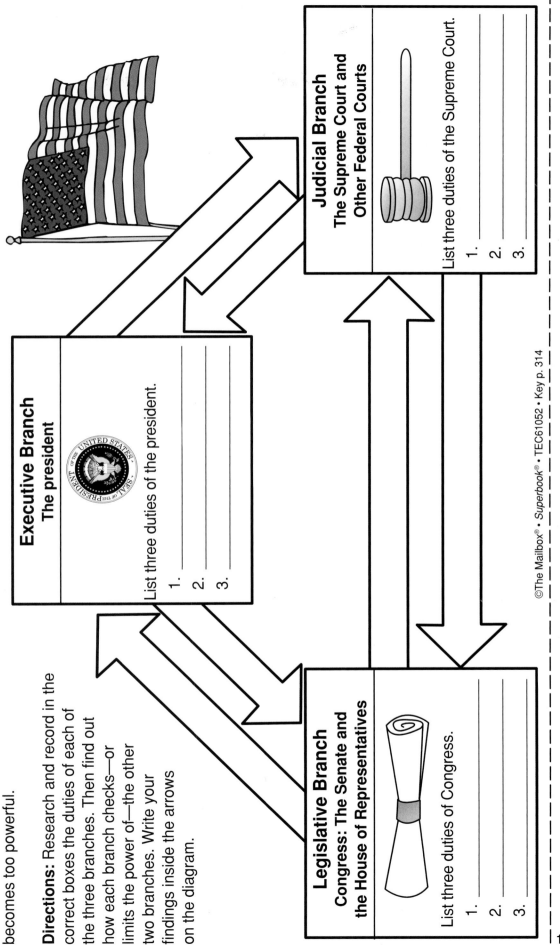

Executive Branch
The president

List three duties of the president.

1. _____
2. _____
3. _____

Judicial Branch
The Supreme Court and Other Federal Courts

List three duties of the Supreme Court.

1. _____
2. _____
3. _____

Legislative Branch
Congress: The Senate and the House of Representatives

List three duties of Congress.

1. _____
2. _____
3. _____

©The Mailbox® • *Superbook*® • TEC61052 • Key p. 314

Note to the teacher: Use with "Branches of Government" on page 180.

181

Amendment Cards

Use with "Which Is Which?" on page 180.

Amendment 1
Basic Freedoms
TEC61052

Citizens have freedom of religion, speech, and the press and the right to assembly and petition. People can worship how they want and say and write what they want. People can gather peacefully and talk about problems they have with the government. TEC61052

Amendment 4
Search and Seizure
TEC61052

A person's property cannot be searched or taken without a warrant. TEC61052

Amendment 5
Rights of the Accused
TEC61052

A person has the right to a fair trial and cannot be accused of the same crime twice. TEC61052

Amendment 6
Right to a Fair Trial
TEC61052

An accused person has a right to a quick and fair jury trial. The government must provide a lawyer for anyone who can't afford one. TEC61052

Amendment 8
Bail and Punishment
TEC61052

A person accused of a crime cannot be treated in a cruel way by the courts. TEC61052

Amendment 13
End of Slavery
TEC61052

Slavery can no longer exist in the United States. TEC61052

Amendment 14
Rights of Citizens
TEC61052

All U.S. citizens have equal rights, and no state can deny citizens their rights. TEC61052

Amendment 15
Voting Rights
TEC61052

No one can be denied voting privileges because of his race. TEC61052

Amendment 19
Women's Suffrage
TEC61052

No one can be denied voting privileges because of her gender. Both men and women can vote in elections. TEC61052

Amendment 26
Voting Age
TEC61052

U.S. citizens age 18 or older may vote. TEC61052

Just the Facts

The Constitution outlines our system of government. It also lists the rights and freedoms of the American people. Complete the passage below by solving each problem.

In _____ (M), (1,088 + 699) men from several states met to write the U.S. Constitution. There were delegates from _____ (I) (180 ÷ 15) states. These states sent a total of _____ (N) (364,353 − 364,298) men to the meeting. They worked for months to write the Constitution.

The final document has _____ (D) (63 ÷ 9) articles. It divides the government into _____ (R) (2.069 + 0.931) branches and explains the powers that each branch has.

Some of the delegates weren't happy with the Constitution. Only _____ (W) (156 ÷ 4) of them signed the Constitution. Of these men, _____ (E) (158 ÷ 79) later became the president. Benjamin Franklin was the oldest person to sign the Constitution. He was _____ (O) (16,622 − 16,541) years old.

The Bill of Rights was added in _____ (A) (199 x 9). Over time, other amendments have been added to the Constitution. There are _____ (J) (621 ÷ 23) amendments right now. An amendment may be proposed if _____ (L) $(\frac{1}{3} \div \frac{1}{2})$ of the states or Congress requests it. It can become a law if _____ (S) $(17\frac{1}{2} - 16\frac{3}{4})$ of the states approve it.

Who is the Father of the Constitution?
To answer the question, write the letter of each answer above on the matching numbered line below.

____ ____ ____ ____ ____
27   1,791 1,787   2 $\frac{3}{4}$

____ ____ ____ ____ ____ ____ ____
1,787 1,791   7   12 $\frac{3}{4}$ 81   55

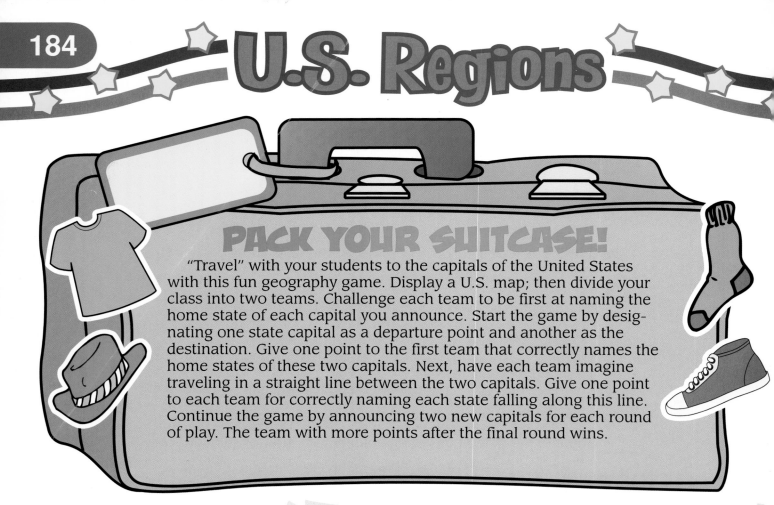

PACK YOUR SUITCASE!

"Travel" with your students to the capitals of the United States with this fun geography game. Display a U.S. map; then divide your class into two teams. Challenge each team to be first at naming the home state of each capital you announce. Start the game by designating one state capital as a departure point and another as the destination. Give one point to the first team that correctly names the home states of these two capitals. Next, have each team imagine traveling in a straight line between the two capitals. Give one point to each team for correctly naming each state falling along this line. Continue the game by announcing two new capitals for each round of play. The team with more points after the final round wins.

PORTRAIT OF A REGION

Looking for a unique activity for motivating students to learn about regions? Form poetry will do the trick! Make one copy of page 187 for each student and distribute them. Also, assign each child a state from the region you are currently studying. Instruct him to use his social studies textbook to find the facts he needs to write a poem on the form provided. Explain that the poem should tell its reader about that assigned state. After each poem has been written, give each student a sheet of drawing paper. Direct him to draw as large an outline of his assigned state as possible on his drawing paper. Then instruct him to copy his poem in the center of the state-outline shape, add illustrations to the poem, and then cut out the outline map that he drew. Post all of your students' poems on a bulletin board titled "Portrait of a Region."

Write All About It!

While studying the geography of the United States, challenge your students to create informative newspapers. Pair your students; then assign each pair a different U.S. region. Give each pair two sheets of drawing paper, the front page of a newspaper, colored pencils, and a copy of page 186 to complete as directed. Display the completed news pages on a bulletin board titled "Extra! Extra! Read All About It!"

Pennsylvania

My region, the Middle Atlantic, is like a crowded mall just one week before the holidays.

My capital is Harrisburg, and my nickname is the Keystone State.

My population is large and includes Italian, German, and Polish descendants.

Tourists come to visit historic Philadelphia and the Pocono Mountains.

My hills and valleys are like a colorful roller coaster track at your favorite amusement park.

My land holds anthracite coal that is as black as the night sky.

I share this land with white-tailed deer and hemlock trees.

Some of my residents work in service industries and eat Hershey's chocolates.

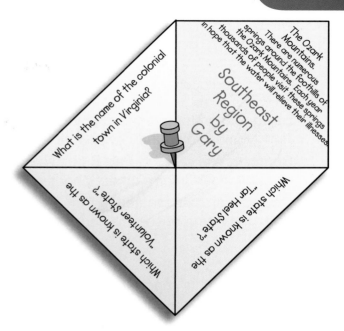

DESTINATION: U.S. REGIONS

Can an imaginary trip actually help your students learn about the regions of the United States? It can with this activity! Give each student a copy of page 188. Then assign her a different region of the United States. Each student imagines that she is planning a trip to her assigned region and fills in each pattern on her reproducible as follows:

 Think about the climate of your region. On the lines of the suitcase, briefly describe from head to toe what you could be wearing on a trip to your assigned region.

 On the shopping bag, name three souvenirs you could bring back from this region.

 On each lens of the sunglasses, name a different tourist attraction that you could visit.

 On the lines of the plate, describe a typical regional meal that you could eat while on your trip.

 On the lines of the pawprint, name three animals that you could see while visiting this region.

Without revealing her assigned region, invite each student to share the information written on her patterns while her classmates guess which region is being described.

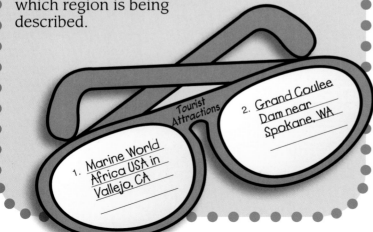

Spinning for Trivia

Is your class ready for some regional trivia? Challenge each student to write four trivia questions about your current region of study. Explain that each trivia question should be accompanied by an answer and an interesting fact related to that answer (see the illustration). After all the trivia questions have been written, give each student an $8\frac{1}{2}$" x $8\frac{1}{2}$" square of drawing paper. The student folds his paper as shown, writing a different trivia question on the outside of each triangular flap. Next, he lifts each flap and writes the answer to the question plus one related, interesting fact on the flap. Then he writes his name and the region's name on the inside square. Mount each trivia square on a bulletin board titled "Spinning for Trivia" by inserting a pushpin through the center of the square, enabling it to rotate. Invite your students to the board to rotate the squares—one triangle at a time—to learn more about your current region of study.

Write All About It!

Directions:

1. Using research materials and your textbook, complete the steps in Part A below to create newspaper articles about your assigned region.
2. Complete the steps in Part B below to design a two-page newspaper layout that will inform others about your region.
3. Copy the articles created in Part A onto the layout created in Part B. Write the name of your newspaper in its designated place.

Part A:

1. Write a weather report that is typical for this time of year.
2. Find out what natural resources are found in this region. Write a short news article about one or more of these resources.
3. Find out what people in this region do for entertainment. Write a short news article that tells about an upcoming event in the region.
4. Design an advertisement for one of the tourist attractions in this region.
5. Write a short news article about an animal found in this region.
6. Find out what types of jobs the people in this region have. Write three classified ads that announce current job openings.

Part B:

1. Study the front page of any local newspaper to see how it is organized. Compare the layout of the front page to that of the other newspaper pages.
2. On a sheet of drawing paper, design a front-page layout. Include space for the name of your paper.
3. On another sheet of drawing paper, create a layout for a second newspaper page.

NAME ____________________

DATE ____________

Write words or phrases about your assigned state to complete each sentence.

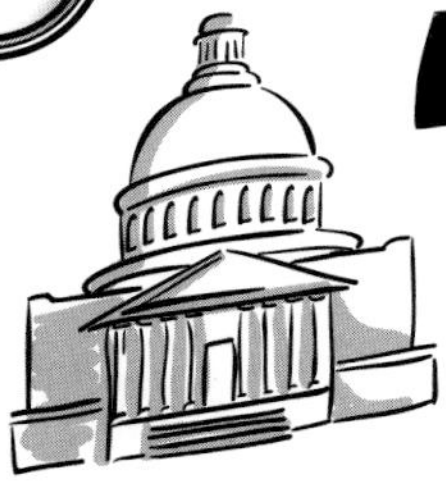

PORTRAIT OF A REGION

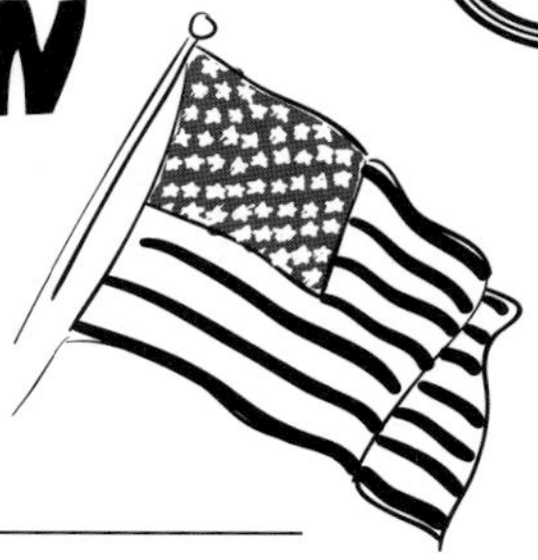

____
name of state

My region, the ____________ (region), is like ____________________

____

____.

My capital is ____________ (capital), and my nickname is ____________ (nickname)

____.

My population is ____________ (adjective) and includes ____________ (nationality)

____________________________________ descendants.

Tourists come to visit ____________ (tourist attraction) and ____________ (tourist attraction)

____.

My ____________ (physical features) are like ____________________

____.

My land holds ____________ (natural resource) that is as ____________ (color) as

____________.

I share this land with ____________ (animal) and ____________ (plant).

Some of my residents work ____________________ (job) and eat

____________________ (popular food from state).

Note to the teacher: Use with "Portrait of a Region" on page 184.

NAME _____

DATE _____

DESTINATION: U.S. REGIONS

Souvenirs

1.
2.
3.

Tourist Attractions

2.

1.

Animals

1.
2.
3.

Clothing

Food

Note to the teacher: Use with "Destination: U.S. Regions" on page 185.

U.S. HISTORY

EXPLORING THE NEW WORLD

Divide your class into cooperative groups; then assign each group a different original colony on which to report. Explain that each group will act as a team of surveyors who should find out as much as possible about its colony and report its observations to the king. Expect each group to research the following topics about its colony: physical features, natural resources, and climate. After each group completes its research, have it present its findings to the royal court—the rest of the class. Have the class discuss whether colonization in each area should be recommended. On the board make a two-column chart presenting reasons for and against the colonization of each area.

What in the World?

Here's an activity that will expose your students to the blending of cultures that occurred when the Old World adventurers discovered the New World. Share with students the foods and plants listed below that were introduced in Europe after explorers brought these items back from the New World. Have each student select one item from the list to research; then have him design a poster advertising that item's attributes and possible uses to his fellow countrymen in the Old World. After each student explains his poster to the class, post it for others to see.

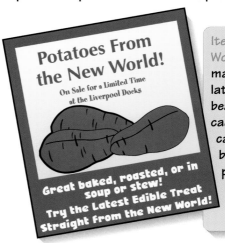

Potatoes From the New World!
On Sale for a Limited Time at the Liverpool Docks

Great baked, roasted, or in soup or stew!
Try the Latest Edible Treat Straight from the New World!

Items From the New World: **corn, potatoes, tomatoes, peppers, chocolate, vanilla, tobacco, beans, pumpkins, avocados, peanuts, pecans, cashews, pineapples, blueberries, sunflowers, petunias, black-eyed Susans, dahlias, marigolds, wild rice**

Colonial Craftsmanship

Investigate the craftsmanship of colonial Americans by having your class research the jobs of various skilled artisans whose work was vital to colonial survival. Direct each student to select a trade from the list below that is of particular interest to her. Then have her research that trade and determine which skills a person would need to be successful at that trade. She uses the information she gathers to develop a "Help Wanted" advertisement for a colonial newspaper. Each ad should include the specific job requirements, salary, and benefits as well as whom to contact for more information about the position.

HELP WANTED: WHEELWRIGHT

Location: Jamestown, Virginia
Job Description: job requires knowledge of the making and repairing of wheels and wheeled vehicles
Salary: based on experience
Benefits: free wheels and meals

Job List: tailor, wheelwright, miller, blacksmith, silversmith, joiner, cooper, tanner, printer, clockmaker, cabinetmaker, pewterer, whitesmith, hatter, fuller, glassblower, cordwainer, cobbler, gunsmith

The Path to Revolution

Use this informative cause-and-effect activity to familiarize your students with the events that paved America's path to revolution. Begin by recording each of the events below at the top of a different stone-shaped cutout. In chronological order, discuss with your class each event (the cause) and how colonists reacted to it (the effect). Then record the effect of each event on the bottom portion of its stone. Attach the stones in chronological order to your classroom wall to create a visual reminder of the events that caused the American Revolution.

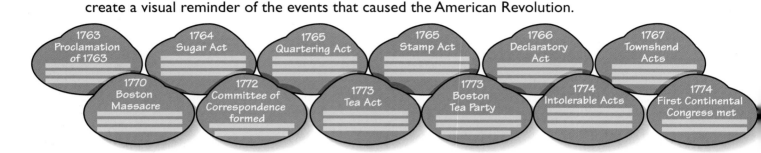

1763 Proclamation of 1763

1764 Sugar Act

1765 Quartering Act

1765 Stamp Act

1766 Declaratory Act

1767 Townshend Acts

1770 Boston Massacre

1772 Committee of Correspondence formed

1773 Tea Act

1773 Boston Tea Party

1774 Intolerable Acts

1774 First Continental Congress met

A Revolutionary Idea

The exciting characters in this activity are sure to spark your students' interest in the Revolutionary War! Provide each student with a copy of the hat pattern on page 192. Write the list of famous American Revolutionary figures below on poster board. Then have each student select one person from the list to research, finding out the individual's date and place of birth, plus information about his education, his role in the Revolution, his accomplishments, and the date of his death. Instruct each student to record his findings on the hat pattern; then have him color and cut out the hat. Display the hats on a bulletin board titled "Famous Figures of the American Revolution."

Abigail Adams
John Adams
Samuel Adams
Benedict Arnold
Crispus Attucks
Margaret Corbin
Charles Cornwallis
Benjamin Franklin
Horatio Gates
George III
Nathanael Greene
Nathan Hale
John Hancock
Mary "Molly Pitcher" Hays
Patrick Henry
John Jay
Thomas Jefferson
John Paul Jones
Marquis de Lafayette
Francis Marion
William Moultrie
Thomas Paine
Paul Revere
Betsy Ross
Baron von Steuben
George Washington

FIRSTHAND INFORMATION

Historical records, diaries, letters, and government documents not only offer important facts, but they also tell a story of what life was once like. With the help of your school's media specialist, find history books that contain examples of primary sources. Tell students that primary sources consist of historical records, diaries, letters, and government documents; then share the examples you collected. Challenge students to use the primary sources and what they know about a specific time period to write a journal entry. Explain that each journal entry should be written as if it were penned by a person living during that era, with specific details about daily life—including references to appropriate dress, education, religion, politics, and transportation. If desired, create aged-looking journal paper by soaking sheets of copy paper in tea and allowing the paper to dry. Have students copy their entries onto the treated paper; then bind them in a class book.

April 19, 1775

Today marked the beginning of the war between the colonists and Great Britain. We can no longer be oppressed by the tyrant King George. Hence, we must defend our rights and gain our freedom from his control. If war be the only way to accomplish this goal, then we must go forth no matter what the cost.

Inventor and Invention	Life Before	Life After
Henry Ford automobile		
Thomas Alva Edison electric light phonograph motion picture camera and projector		
Alexander Graham Bell telephone		

OFF TO WORK WE GO

Familiarize your students with the Industrial Revolution by introducing them to some of its key players. Explain to your students that during the Industrial Revolution, lots of new machines were invented that changed the nature of American life. Challenge your students to scour their social studies texts and reference materials to contribute to a class list of American inventors and inventions. Compile and duplicate this list for every student. Next, have each student fold a sheet of paper into thirds and label the three resulting sections "Inventor and Invention," "Life Before," and "Life After." Have each student record the inventors and their inventions from the class list in the "Inventor and Invention" column of his chart. Then instruct each student to think about what life would have been like before and after each invention and record his thoughts in the appropriate column.

A Nation Divided

Explore the complicated issues that led to the onset of the Civil War with this critical-thinking exercise. Divide your class into two groups—the North and the South. Then make a three-column chart on the board as shown. In the first column of the chart, record the suggested events or issues listed below that contributed to the deterioration of relations between the Northern and Southern states prior to 1861. Subdivide the Northern and Southern groups into smaller cooperative groups of two to three students. Assign one coopera- tive group from each side the same topic to research from its perspective.

After the groups have researched, have them present their Confederate or Union viewpoints, in turn, to the class. As the groups present their positions, record relevant infor- mation on the board as shown. Ask students to analyze why the two sides held such different positions on the issues and how such differ- ences could have caused the two regions to go to war against each other.

Suggested Topics
- The Compromise of 1850
- The Fugitive Slave Law
- The impact of Uncle Tom's Cabin by Harriet Beecher Stowe
- The abolitionist movement
- Lincoln's election to the presidency
- The Kansas-Nebraska Act
- The Dred Scott decision
- The raid on Harpers Ferry
- The secession of South Carolina from the Union

Event/Issue	North	South
Fugitive Slave Law	The North was against the law because they were against returning es- caped slaves to their owners. Abolition- ists established the Underground Railroad to help slaves escape to freedom.	The South was for the law be- cause it forced the return of all escaped slaves.

Check out the skill-building reproducibles on pages 193–194.

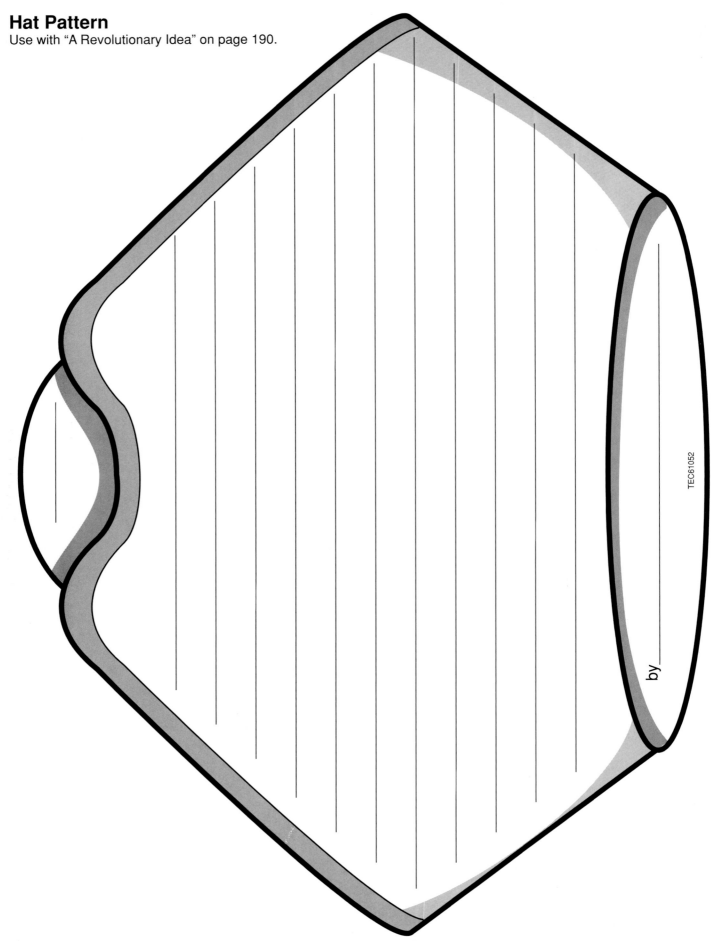

by _____

TEC61052

MAPPING OUT THE 13 COLONIES

Find each item listed in the word bank and label
it on the map. Then answer the questions.

Word Bank

Atlantic Ocean	New Jersey
Connecticut	New York
Delaware	North Carolina
Georgia	Pennsylvania
Maryland	Rhode Island
Massachusetts	South Carolina
New Hampshire	Virginia

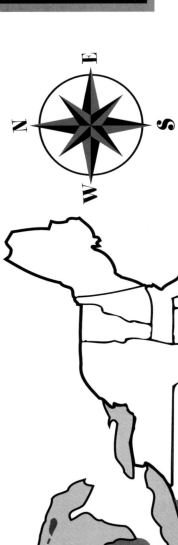

1. What colony is north of Pennsylvania? _____

2. What colony is farthest south? _____

3. What colonies make up the New England colonies? _____

   _____, _____, _____, _____

   Color these colonies yellow.

4. What colonies make up the Middle Colonies? _____, _____,

   _____, _____ Color these colonies red.

5. What colonies make up the Southern Colonies? _____, _____,

   _____, _____, _____ Color these colonies blue.

A NATION DIVIDED

Select _____ projects from the list below to learn more about the Civil War.

1. Many soldiers fighting in the Civil War kept journals. Imagine that you are a Union or Confederate soldier. Write three journal entries about your wartime experiences.

2. Mathew Brady was a famous Civil War photographer. Design a page of Civil War events that might have appeared in one of Brady's photo albums. Be sure to include a detailed caption under each photo.

3. The Underground Railroad was not under the ground, and it wasn't a railroad. Research to find out exactly what the Underground Railroad was, and why it was important to so many people during the Civil War.

4. During the Civil War, the United States was a divided nation. On an outline map of the United States, color the Union states blue and the Confederate states gray.

5. During the Civil War, hot-air balloons were used by the military. Find out the purpose of these balloons. Then make a diorama with a scene that includes a hot-air balloon.

6. The battles of the Civil War took place in many different locations. On a map of the United States, label the sites of at least ten major Civil War battles.

7. The Union forces were led by General Ulysses S. Grant, and the Confederate forces were led by General Robert E. Lee. Research one of these two men and write a short biography about him.

©The Mailbox® • Superbook® • TEC61052

Note to the teacher: Before duplicating, write the number of projects you want each student to complete. Then make a copy of the contract for each student.

194

Graphic Organizers

Forecasting Chart

After introducing a character's conflict in a story or an environmental issue, provide each student with a copy of the organizer on page 197. Have him complete the organizer based on the information he has learned and then compare his answers with another student's. Have the pair decide who has the best course of action and share the results with the class.

Storyboard

Have pairs of students complete the organizer on page 198, recording the topic or story title in the space provided. Then have the duo write a brief description of the main event that begins the story in the first box. Have them write a description of the event that ends the story in the last box. In the remaining boxes, have the students describe other important parts of the story in order.

WHO, WHAT, WHEN, WHERE, WHY, AND HOW WEB

Use the organizer on page 199 to brainstorm before writing a story or to review facts after reading a nonfiction article. Have each student write the title and then answer the questions that follow. Finally, have the student use the information recorded to write her story or a summary paragraph.

FORECASTING CHART

NAME Stan
DATE September 9

ROBOT

Topic or title:

The Lion, the Witch and the Wardrobe

What is the problem?

Lucy's brothers and sister do not believe she went to Narnia and met Mr. Tumnus.

What is a possible effect of the problem?

Lucy's siblings may never believe anything she says ever again.

What is another possible effect?

They will think she has lost her mind.

What could change the possible outcomes?

If her brothers and sister visit Narnia themselves, they would finally believe her.

What should the plan of action be?

Lucy should figure out how the wardrobe works and get her brothers and sister to go to Narnia. Maybe she can trick them to get them in the wardrobe.

NAME Taylor
DATE May 2

WHO, WHAT, WHEN, WHERE, WHY, AND HOW WEB

Bank Shot

Title: Green Hair, Blue Hair

When?
last weekend at a slumber party

Who?
all of my friends, my best friend Stephanie, and me

What?
I woke up to find that my hair was green and blue.

How?
My friends were mad at me.

Why?
I had spread rumors about them around school.

Where?
at Stephanie's house

Plot Diagram

Encourage small groups of students to retell a story or historical event using the organizer on page 200. Have each group write the title and then plot the main events in each corresponding section. Then have the group use the organizer to retell the story to the class.

WORD WEB

Explore unfamiliar words while reading by using the organizer on page 202. Provide each student with several copies of the organizer. For each new word she reads, she records the word, her definition, and the dictionary's definition. She then describes what the word reminds her of. Finally, she draws a picture that goes with the word and its meaning.

Chain of Events Chart

To review a chapter from a novel, provide each student with a copy of the organizer on page 201. After recording the topic, the student writes the starting event in the corresponding space. In the next space, he writes about what the first event caused. In the last space, he writes about the second event's outcome. If desired, have the student complete a copy of the organizer after each chapter and then use them to review for the final test.

NAME _____

DATE _____

ROBOT

Topic or title:

What is a possible effect of the problem?

What is the problem?

What is another possible effect?

What could change the possible outcomes?

What should the plan of action be?

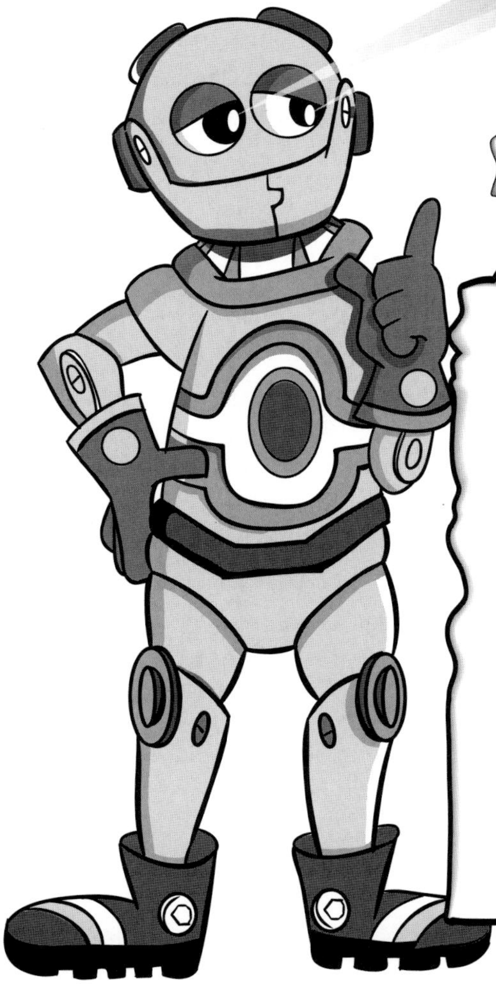

NAMES _____

DATE _____

AND THEN...

Topic or title: _____

First,

Second,

Third,

Fourth,

Fifth,

Sixth,

Note to the teacher: Use with "Storyboard" on page 195.

Bank Shot

Title: _____

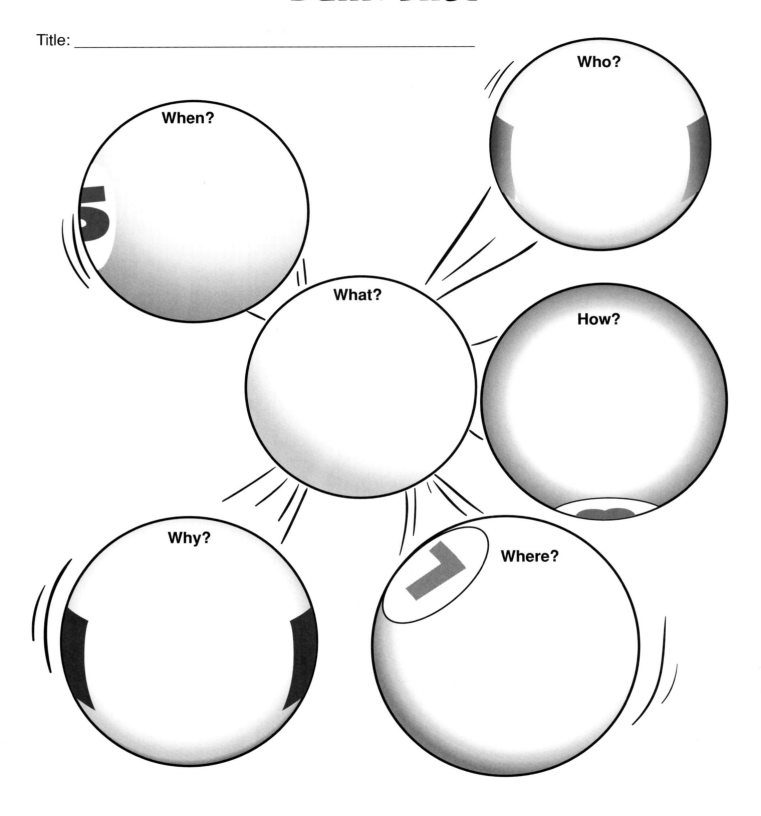

Note to the teacher: Use with "Who, What, When, Where, Why, and How Web" on page 195.

199

NAMES _____

DATE _____

200

Off-Road Adventure

Title: _____

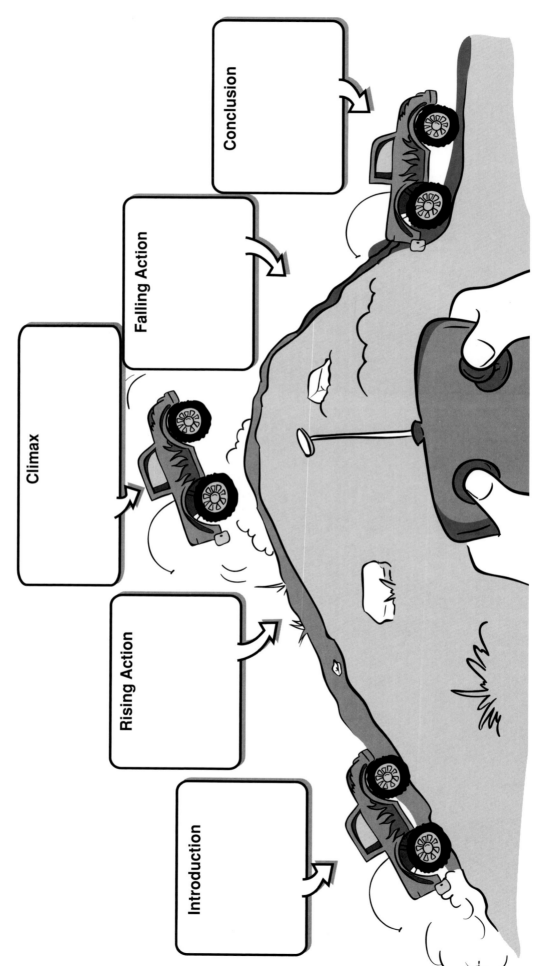

Introduction

Rising Action

Climax

Falling Action

Conclusion

Note to the teacher: Use with "Plot Diagram" on page 196.

Ollie Oops!

Topic

The First Event

The first event caused

This caused

DATE _____

The SCENE Magazine

Word:

I **think** the word means this:

The word **reminds me** of this:

Here's a **picture** of the word:

Cool Vocab

$4.95

The **dictionary** says the word means this:

Language Arts Centers

Author's Inspiration Station

Put all of a story's elements at students' fingertips with this center idea. On a copy of page 205, color each story-element column a different color. If desired, laminate the page for durability. Post the chart in a writing center and instruct each student to pick one story element from each column to use in writing a story. This center will offer a quick remedy to any of your young authors who suffer from writer's block!

CHARACTERS	PLOT	SETTING	THEME
Scout Max Flash	Two characters search for the missing one.	The wilderness	Acting without thinking often brings trouble.

Who? What? When? Where? Why?

Use this great center to introduce students to the five Ws of a newspaper article. Stock the center with newspapers, index cards, highlighter pens, and pencils. To use the center, each child looks through the newspapers for an interesting news article. He reads the article and uses a highlighter pen to mark the article's five Ws. Next, he writes the article's headline at the top of an index card. Then he writes the article's five Ws on the index card. To display students' completed cards, post them on a bulletin board titled "News in Brief."

Springfield Gazette

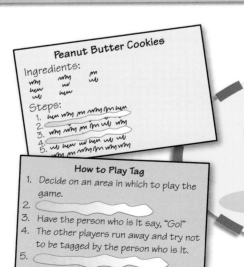

Peanut Butter Cookies

Ingredients:

Steps:
1.
2.
3.
4.
5.

How to Play Tag
1. Decide on an area in which to play the game.
2.
3. Have the person who is It say, "Go!"
4. The other players run away and try not to be tagged by the person who is It.
5.

WHAT'S NEXT?

Motivate students to be clear and concise when writing directions with this writing center idea. Photocopy several simple sets of directions similar to the ones shown. Whiteout two or three steps from each set of directions. Then place several copies of the directions at the center along with an answer key containing the missing steps. Instruct each student using the center to think about the sequence of events before and after each missing step. Have her complete each set of directions by filling in the missing steps; then she checks her answers with the key.

Order Up!

Serve up some main-idea practice with this easy activity. Cut a sheet of construction paper into one-inch strips. Select a paragraph from a textbook or novel your class is reading; then copy each sentence from the paragraph onto a separate paper strip. Shuffle the strips and place them in a numbered envelope. Repeat the procedure with several additional paragraphs. Then make an answer key, giving the correct order for each paragraph. Place the envelopes and the answer key in a classroom center. Challenge each student who visits the center to select an envelope and find the main idea. Have the child put the remaining sentences in the correct order after the main idea and then check her work with the answer key.

Making a peanut butter sandwich is easy.

First, get two slices of bread.

Next, spread peanut butter on one slice.

Then place the two slices of bread together and cut the sandwich.

Finally, pour a big glass of milk and enjoy!

#3

LOCATING IMPORTANT DETAILS

Help students learn how to write a summary by focusing on the key words in paragraphs. Place several copies of page 206 at a center. To use the center, a student reads a selection from a text and then records the most important words in each paragraph in the keys on a copy of the page. Then he closes his book and writes one or two sentences on the bottom half of the page that use those key words to summarize what he's read. If the assigned reading is a long one, divide it into smaller sections and have each student summarize only a certain number of paragraphs. Studying the resulting notes will be a valuable way for students to review a reading assignment before a test.

Chain of Events

Use this 3-D center to help students sequence book events after they've read a story. Place 1" x 6" strips of construction paper at the center. Each student using the center writes each of the following items on a separate strip—her name, the book's title, the author's name, and each of the major events in the story she read. Then she staples the strips to make a chain that shows the sequence of events in the story. Hang students' chains from your classroom ceiling to create an eye-catching display.

Story Elements

CHARACTERS	PLOT	SETTING	THEME
Scout Max Flash	Two characters search for the missing one.	The wilderness	Acting without thinking often brings trouble.
Junior Princess Mr. Shortcut	Someone has stolen the president's car.	A character's backyard	Better late than never.
Willy Jones The Witch Wendy Walsh	The characters are on an adventure.	An underwater hideout	Honesty is the best policy.
Gus Caesar The Shadow	The characters have a wonderful vacation in a surprising place.	Another planet	You can't judge a book by its cover.
Clancy Ms. Fancy Sunny	The characters find a treasure and decide what to do with it.	An ice palace	The best things in life are free.

©The Mailbox® • *Superbook*® • TEC61052

Note to the teacher: Use with "Author's Inspiration Station" on page 203.

 # Keys to Success

Topic: _____

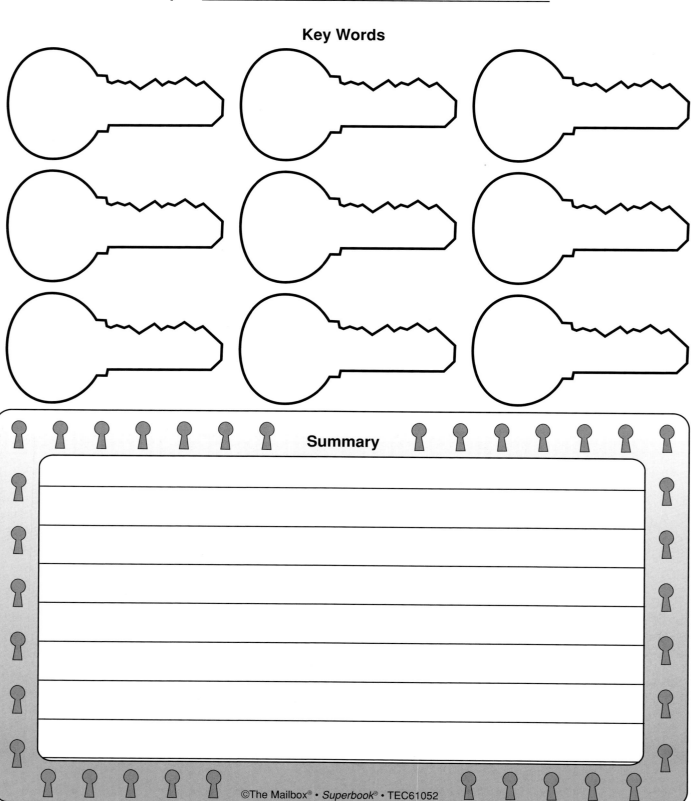

Key Words

Summary

©The Mailbox® • Superbook® • TEC61052

206 **Note to the teacher:** Use with "Locating Important Details" on page 204.

MATH CENTERS

The Price Is Almost Right

Use this center game to reinforce students' estimation skills. Stock a center with several mail-order catalogs, pencils, scrap paper, calculators, game pieces, a die, and a copy of the gameboard on page 209. Copy the directions below and post them at the center.

Directions for 2–4 players:
1. Each player gets one game piece, one sheet of scrap paper, a pencil, a calculator, and a catalog.
2. The first player rolls the die and moves his game piece that number of spaces on the gameboard. Using a catalog, he follows the directions in the space on which he lands and records an estimated answer on his paper.
3. Then he finds the exact answer and records the difference between it and his estimate.
4. Once all players reach Finish, each player totals his differences. The player with the smallest total wins.

Lock It Up!

Attach a combination lock to a lock box. Create math problems with answers that match the numbers of the combination. Direct students using the center to solve the problems and then check their answers by trying to "crack" the safe. Place stickers or candy inside the locked box as a reward for students who successfully open the lock. If you purchase a lock with a programmable combination, you can change the center by simply changing the code and creating new problems.

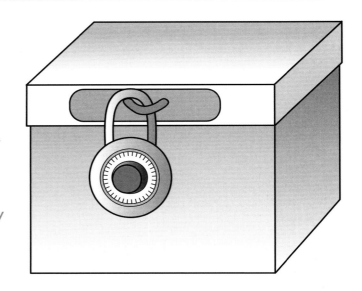

My, How Time Flies!

Students can practice calculating elapsed time at this center. Program a copy of page 210 with everyday home and school activities such as waking up, eating breakfast, and going to recess. Starting with lunch, sequentially list activities that can be completed that day or the next morning. Before lunch, give each child who will use the center a copy of the programmed page to start filling in at lunchtime.

At the center the next day, have small groups of students use their members' completed charts to answer questions similar to the ones shown below.

Sample Questions:
Which person arrived home from school in the least amount of time?
Who spent the longest amount of time eating?
Who slept the longest? Who slept the least? Find the difference between the two times.
What is the total amount of time the members of the group spent on homework?

NAME _____
DATE _____   ELAPSED TIME

My, How Time Flies!

Activity	Start Time	Stop Time

Problem Plates

Serve up great problem-solving skills by placing a supply of colored pencils and paper plates at a center. Each member of a small group writes a different number in the center of a plate. Next, he uses various operations to create as many problems as he can that have his number as the answer. He also writes a word problem on the back of his plate that corresponds to one of the problems he created. Group members trade plates, solve the word problems, and then turn the plates over to check the answers.

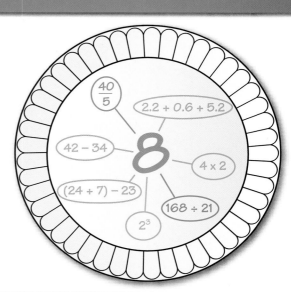

$\frac{40}{5}$ $2.2 + 0.6 + 5.2$ $42 - 34$ **8** 4×2 $(24 \div 7) - 23$ $168 \div 21$ 2^3

My average is 4.5!

My average is 5! I win this round!

HIGH CARD WINS!

Pairs of students playing this center game will use a deck of cards and a timer to find averages! Label all face cards and aces with a different number value as shown. The students shuffle the deck and then set the timer for ten minutes. Each player draws two cards, places them faceup in front of her, and then uses mental math to find the average of her two cards. The player with the higher average wins the round and collects both sets of cards. The students play additional rounds until all the cards have been used or time is up. Each player then uses a calculator to find the average of all the cards she collected during the game. The winner is the child with the higher overall average.

You've Won the Sweepstakes! Roll Again!

You're an Heir! Move Ahead 3 Spaces.

Bankrupt! Lose a Turn.

Held Up by a Bank Robber! Return to Start.

Find an item in your catalog that you can't use. If someone gave you 13 of that item, how much money would you get when you returned them?

Purchase a great outfit for yourself. Be sure not to spend more than $145.

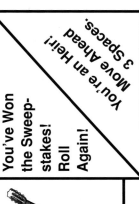

Find cool outfits for the four members of your band. You have $444 to spend.

Find the most expensive item on the first two pages of your catalog. How much would four of that item cost?

Find an item that costs less than $10. How many of that item could you purchase for $100?

Find an item in your favorite color. If you bought six of that item, how much would it cost?

Find the last item in your catalog. If you had $135 to spend, how many of that item could you buy?

Find the least expensive item on the first two pages of your catalog. How many of this item could you buy if you had $100?

Find an item that makes life easier. Buy one for each of your ten friends. Don't spend more than $100.

Find an item in your favorite color. If you bought six of that item, how much would it cost?

Find an item in your favorite color. Buy a gift for your dog and a gift for your cat. What is the difference between the two prices?

You have $67 to spend. Find three toys to buy.

You need to buy a gift for each of your eight brothers! You have $108 to spend.

Find gifts for each of your teachers. Don't spend more than $50.

Purchase three items that would be great to use outdoors.

Start

You've Won the Sweepstakes! Roll Again!

You're an Heir! Move Ahead 3 Spaces.

Held Up by a Bank Robber! Return to Start.

Bankrupt! Lose a Turn.

finish

©The Mailbox® • Superbook® • TEC61052

Note to the teacher: Use with "The Price Is Almost Right" on page 207.

 # My, How Time Flies!

Activity	Start Time	Stop Time

Note to the teacher: Use with "My, How Time Flies!" on page 208.

Games

Number Lineup

Put place-value skills on the line with this interactive game. Divide your class into teams of 13 players. Give each team a copy of page 216 to cut apart and hold. (If teams with fewer players are needed, have each player hold more than one card.) Next, call out a number requiring the use of all 13 cards. Have teams form that number by lining up in the appropriate order as quickly as possible. The first team to correctly form the number wins. Play additional rounds as time permits. To vary the game, write a number's word or expanded form on the board instead of saying the number aloud. **Place value**

Quick Draw!

Review geometric shapes with this fast-paced drawing game. Divide your class into even teams. Number the players on each team; then supply each team with small sheets of scrap paper, a pencil, and—if desired—a ruler and a protractor. To play, call out a number and a geometric term (see the list). Have each player with that number draw that shape on scrap paper as quickly as possible. If the player does not know what to draw, allow coaching from his teammates. After he completes his drawing, have him quickly run the paper to you. Give the first team to give you a correct drawing two points and other teams with correct drawings one point. Continue play in this manner until all the items have been drawn. The team with the most points wins. **Geometry**

Geometric Items to Draw: point, plane, line AB, ray CD, line segment EF, parallel lines, intersecting lines, perpendicular lines, acute angle CAB, obtuse angle EFG, right angle ABC, acute triangle, right triangle, obtuse triangle, equilateral triangle, square, rectangle, pentagon, hexagon, octagon, parallelogram, rhombus, trapezoid, shape with only one line of symmetry, shape with two lines of symmetry, shape with three lines of symmetry, rectangle with perimeter of 10 cm, rectangle with area of 10 cm², etc.

Tic-Add-Toe

Pair your students; then have each pair draw a game grid on paper. Direct each player, in turn, to write a digit 0–9 on the grid instead of an X or an O. Explain that the object of the game is to create an addition or subtraction sentence in one row, column, or diagonal. Explain further that the player who places the third digit and completes the number sentence gets one point. For example, the player who places a 9 in the upper right corner of the grid shown would receive one point because $3 + 6 = 9$. Allow students to play as many rounds as time permits; then declare the player with the most points the winner. **Addition and subtraction**

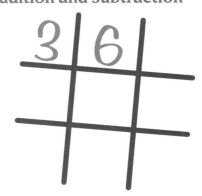

Basic-Facts Circle

Get your students moving with this fun review of basic multiplication and division facts! Write each of the following numbers on a different index card: 1, 2, 3, 4, 5, 6, 7, 8, 9, 10, 12, 14, 15, 16, 18, 20, 21, 24, 27, 28, 30, 32, 35, 36, 40, 42, 45, 48, 50, 54, 56, 60, 63, 70, 72, 80, 90. Have your students sit in a circle; then pass out all the cards (some students will have more than one card). Then follow the directions below.
Basic facts

7   6   42

To play:

1. Have each student hold his cards so that the numbers face outward and are visible to everyone in the circle.
2. Call out a basic multiplication or division fact. Have the two players with those numbers on their cards get up and run to the player holding the solution that will complete the basic fact.
3. After those two students find the solution, instruct them to return to their places in the circle; then have each player pass his cards to the player on the right.
4. If by chance a student holds two or three of the cards needed to complete a basic fact, call out a different basic fact for that round and direct that player to trade one of his cards with another player so that fact can be used later.
5. Continue play by saying the next basic fact. To vary the game, call out a basic fact and have the player holding the answer card go and stand in the center of the circle. Or call out a number and challenge students to suggest possible equations that will equal that number.

"Equiz!"

Strengthen your students' basic-operation skills with this quick equation game. Write the digits 0–9 on the board. Also draw on the board a blank version of the chart below. Have each pair of students copy the blank chart from the board on a sheet of paper. To play, direct Player 1 to write any five digits from 0–9 in the chart. Have Player 2 use as many of those five digits as he can—without repeating any digit—to form a correct number sentence and write it in the chart. Explain that the basic-operation symbols +, −, ×, and ÷ can be used as often as needed, but that the equal symbol can be used only once. Also explain that each player earns one point for every digit he uses in a correct equation. Continue play by having Player 2 list five digits in the chart for Player 1 to use. End the game after a set amount of time or when both players have had an equal number of turns. The player with more total points wins. **Basic facts**

Player	Digits	Equation	Points
1	1, 2, 3, 5, 0	$1 \times 2 + 3 = 5 + 0$	5
2	3, 6, 2, 4, 8	$6 \div 3 + 2 = 8 - 4$	5

Silly-Dilly Sentences

Create a class set of game cards by writing different adjectives, adverbs, verbs, and nouns on separate index cards. Divide the class into four teams. Shuffle the cards; then distribute the cards for Round 1, one card for each student.

To play:

1. Direct all students whose cards have nouns to go to one corner of the room, those with adjectives to a second corner, and so on with verbs and adverbs.

2. In turn, have every student in each corner read aloud the word on his card so that the class can determine whether he has classified his word correctly or not.

3. Give each team one point for every correctly classified word.

4. Have the class reclassify any word that was grouped incorrectly; then direct the student holding that card to move to the correct corner of the room.

5. Play additional rounds as time permits; then declare the team with the most points the winner.

Continue the activity by forming smaller groups. Have four students (one from each corner of the room) work together in a small group. Challenge each small group to use its four words, adding articles such as *a, an,* or *the* as needed, to create a silly—but complete—sentence for you to record on the board. **Parts of speech**

The enormous shoe danced carefully.
adj.   noun   verb   adv.

Build-a-Sentence Relay

Divide your class into teams of five to six students. Explain that the object of the game is to be the first team to write a complete sentence on the board. Direct the first player on each team to go to the board, write one word, and return to his team. In the same manner, instruct each remaining member of the team to contribute one word or punctuation mark to form a complete sentence. If a complete sentence—including its end punctuation—has been formed when the last team member takes his turn, have that team indicate that fact by sitting down. The first team to complete the task wins that round. If a complete sentence has not been written after every team member has had a turn, require that team to play until it does have a complete sentence. Appoint a new player to start the next round, explaining that a different sentence must be written. For a more challenging game, require the first player to write a word other than the first word of the sentence. Or have team members write the sentence backward, beginning with the first player writing the last word in the sentence! **Sentences**

Team 1	Team 2
Saturdays are for	Mom told my

Shaping Up With Spelling

Have each child write a different spelling word on an index card. Collect the cards. Next, write the motions listed below on the board and practice them with your students. Divide your class into teams of six to eight students; then have each team stand in a line. **Spelling**

To play:

1 Divide the game cards into as many sets as you have teams. Then place each set face-down in a designated spot at an equal distance from each team.

2 On your signal, Player 1 on each team runs to the pile of cards, takes the top card, runs back to his team, and hands the card faceup to Player 2.

3 Player 2 says the word aloud to Player 1; then Player 1 spells the word aloud while performing the different motions assigned to each letter.

4 After spelling the word, Player 1 takes the card from Player 2 and sits down.

5 Player 2 runs to the pile and repeats the process with Player 3 on his team.

6 Continue play in this manner until every player on the team has spelled a word and sat down. The first team to complete these tasks as directed wins.

7 Play additional rounds by having the teams exchange their sets of cards.

Motions for Spelling a Word

First letter: Squat down.
Second letter: Stand up.
Third letter: Raise right arm.
Fourth letter: Raise left arm.
Fifth letter: Clap hands.
Additional letters: Repeat each motion in the same order.

Describe It!

Distribute old magazines to your students. Direct each child to cut out pictures of objects and food items and then mount each picture on a different sheet of construction paper. To play the game, select one student to be It and have him stand behind you in front of the classroom. Next, hold up a picture for class viewing in a way that prevents It from seeing the picture. Instruct It to call on five different classmates to suggest a specific adjective that describes the picture being held. Then have It try to guess what the picture is. If he succeeds, allow him to choose one of the five students who supplied adjectives to replace him as It. If he guesses incorrectly, allow him to call on five more students to offer different adjectives that might help him guess the word. **Adjectives**

Truth or Consequences

To review for a test, add a fun twist that will get your students' hearts a-pumpin' and the oxygen a-flowin'! Before playing the game, write several fun-to-do consequences on slips of paper (see the suggested list) and place them in a paper bag. Divide your students into teams. Ask review questions of each team. If a team gives an incorrect response (doesn't tell the truth), instruct one of the team members to draw a slip of paper from the consequences bag. Then have the whole team perform that stunt. As a variation, collect an object from each student before starting the game. Whenever a team answers a question correctly, allow one team member to reclaim his object! **Skill review**

Fun-to-Do Consequences

- Run in place for ten seconds.
- Do five jumping jacks.
- Touch your toes as you spell your name aloud—backward—five times.
- Hop on one foot five times.
- Walk in place as you count backward from 100 to 85.
- Stand on your tiptoes as you count by threes from zero to 33.

Money Hungry

Capitalize on students' interest in working with money the next time you review a unit with your class. Write review questions on slips of paper (or have students create the questions and put them on paper); then assign each question a monetary value according to its level of difficulty. Fold the slips of paper and place them in a container such as an old piggy bank. Divide your class into teams of three to five students and have them take turns drawing questions from the container. For every correct answer, reward each team play money equal to the monetary value of its question or keep a running total of the values on paper. Declare the team with the most money at the end of the game the winner. **Skill review**

$10.00 Question

Identify the adverb in this sentence:
She has to leave for the airport soon.

Categories

Prepare (or have your students prepare) clue cards for identifying different topics studied throughout the year. Stipulate that each card have three words or phrases on it that help identify a specific category (see the chart). Divide your class into teams of three to five players; then follow the steps below to play the game. **Skill review**

Words	Category
guide words, pronunciation key, entry words	parts of a dictionary
Boston Tea Party, Sugar Act, Stamp Act	causes of the American Revolution
veins, arteries, blood	parts of the circulatory system

1. Say the words on one of the cards to the first team.
2. Allow that team's members about ten seconds to name a specific category.
3. If the first category named is not specific enough, allow the team an additional 15 seconds to revise its answer. For example, if the clues are *humerus, radius,* and *ulna,* and a team's guess is "Bones of the body," you could say, "Think of a more specific category," giving that team a chance to say, "Arm bones."
4. If the named category is correct, give that team three points; if incorrect, pass the play to Team 2, giving them two points for a correct guess.
5. Should Team 2 answer incorrectly, give Team 1 another chance to win just one point for answering correctly. Then announce the next set of clues to a different team.
6. Play for a set amount of time. The team with the most points at the end of that time wins.

Check out the skill-building reproducibles on pages 217-218.

Game Cards

Use with "Number Lineup" on page 211.

0 TEC61052	**1** TEC61052	**2** TEC61052
3 TEC61052	**4** TEC61052	**5** TEC61052
6 TEC61052	**7** TEC61052	**8** TEC61052
9 TEC61052	**.** TEC61052	**,** TEC61052 **,** TEC61052

NAMES

DATE

Complete the Laps

Code
Even = larger
Odd = smaller

Directions for two players:

1. Player 1 rolls the die and circles "larger" or "smaller" for Lap 1, according to the code. (If "larger" is circled, the player with the larger decimal wins Lap 1. If "smaller" is circled, the player with the smaller decimal wins.)

2. Player 1 rolls the die again and writes the number rolled in one of his blanks for Lap 1. Player 2 rolls the die and writes the number rolled in one of his blanks for Lap 1.

3. Each player repeats Step 2 and writes the number rolled in the other blank for Lap 1.

4. Players compare numbers to determine who wins the lap. The winner colors his flags for that lap. If players write the same number, they both color their flags.

5. Play continues in this manner through Lap 10. The player with more colored flags wins. In case of a tie, repeat Lap 10.

Player 1		Player 2
_ , _ _ . _ _	larger/smaller	_ , _ _ . _ _
_ , _ _ . _ _	larger/smaller	_ , _ _ . _ _
_ , _ _ . _ _	larger/smaller	_ , _ _ . _ _
_ , _ _ . _ _	larger/smaller	_ , _ _ . _ _
_ _ . _ _	larger/smaller	_ _ . _ _
_ _ . _ _	larger/smaller	_ _ . _ _
_ _ . _ _	larger/smaller	_ _ . _ _
_ . _ _	larger/smaller	_ . _ _
_ . _	larger/smaller	_ . _
0 . _	larger/smaller	0 . _

Player 1: Lap 10 · Lap 9 · Lap 8 · Lap 7 · Lap 6 · Lap 5 · Lap 4 · Lap 3 · Lap 2 · Lap 1

Player 2: Lap 10 · Lap 9 · Lap 8 · Lap 7 · Lap 6 · Lap 5 · Lap 4 · Lap 3 · Lap 2 · Lap 1

Note to the teacher: Students will need a die to play this game.

NAMES _____

DATE _____

218

Synonym-Antonym Roundup

Code
Even number = Write a synonym.
Odd number = Write an antonym.

Directions for two players:

1. Player 1 rolls the die and then writes a synonym or an antonym for the Round 1 word, according to the code. If Player 1 writes a correct word, he records as his score the number of letters in his answer. If Player 1 can't think of an answer or writes an incorrect word, his score for that round is zero.
2. Player 2 rolls the die and takes a turn in the same manner.
3. Players cannot repeat words already written.
4. Play continues with players taking turns through Round 10. Then each player totals his score. The player with more points wins.

Player 1:

Round	Word	Synonym	Antonym	Score
1	big			
2	hard			
3	good			
4	neat			
5	find			
6	funny			
7	walk			
8	loud			
9	plain			
10	full			
			Total	

Player 2:

Round	Word	Synonym	Antonym	Score
1	big			
2	hard			
3	good			
4	neat			
5	find			
6	funny			
7	walk			
8	loud			
9	plain			
10	full			
			Total	

©The Mailbox® • Superbook® • TEC61052

Note to the teacher: Students will need a die to play this game.

DIFFERENTIATION Tips

Highlighting Tips

Students will highlight the way to better understanding with a few quick and easy tips!

- Have a child highlight key words in directions.
- Have a student highlight operation signs, decimal points, or placeholders in math problems.
- Modify multiple-choice tests by highlighting the correct answer and one incorrect answer.
- Have a child highlight important vocabulary words.
- Highlight any questions a student needs to review before turning an assignment in for a final grade.

Spelling Choices

Meet the spelling needs of several different students at once by providing each with a copy of page 222. Have the student copy his spelling words in the space provided. Then assign him a specific number of activities to complete by the end of the week. As he completes an activity, have him color the matching space and then place the assignment in a folder. Before he takes his spelling test, have him turn in his sheet and folder of work.

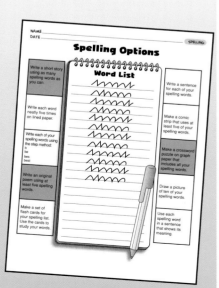

MEETING MATH NEEDS

Give a short pretest at the beginning of each new math unit to determine the learning needs of each student. Assign each child to a group based on the test results. Next, prepare different packets of textbook pages and reproducibles for each group. Each day, distribute the packets and meet with each group for a minilesson while other students work quietly. If a child masters a set of skills or needs more reinforcement on it, simply assign her to a different group.

Lesson Plan Stickers

Incorporate student modifications in your weekly lesson plans with this teacher-friendly solution! On your computer, program each label on a sheet of large adhesive labels with a different student's initials and a list of his required modifications. Then print a sheet of the labels and affix one to each new week in your planbook. As you make preparations, simply refer to the labels to remind you of the needed modifications.

B. K. (ESL)—abbreviated spelling list, test read-aloud, sit near teacher

B. M. (504 plan)—large print, highlighter, extended time on tests, sit near front of room

H. B. (resource reading)—abbreviated assignments, books on tape, peer tutor, small-group instruction

J. S. (gifted/talented)—enrichment activities, advanced reading

P. W. (resource math)—extended time on tests, peer tutor

An Array of Resources

Be prepared for students' needs by partnering with teachers below and above your grade level and agreeing to share reproducible skill-practice materials. When a student needs reinforcement, extra practice, or reteaching, you'll always have a reproducible appropriate for her needs!

WHAT'S YOUR INTEREST?

When it's time to begin a new unit of study, gather center materials and reproducibles based on three or four different themes. Place the materials in a labeled basket or box. When it's time for students to practice or reinforce skills, they can choose activities from the theme that interests them most. To make the practice pages even more inviting, copy them onto different-colored paper.

Fractions

Ten-Point Tests

Give students flexibility by designing tests based on the ten-point system. At the end of a unit, develop a test that has questions with varying difficulty. Then assign a point value of two, three, or four to each question. Distribute the test copies and tell students they can choose the questions they would like to answer, but the questions they answer must total ten points.

Ten-Point Test

(2 points) 1. Who is the fastest hole digger in Stanley's group?

(2 points) 2. How does Kate Barlow die?

(2 points) 3. What does Stanley's father invent and Clyde Livingston advertise on television?

(3 points) 4. Why do you think the boys at Camp Green Lake use nicknames?

(3 points) 5. What is the importance of yellow-spotted lizards throughout the book?

(4 points) 6. Why do you think Louis Sachar titled the book *Holes*?

GOAL SETTING

Help each student succeed week by week by having him fill out a copy of page 223. First, have the student complete each section of the page with his current spelling list, math facts or terms, and vocabulary words. Then have him write a goal he would like to achieve by the end of the week. Each day, have the student use the bottom portion of the page to reflect on his accomplishments or something he needs to improve. If desired, have the student hole-punch his page and place it in a folder. Throughout the week, have him refer to his goal and lists as needed.

Speedy Record Keeping

Track student progress during small-group time by creating a grid similar to the one shown. For each group, program the chart with student names and skills or goals for the group. When working with the small group, make notes in each appropriate space to keep track of each student's individual needs.

Literature Circle Group April 2–6	Reads fluently	Identifies main idea	Understands cause/effect	Summarizes	Understands vocabulary
Dustin	rarely	✗	✗	✔	✗
Georgetta	text too difficult	✔	✗	needs prompts	✗
Ally	✔	✔	sometimes	not yet	✗
Eric	reads without errors	✔	good understanding	✔	✔
Nash	✔	needs prompts	✗	✔	✔

Spelling Options

Word List

Write a short story using as many spelling words as you can.

Write each word neatly five times on lined paper.

Write each of your spelling words using the step method:
b
be
bes
best

Write an original poem using at least five spelling words.

Make a set of flash cards for your spelling list. Use the cards to study your words.

Write a sentence for each of your spelling words.

Make a comic strip that uses at least five of your spelling words.

Make a crossword puzzle on graph paper that includes all your spelling words.

Draw a picture of ten of your spelling words.

Use each spelling word in a sentence that shows its meaning.

NAME

DATE

Reaching for Goals

Week of _____

My Goal: _____

My Spelling List

My Math Facts and Terms

My Vocabulary Words

What I Did Well

What I Need to Work On

Monday:

Tuesday:

Wednesday:

Thursday:

Friday:

©The Mailbox® • Superbook® • TEC61052

Note to the teacher: Use with "Goal Setting" on page 221.

Assessment

Positively Colorful Writing

Put a positive spin on assessing student writing with the help of colorful ink pens. When grading a student's paper, use different colors to mark things the student did well. For example, use a green pen to circle correct punctuation, use a red pen to underline descriptive adjectives, and use a blue pen to circle vocabulary words. At a glance, both you and your students will be able to see what they are doing well!

It was a wet and chilly November night. All the kids were fast asleep. Mom and Dad were sitting at the kitchen table discussing important things. I slowly crept out of bed, carefully avoiding the one creaky floorboard in the middle of the room. I pressed my hands against the icy windowpane and pushed the window open.

Topic: ~~~~~~ ~~ ~~

Know	Want to know	Learned

What We Know

Create and laminate a large KWL chart as shown. Using a dry-erase marker, label the chart with a topic that is being introduced. Invite students to share any information that they already know about the topic. Write each of their responses on a sticky note and place it in the first column. Next, have the students ask questions that they hope to answer during the unit of study. Record these on sticky notes as well and place them in the second column. Then place a supply of new sticky notes next to the chart. As students gather information, encourage them to record the knowledge on new sticky notes and place them in the third column. If a student learns the answer to one of the questions in the second column, have him write the answer under the question and move the sticky note to the third column. Challenge students to answer all the questions in the second column before the unit of study is over.

Your Opinion Counts

When it's time to fill out report cards, let students' opinions be included. Provide each student with a copy of page 226. Meet with her one-on-one to discuss and fill out the form, or let her complete the form on her own. Review the completed form and then send it home with the student's report card. A parent is sure to appreciate the unique perspective on her child's grades.

Your Opinion Counts

Name __Sophie__

Date __December 20__

What grades would you give yourself for this grading period?

Subject	Grade	Subject	Grade
Math	A	Social Studies	B
Reading	A	Music	B
English	B	P.E.	A
Spelling	B	Art	A
Writing	A–	Behavior	B+
Science	A+	Spanish	B

What was your biggest achievement this grading period? __I made an A on all of my math tests.__

What do you need to work on next grading period? __I need to practice my spelling words more.__

How do you feel about school? (Color one.)

Love it　　Like it　　Neither like nor dislike it　　Dislike it

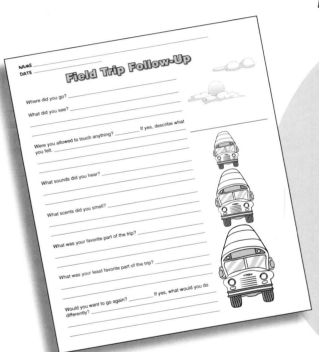

Field Trip Follow-Up

NAME _____
DATE _____

Where did you go? _____

What did you see? _____

Were you allowed to touch anything? _____ If yes, describe what you felt. _____

What sounds did you hear? _____

What scents did you smell? _____

What was your favorite part of the trip? _____

What was your least favorite part of the trip? _____

Would you want to go again? _____ If yes, what would you do differently? _____

Field Trip Follow-Up

Use this assessment activity after returning from a field trip. Give each child a copy of the form on page 227. Instruct her to complete each section based on what she observed while on the field trip. If desired, allow each student to share her responses with the class before displaying them on a board next to photographs taken on the trip.

Multiple-Choice Assessments

Help students remember to read all multiple-choice answers before choosing an answer with this assessment tip! Provide each small group with several multiple-choice questions. In addition to having the group circle each correct answer, have it also write a brief explanation stating why the remaining answers are incorrect. Reward each group with one point for each correct answer and two bonus points for each correct explanation.

5. Which polygon has more than five sides?
   A. pentagon
   B. triangle
   C. octagon
   D. square

   A. A pentagon only has five sides. The question asks for more than five.
   B. A triangle only has three sides.
   D. A square only has four sides.

Your Opinion Counts

Name _____

Date _____

What was your biggest achievement this grading period? _____

What do you need to work on next grading period? _____

How do you feel about school? (Color one.)

☺	☺	😐	☺
Love it	Like it	Neither like nor dislike it	Dislike it

What grades would you give yourself for this grading period?

Subject	Grade	Subject	Grade
Math		Social Studies	
Reading		Music	
English		P.E.	
Spelling		Art	
Writing		Behavior	
Science			

Note to the teacher: Use with "Your Opinion Counts" on page 225.

NAME ______________________________

DATE ______________

Field Trip Follow-Up

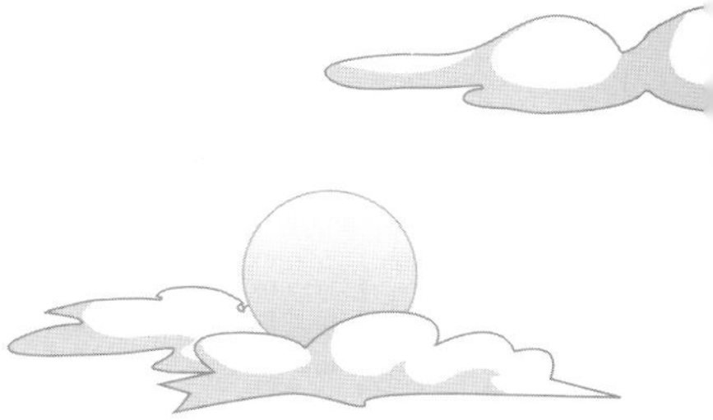

Where did you go? ______________________________

What did you see? ______________________________

____

____

Were you allowed to touch anything? __________ If yes, describe what you felt. ______________________________

____

____

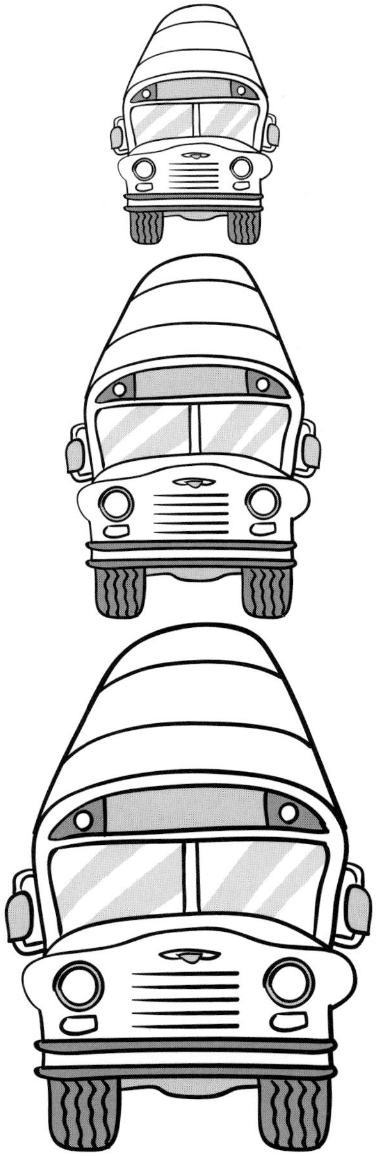

What sounds did you hear? ______________________________

____

____

What scents did you smell? ______________________________

____

____

What was your favorite part of the trip? ______________________________

____

____

What was your least favorite part of the trip? ______________________________

____

____

Would you want to go again? __________ If yes, what would you do differently? ______________________________

____

____

Note to the teacher: Use with "Field Trip Follow-Up" on page 225.

TEST-TAKING TIPS

Building Great Habits!

After reviewing various test-taking strategies, provide each student with a copy of the construction hat pattern on page 230. Have each student label the hat with her name and then decorate it as desired. On a separate sheet of paper, have the student then make a list of other test-taking strategies that she likes to use or that she feels will help others in the class. Finally, have the student glue her hat to the top of her paper. Display the hats on a board under the title "Building Great Test Habits!" Encourage students to refer to the board as needed to practice test-taking skills.

Brooke

1. Pay attention to what the question is asking.
2. Highlight important information for each answer.
3. Rule out unreasonable answer choices.
4. Double-check your work.
5. Take your time.

I'm Working

I'm Working.

Carlie

Help children understand the need for quiet during testing by creating testing folders for each child. Give each child a colorful file folder and have her write "I'm Working" and her name on one side as shown. Collect the folders and then, on testing days, redistribute them. Direct each child to set up her folder on her desk, creating a wall that she can work behind. Explain to students that when the folders are up, no one may talk or get out of his seat. This serves as a great reminder to students that although each child works at his own pace, each student should respect the others' right to work in a quiet, still environment.

Answer Sheet Quiz

Review with students the importance of using an answer sheet correctly with the help of this handy quiz sheet. Before taking a standardized test, provide each student with a copy of page 231. Have each child read and answer each multiple choice question. Then have him color in his answer choice on the grid to the right. Once all students have completed the page, review and discuss the correct answers as a class.

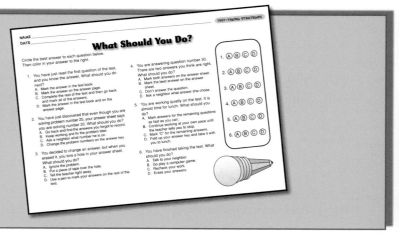

Make Your Mark

To begin, have each student pick her five favorite test-taking tips. Then provide her with a construction paper bookmark. Have her write a checklist on the bookmark, listing each of her five strategies. Then laminate the bookmark. As the student completes quizzes and practice tests, have her use her bookmark to mentally check off the different strategies used.

Test Strategies to Use:

- ☐ 1. Carefully read directions.
- ☐ 2. Underline important information.
- ☐ 3. Identify key vocabulary words.
- ☐ 4. Rule out unreasonable answer choices.
- ☐ 5. Reread anything that is confusing.

Eat a good breakfast.

Focus on the question being asked.

Follow the directions.

Organize your thoughts on written answers.

Recheck your answers.

Try your best.

Just What the Doctor Ordered

Label several large craft sticks with different test-taking tips. Then place the sticks in a jar and label it as shown. Prior to any test, have a volunteer draw one stick from the jar and then read the tip aloud. Discuss the importance of the tip before setting it aside and having another student draw the next craft stick.

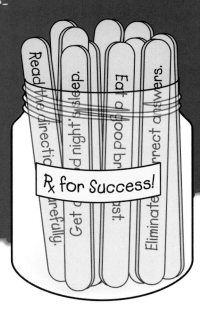

Three Cheers!

Cheer students to testing victory with this simple activity. Have small groups of students create a mnemonic device to help remember important information about taking a test. Then have each group present its mnemonic to the class using arms and legs to spell out each letter of the device.

Construction Hat Pattern

Use with "Building Great Habits!" on page 228.

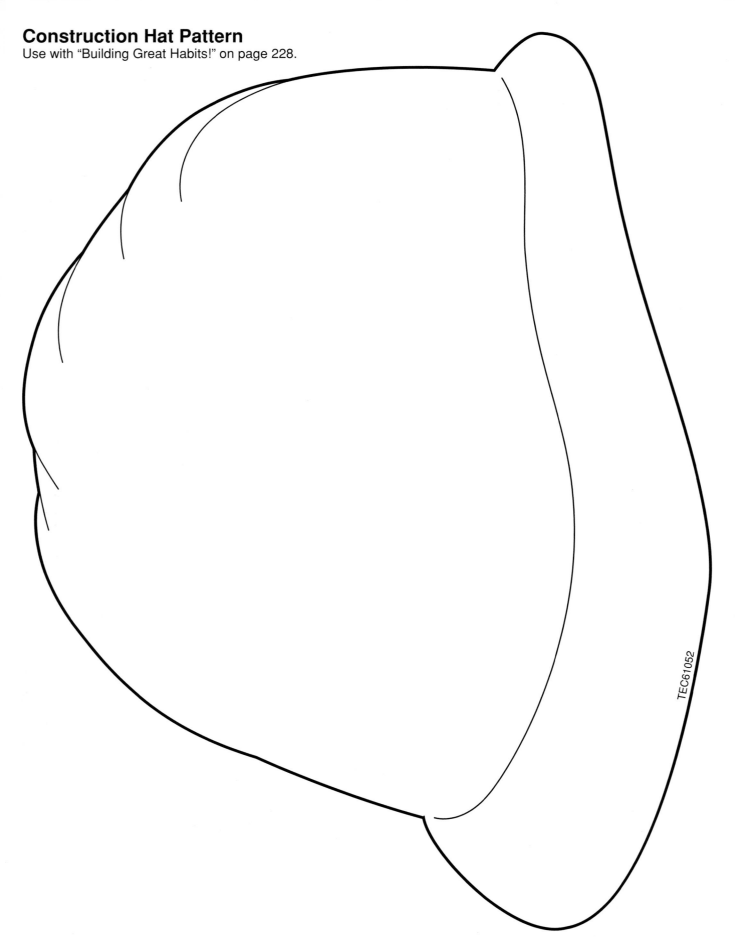

TEC61052

NAME

DATE

What Should You Do?

Circle the best answer to each question below.
Then color in your answer to the right.

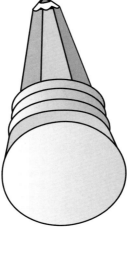

1. A B C D

2. A B C D

3. A B C D

4. A B C D

5. A B C D

6. A B C D

1. You have just read the first question of the test,
   and you know the answer. What should you do
   next?
   A. Mark the answer in the test book.
   B. Mark the answer on the answer page.
   C. Complete the rest of the test and then go back
      and mark all of the answers.
   D. Mark the answer in the test book and on the
      answer page.

2. You have just discovered that even though you are
   solving problem number 25, your answer sheet says
   you are solving number 20. What should you do?
   A. Go back and find the answers you forgot to record.
   B. Keep working and fix the problem later.
   C. Ask a neighbor what number he is on.
   D. Change the problem numbers on the answer key.

3. You decided to change an answer, but when you
   erased it, you tore a hole in your answer sheet.
   What should you do?
   A. Ignore the problem.
   B. Put a piece of tape over the hole.
   C. Tell the teacher right away.
   D. Use a pen to mark your answers on the rest of the
      test.

4. You are answering question number 30.
   There are two answers you think are right.
   What should you do?
   A. Mark both answers on the answer sheet.
   B. Mark the best answer on the answer
      sheet.
   C. Don't answer the question.
   D. Ask a neighbor what answer she chose.

5. You are working quietly on the test. It is
   almost time for lunch. What should you
   do?
   A. Mark answers for the remaining questions
      as fast as you can.
   B. Continue working at your own pace until
      the teacher tells you to stop.
   C. Mark "C" for the remaining answers.
   D. Fold up your answer key and take it with
      you to lunch.

6. You have finished taking the test. What
   should you do?
   A. Talk to your neighbor.
   B. Go play a computer game.
   C. Recheck your work.
   D. Erase your answers.

©The Mailbox® • Superbook® • TEC61052

Note to the teacher: Use with "Answer Sheet Quiz" on page 228.

English Language Learners

Take-Home Kit

To help English language learners participate in at-home reading projects, put together a kit that can be checked out along with the book. Inside a large resealable plastic bag, place the student's book, simplified project guidelines, and supplies the child will need to complete the project. Then, before sending the kit home, review the instructions with the student, pointing out that the materials are included. Encourage the child to bring in his project a day or two early to check for any missed details or ask any questions.

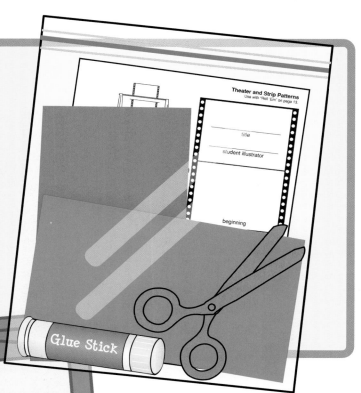

Listen to Me

Boost reading skills and help each English language learner share her school success. After reading a selection with a child, guide her to record herself as she reads the selection aloud. Then send the tape and the selection home in a plastic resealable bag. At home, the student can replay the tape for her family and then read along with it to build her reading skills!

In a Snap

When your English language learner is ready to start writing, have her use pictures to get started. Collect several interesting pictures from old magazines and cut several small sticky notes into narrow strips. Next, have the child choose a picture and glue it to a sheet of construction paper. Guide the student to label colors, objects, and actions in the picture using the sticky-note strips. Then help the child use the labels to describe the picture or write a story about what is happening in the picture and glue it to the picture's flip side.

I Spy

Increase classroom vocabulary by playing quick rounds of I Spy with students. Start the game by stating, "I spy something [adjective]." The first child to correctly guess the object you describe then gets to "spy" another object for his classmates to guess.

I spy something blue.

A bird!

A book!

The sky!

Locomotion

Get students on their feet to help them remember new vocabulary words. For each new word, have one child make a motion that he associates with that word and its meaning. Then, as a class, make that same motion each time the word is reviewed. If desired, play soft music in the background to really get students in the mood to make vocabulary locomotion!

athlete

Stop, Think, Write!

Help familiarize ELL students with the writing process by using a traffic light poster. On a large sheet of black construction paper, glue one red, one yellow, and one green circle. Label each one as shown. To use the traffic light, first have each student plan the who, what, when, where, and why of his story. Then have him carefully plan the beginning, middle, and end of the story. Finally, the student goes for it and writes the complete story! If desired, have each child use a copy of the graphic organizer on page 234 in conjunction with the traffic light poster.

Plan the 5 Ws.

Plan the beginning, middle, and end.

Go write your story!

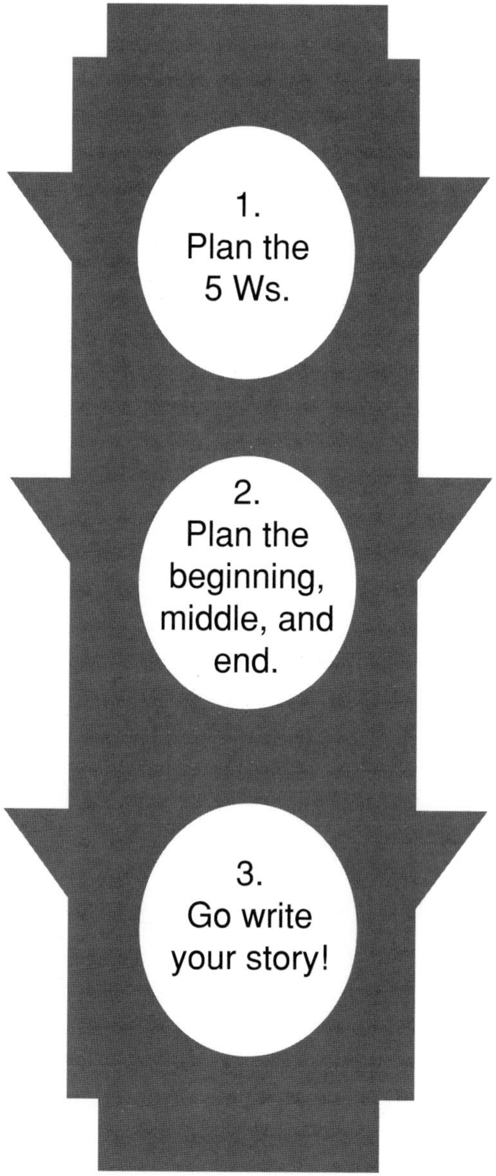

STOP, THINK, WRITE!

Title: _____

1. **Who?** _____

   What? _____

   When? _____

   Where? _____

   Why? _____

2. **Beginning:** _____
   _____

   Middle: _____
   _____

   End: _____
   _____

3. **Now use the information recorded above to write your story on another sheet of paper.**

1.
Plan the
5 Ws.

2.
Plan the
beginning,
middle, and
end.

3.
Go write
your story!

©The Mailbox® • *Superbook*® • TEC61052

NAME

DATE

Bursting With Information!

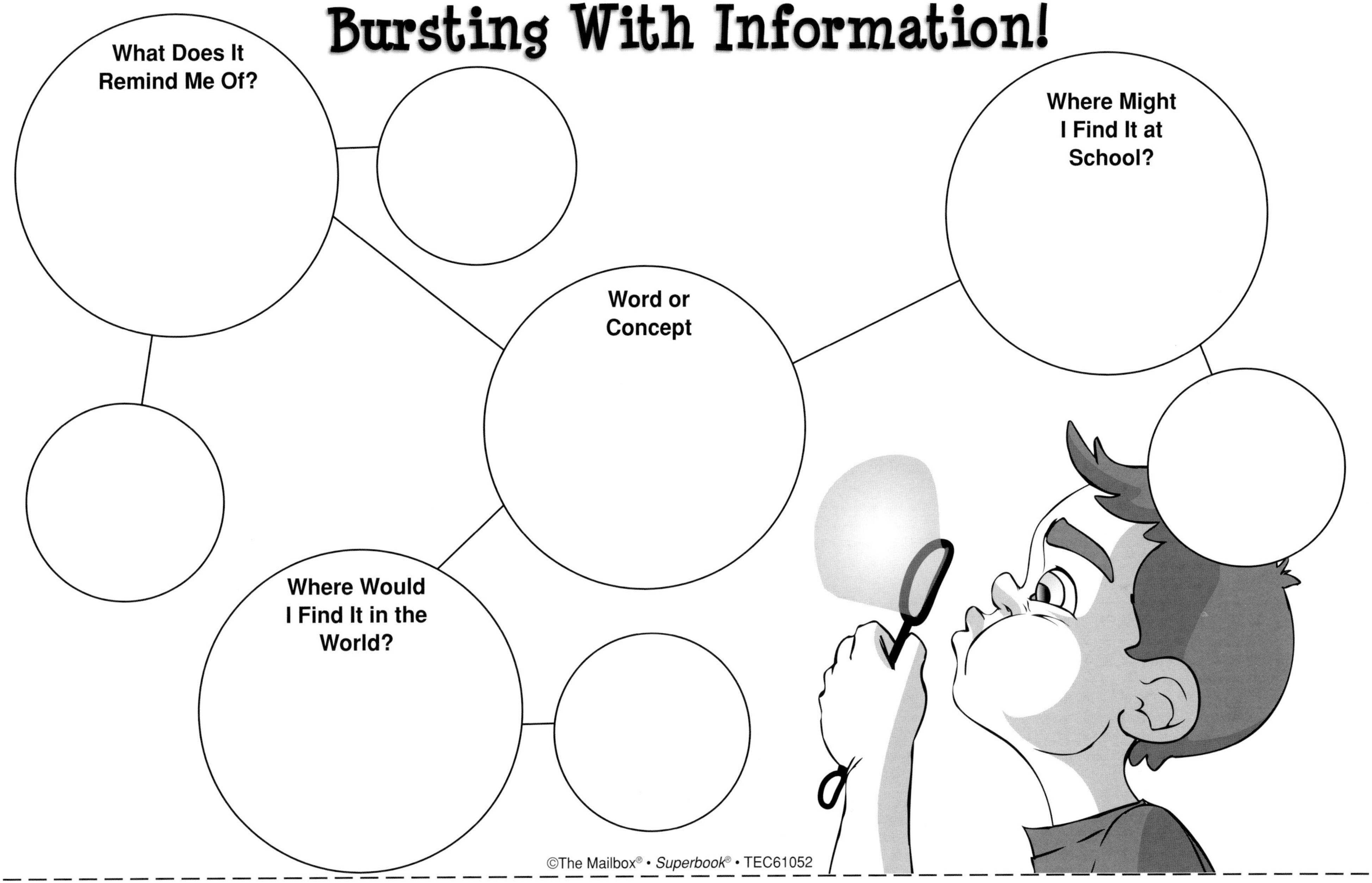

Where Might I Find It at School?

Word or Concept

What Does It Remind Me Of?

Where Would I Find It in the World?

Note to the teacher: Use this page to introduce new vocabulary or concepts to students or use it to review before a test.

How Do You Feel?

✏️ Draw a picture for each sentence.

This is a time
when I felt **happy.**

This is a time
when I felt **sad.**

This is a time
when I got **mad.**

This is a time
when I was **confused.**

Bulletin Boards

Perking Up Your Background Paper

Allow the theme of your bulletin board to inspire your choice of background paper. Gift wrap comes in a variety of designs, patterns, and colors that can enhance a bulletin board display. For example, cover a board with birthday wrap to feature your students' birthdays. Or add some sparkle to a seasonal display with a background of holiday wrap. Create other interesting displays with the following background-paper materials:

* newspaper
* calendar pages
* wallpaper
* plastic tablecloths

* road maps
* fabric
* colored cellophane
* bedsheets

Beautiful Borders

Looking for just a touch of color to add to a bulletin board with a solid-colored background? Accomplish this by creating colorful borders! Choose any material from the list above. Trace several strips of precut border onto your choice of material. Laminate the strips for added durability before cutting them out, if desired. Interesting borders can also be made using doilies, cupcake liners, dried leaves, die-cut shapes, and student-decorated adding-machine tape.

DISTINCTIVE-LETTERING DESIGNS

A bulletin board's title can be a work of art in itself. Add pizzazz to your board's letters by cutting them from any of the materials below using pinking shears or other specialized scissors.

* wallpaper samples
* greeting cards
* foil
* posters
* corrugated cardboard

* sandpaper
* newspapers
* magazine pages
* paper bags

File It for Next Year

Before you take down a bulletin board, photograph it! Then store the photo in an appropriately labeled folder or album. You'll have a wonderful collection of bulletin board ideas from which to choose in the future, plus a handy reference of all your completed displays.

From construction paper, cut a different large geometric shape for each subject area. Then label each shape with titles of some upcoming units. Whether you're starting off the school year or preparing for open house, this board will ensure that your classroom is in great shape!

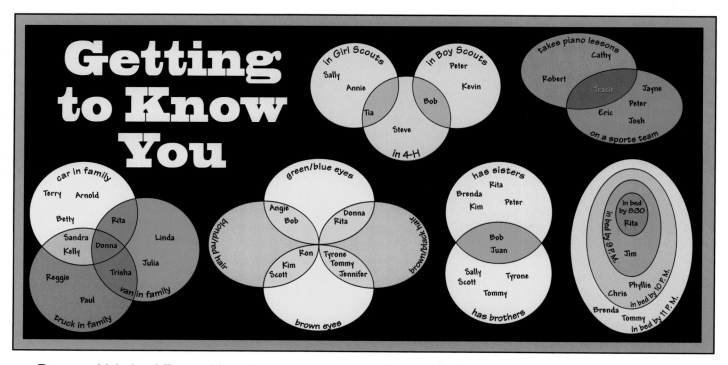

Draw and label a different Venn diagram on separate sheets of white construction paper, making the circles as large as possible and coloring them as shown. Direct each student to sign her name in an appropriate circle on each diagram with a black marker. Then display the diagrams on a bulletin board as shown. Afterward, pose questions that challenge your students to glean information from the diagrams, such as "How many more students like peanut-butter-and-jelly sandwiches than ham-and-cheese sandwiches?"

Use this display to encourage students to harvest math strategies and become better problem solvers. Overlap various sizes of pumpkin cutouts to create a full-grown patch. On each of the smaller pumpkins, post a different problem-solving strategy. Display examples of student work on the larger pumpkins. For a quick reference, have each student assemble a copy of the strategy booklet on pages 152–154.

Enlarge the mummy pattern from page 248 and display it on a board that has strips of white gauze or paper stapled across the background. Surround this ghoulish creature with student-written book reviews and recommendations. Invite each child to share his synopsis and unmask the mystery of a good book.

Give each student an index card on which to write a favorite recipe or a description of a family tradition. Next, direct her to use markers, crayons, and construction paper to decorate a paper lunch bag so that it resembles her home. Instruct her to cut out a window from the front of her house and tape her card to the back of this opening so that the card is visible from the front. Then post the bags along a winding road as shown.

Celebrate the holiday season with wishes for harmony in the world. Have each student write a personal wish for joy or peace on an index card. Instruct him to draw and cut out a dove. Then he tapes the card to the dove and attaches it to a bulletin board as shown.

Cover a board with white paper; then draw the skeleton of a large pine tree with a brown marker. Paint green boughs on the tree using a semidry paintbrush. Have students make paper ornaments and personalize them with acronyms using their names. Staple the ornaments to the tree after it dries.

Cover and title a board as shown, positioning a dreidel in each corner and a large Star of David with a menorah in the center. Discuss the history and symbolism of Hanukkah with your students. Have each student make a six-pointed star and cut it out. Have the student write his name in the center of the star and a fact about this holiday on each of the star's six points. After each child has decorated his star, add it to the board.

End the calendar year with a year-in-review bulletin board. Have your students bring in magazine covers and information from the Internet related to important events of the past year. Divide your students into groups; then give each group a different magazine cover or Internet article and an index card on which to summarize that event. Display the summaries and their corresponding magazine covers or front pages on a board as shown.

After winter break, have each student write about a person who did something nice for him during the holidays. Make several enlargements of the penguin from the notecard on page 249. Color the penguins and display them along with your students' writings on a snowflake-bordered board as shown. Afterward, give each student a copy of the penguin-shaped notecard from page 249 on which to write a special thank-you note to his person.

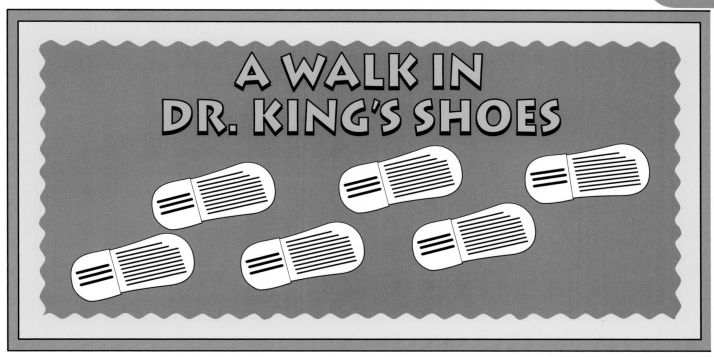

Divide your class into six groups. Assign each group a different event from Dr. King's life: leading the Montgomery bus boycott, founding the Southern Christian Leadership Conference, delivering the famous "I Have a Dream" speech, receiving the Nobel Peace Prize, supporting the Voting Rights Act of 1965, or being assassinated on April 4, 1968. Have each group research its assigned event and write a brief description of it on a copy of the shoe pattern from page 250. Then arrange each group's event in chronological order on a bulletin board as shown.

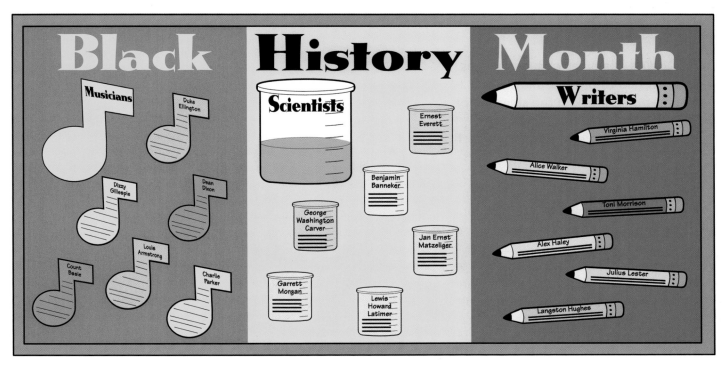

Have each student choose a different Black American from the field of music, science, or literature to research. Direct the student to summarize that person's contributions in a sentence or two on a copy of a corresponding pattern from page 251. Post each student's summary on its matching red, yellow, or green section of the bulletin board as shown.

Have your students brainstorm a list of favorite characters from books they've read. Afterward, ask each student to choose a character and have that character send a special valentine to another character from the same story. To make the valentine, each student decorates a heart shape cut from red or pink paper. On the front of the valentine, he writes his special message from one character to the other. On the back of the valentine, the student writes the title and author of the book from which his characters come. Display the completed valentines on a bulletin board, as shown, with some of the books they mention nearby.

Discuss examples of superstitions that are said to bring bad luck, such as stepping on a crack in the sidewalk or walking under a ladder. Next, brainstorm a list of good-luck charms, such as four-leaf clovers, rainbows, rabbits' feet, horseshoes, or the number 7. On a copy of the four-leaf clover pattern from page 252, challenge each student to write about either a superstition, a lucky charm, or a topic such as "The Luckiest Thing That Ever Happened to Me." After your students decorate and cut out their clovers, display the projects on a bulletin board with cutouts of good-luck charms as shown.

White
fluffy clouds and
bouncing sheep...

Rosy red roses, leaves in the fall, cardinals...
Golden orange the sun beats down, tigerlike...
Yellow sunshine, daffodils, bumblebees, and...
Green is the color of grass in the spring...
Bluebells ring and bluebirds sing...
Purple cows I never saw...violets, grapes, and...

Colorful Poetry

Integrate poetry into a springtime bulletin board. Read aloud several poems about color from *Hailstones and Halibut Bones* by Mary O'Neil. Afterward, divide your students into groups; then have each group write its own poem about color. Next, give each group a strip of wide-arched bulletin board paper that matches the color in the students' poem. Direct each group to copy its poem in large letters onto the colored strip of paper. Assemble the strips on a bulletin board so that they extend from a large white cloud and represent a rainbow as shown.

BLOOMING GOOD NOUNS

Singular — student
Singular Possessive — teacher's
bike
dog's
Plural — women
books
Plural Possessive — groups'
fans'

Usher in spring with a display that is as practical as it is pretty. Staple four pieces of green yarn and four flower centers to a board as shown. Give each student four petals or leaves and have him write a singular, singular possessive, plural, or plural possessive noun on each one. Then ask him to attach the petal or leaf to the matching flower center or stem.

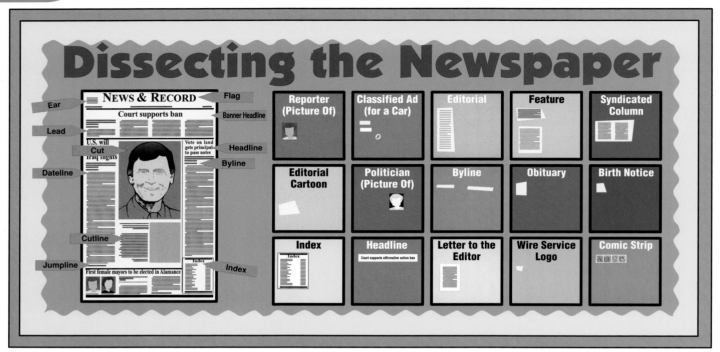

Examine the parts of a newspaper with a scavenger hunt that becomes an educational display. Collect one newspaper for each pair of students. Also label and post the front page of a newspaper and 15 construction paper signs as shown. Give each pair of students one newspaper. The pair uses the newspaper's index to find an example of each topic, cuts it out, and staples it to the appropriate sign. (Staple only the top edge of a large example so that other samples can be viewed simply by lifting one layer at a time.)

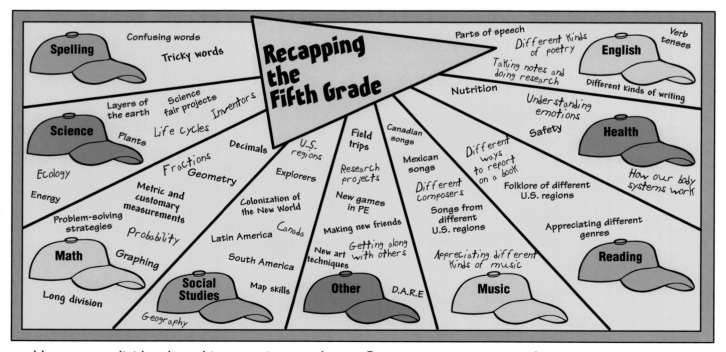

Use yarn to divide a board into sections as shown. Cut out a sports pennant from construction paper, write the board's title on it, and position the pennant in the center of the board. Enlarge and duplicate an appropriate number of baseball caps from the pattern on page 249. Color and program each cap with a different subject. During free time, have your students use markers to write specific things learned about those subjects throughout year in each section.

Enlarge the hippo pattern from page 253 and position it on a board as shown. Each week, reward any student who's shown improvement and/or made a top score in any subject area by posting his work on this attention-getting bulletin board.

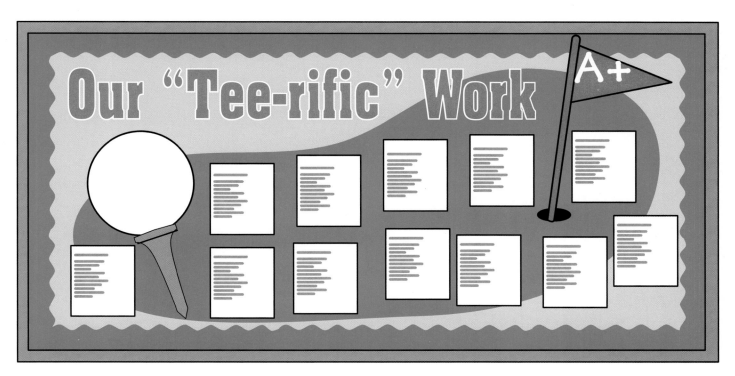

When a student achieves a good score on a paper, show her how "tee-rific" that is by posting her paper on a special bulletin board. Cut a fairway from green bulletin board paper, a flag and pole from red paper, a golf tee from brown paper, and a golf ball from white paper. Assemble the board as shown; then challenge all your students to try for a hole in one!

Mummy Pattern

Use with "Wrapped Up in a Good Book" on page 239.

TEC61052

Penguin Notecard Pattern
Use with "A Blizzard of Blessings" on page 242.

TEC61052

Hat Pattern
Use with "Recapping the Fifth Grade" on page 246.

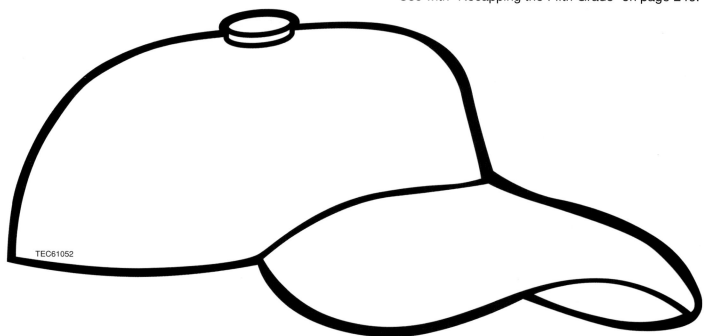

TEC61052

Shoe Pattern

Use with "A Walk in Dr. King's Shoes" on page 243.

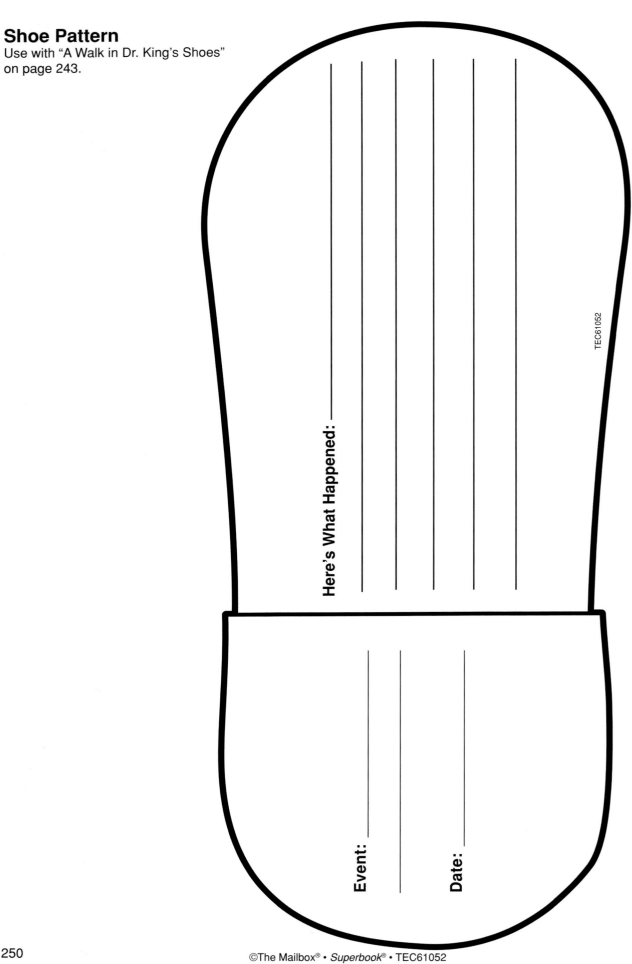

Here's What Happened: _____

Event: _____

Date: _____

TEC61052

Note, Beaker, and Pencil Patterns

Use with "Black History Month" on page 243.

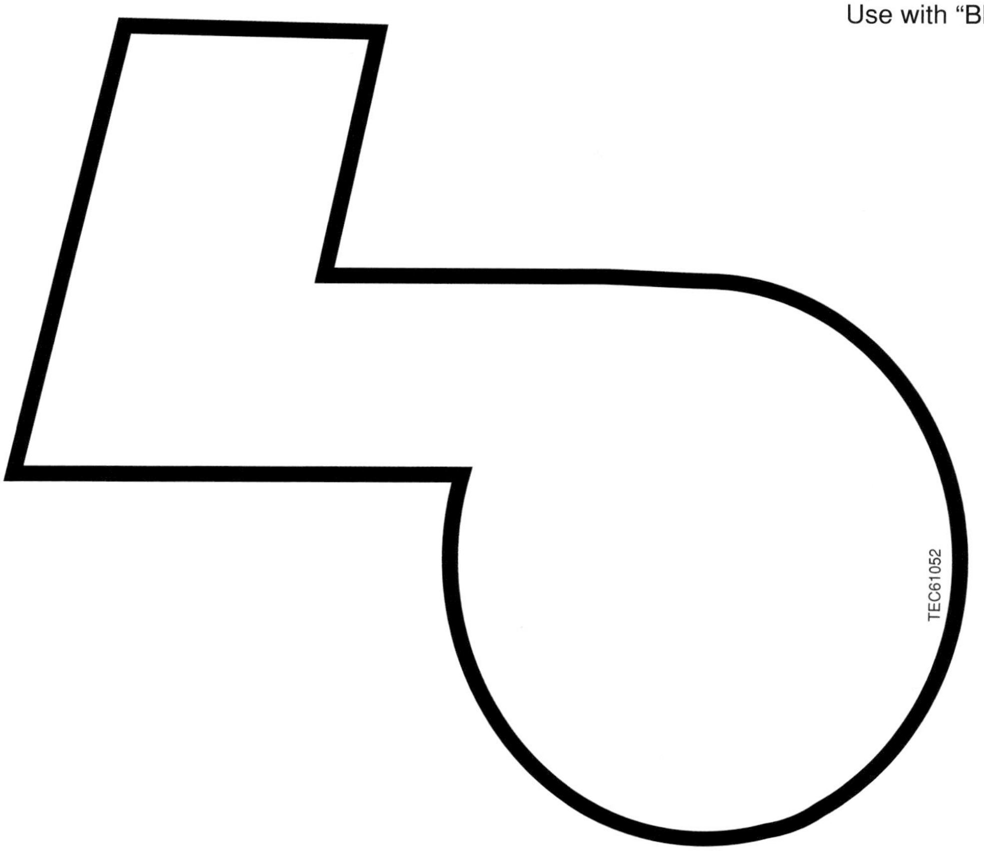

TEC61052

TEC61052

TEC61052

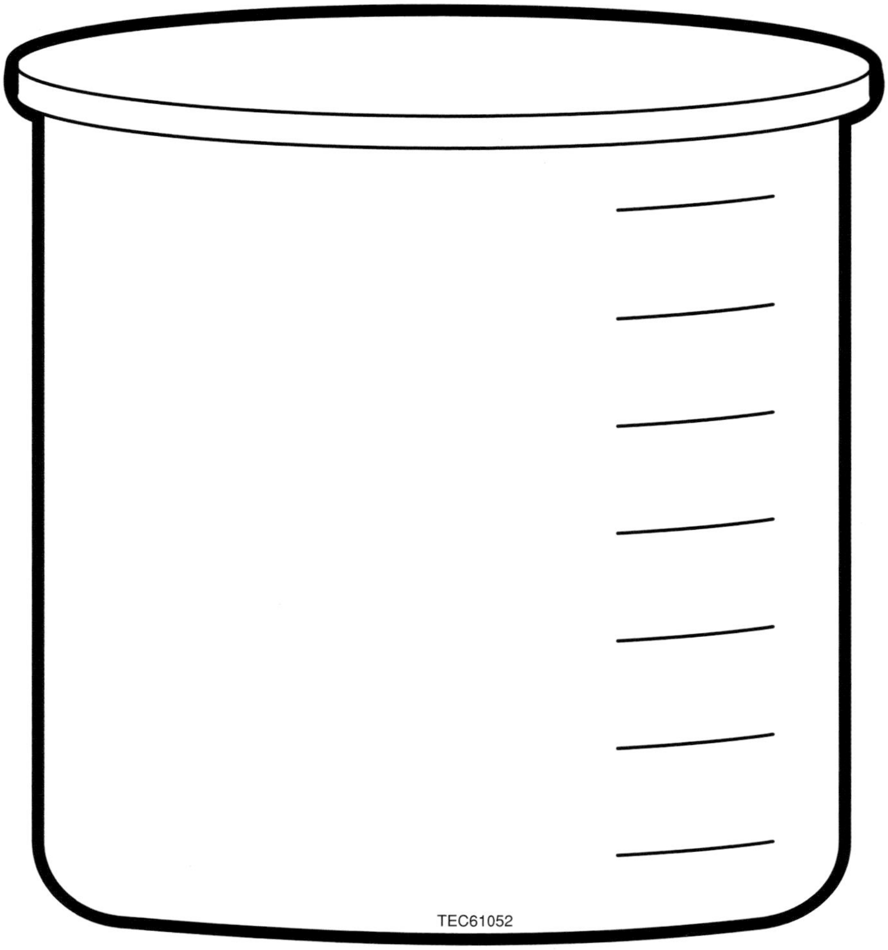

Clover Pattern
Use with "Lucky Charms" on page 244.

Name _____

©The Mailbox® • Superbook® • TEC61052

Classroom Management

Ball Toss

Use this quick and easy trick whenever you want to make it clear whose turn it is to talk. Buy an inexpensive sponge ball and keep it handy throughout the day. Whenever a discussion becomes too lively, toss the ball to a student and explain that only the person with the ball has permission to speak. That student now has the floor to ask a question or make a comment without any interruptions from the other students. When he is finished speaking, have that student pass the ball back to you so you can then toss it to another student. Continue in this manner until everyone has had a chance to speak.

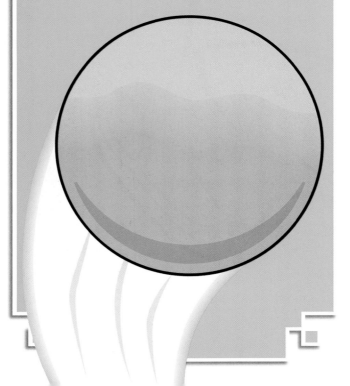

Quick Cleanups

Keep a pop-up dispenser of inexpensive baby wipes in your classroom for a quick and easy way to clean overhead transparencies. (Be sure to get wipes without lotion.) These handy wipes are also great for cleaning hands, faces, little messes, desk surfaces, and tabletops!

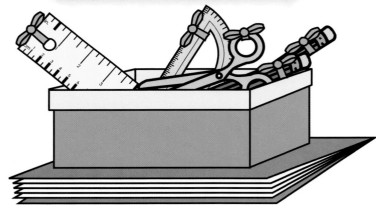

Borrower's Stash

A "borrower's stash" is a great idea for forgetful students. Fill a basket, box, or plastic tub with pencils, pens, scissors, protractors, and other items. Tie colorful ribbons to each item to easily identify it as belonging to the classroom stash. Place the stash on top of a file folder containing loose-leaf paper in an easy-to-reach spot in the classroom. Tell your students that the items belong to the classroom and are for their use when they've forgotten to bring an item or have run out of a particular supply. The ribbons will serve as gentle reminders for students to return items to the stash when finished so the supplies will be available when needed by other students.

Keeping Track of Supplies

Keep track of grade-level supplies with this simple trick. Have each teacher at your grade level choose a different color nail polish and use it to mark dots on those items that are shared throughout the year. These simple color dots will help ensure that protractors, Geoboards, scissors, and other supplies get returned to the right rooms by the end of the day, week, month, or year. If a teacher moves away, have the new teacher use the same color nail polish as the previous teacher. This alleviates the confusion of having the previous teacher's name on classroom supplies.

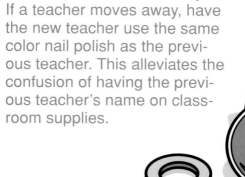

Good-Neighbor Reports

Update absent students on missed activities with this simple note-taking system. Copy a supply of the reproducible on page 259 to keep handy in the classroom. Each day a student is absent, assign a classmate to fill out a "Good-Neighbor Report." Instruct the selected student to be concise and specific when writing up that day's assignments. At the end of the day, have the recorder put the completed sheet in a three-ring binder labeled "Good-Neighbor Reports." Briefly look over the completed sheet to be sure no assignments were left off the sheet. Praise the recorder for a job well done, or give some pointers on how to write better notes next time. Direct each student returning from an absence to read the appropriate reports to find out which assignments he missed and what he needs to complete.

Put It in Writing!

Need an easy way to help settle student arguments? Have each student take time out to cool off and write down exactly what happened, including emotions and events that led up to the incident. Chances are good that by the time each student has recorded his version of the story, tempers will have cooled. If the students still need your intervention, read each student's account of the situation and then discuss the versions with the students involved. Not only does this strategy help clarify the situation, but it also allows each student involved to tell his side of the story.

It all started when Sally called me a...

Thrifty Containers

When distributing small game pieces, manipulatives, or food items to your students, coffee filters serve as inexpensive, one-time containers. Place a filter on each student's desk to prevent rolling or misplaced pieces, or to contain messy crumbs. When it's time to clean up, the scraps, crumbs, and leftovers can be neatly disposed of inside the filter. Used filters that are still clean can be recycled for another activity.

What's Your Name?

Not being able to call students by their names can frustrate a substitute and your students. Avoid this problem by having your students create decorative nametags for their desks. Give each student a large unlined index card; then have him fold it in half lengthwise so that it stands like a tent card. Have the student use a black marker to write his first name on both sides of the card. Allow him to decorate his card any way he chooses as long as his name is still clearly visible. Collect the nametags and store them with your substitute notebook. Instruct your substitute to have one student pass out the nametags for students to place on their desktops. At the end of the day, have the substitute collect the nametags so that they'll be ready to use the next time you have a substitute.

Mark

A Helping Hand

Let your substitute know that he has a helping hand close by! On a hand-shaped cutout, write the name of a teacher in a nearby classroom to whom the substitute can turn for answers to questions. Select a teacher who is familiar with your classroom procedures and make her aware that you are suggesting her as a helper. Laminate the hand and tape it to the front of your substitute notebook. This will make your substitute feel more comfortable, and you'll feel better knowing his day will run smoothly.

A Helping Hand
See Mrs. Adcock
in Room 406
about any
questions you
may have.

Parent Survival Guide

Help each parent overcome the challenges of a new year by creating a personalized parent survival guide. Before the beginning of school, duplicate important school and classroom information to include in the guide (see the examples). Also include a brief welcome letter that includes background information about yourself. Next, enlist the help of your students in assembling the guide by following the steps below.

1 Give each student a 12" x 18" sheet of light-colored construction paper and a copy of each page in the guide.

2 Direct the student to fold the construction paper in half, labeling the front to make a cover as shown.

3 Have him decorate his cover with colorful illustrations of appropriate grade-level, survival-type items. Laminate the covers if desired.

4 Have each student design a table of contents; then have him bind the pages of his book using staples or a hole puncher and brads.

5 Allow each student to take the book he assembled home and present it to his parents.

Table of Contents

Welcome Letter	page 1
Staff Directory	page 2
School Floor Plan	page 3
Daily Schedule	page 4
Materials List	page 5
	page 6

How to Survive 5th Grade

Valuable Volunteers

Parents can certainly be valuable resources for your classroom—from helping with art activities or science projects to sharing books with children. Some parents might have talents, hobbies, or occupations they could share with the class. Follow the steps below to put these valuable volunteers to work for you and your students!

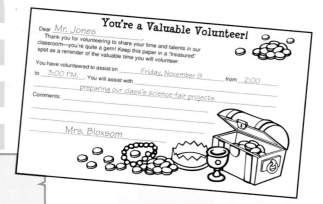

1. Make one copy of "Trackin' Down Treasures" at the top of page 260 to send home to each parent.

2. Have each child ask his parent to indicate an area in which to help.

3. Collect and compile all the information from the returned forms.

4. Schedule designated times each week or month for different parent volunteers.

5. Send home the bottom half of page 260 as a reminder to each parent of the appointed time.

6. Follow up each parent's visit by having students sign a thank-you card to send to each visitor.

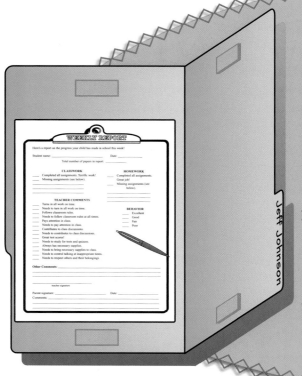

Don't Forget Your Briefcase!

Looking for a way to inform each parent of the progress his child is making and send papers home safely? Then have each student construct a personal briefcase. Obtain a file folder for each student; then write each student's name on the tab of a different folder. Give each student his folder and have him decorate it. Collect the folders, laminating them for durability if desired; then attach two Velcro strips onto the inside flaps of each folder as shown.

Next, make multiple copies of "Weekly Report" on page 261. If desired, also make copies of "Missed Assignments" and "Incomplete Work" on page 262. Each time you send papers home, fill out a report—including a report on missed or incomplete work—for each student; then staple it to the inside flap of his folder. Request that each parent read and discuss the report with his child and then sign and return it in the folder the following day. Collect each student's folder and store it until the next round of papers is ready to go home.

Staying on Schedule

Veteran and novice teachers alike know that sticking to a conference schedule is not always easy. Adhere to your schedule by posting a sign on your door that asks each parent to knock when it is his scheduled conference time. Inform each parent of your procedure at the start of the conference and explain that if additional time is needed, you can schedule another conference as soon as possible. What a great way to ensure that your schedule stays on track and parents are not left waiting too long!

WELCOME PARENTS!

Please knock if it is past your scheduled conference time. For your convenience, we want to adhere to the schedule as closely as possible. Thank you,
Mrs. Kreger

Student code of conduct

10 Ways To Help Your Child In School

Is Your child Gifted?

Got a Minute?

Provide parents who arrive early for scheduled conferences with interesting reading material to help pass the time. Prior to conference day, make copies of class newsletters, outlines of school policies, home-learning activities, and articles about learning disabilities, cooperative discipline, gifted programs, and other topics of interest. Also include several order forms for children's books and children's magazines for young readers. Parents will appreciate the opportunity to do something constructive while they wait.

Scheduling Solution

Parents' work and child-care schedules often make it difficult to schedule conferences at convenient times. Make this task easier by asking for parental input before scheduling any conference. One week prior to the conferences, send home a note requesting parents to suggest several workable conference times. From the responses, select a time from each parent that best fits your conference schedule. Send a confirmation form to each parent honoring one of the specific times he suggested (see the forms on page 263). Allowing parents flexibility in scheduling conferences is just one more way you can keep the lines of communication open.

Conference Request

Dear <u>Mrs. Willett</u>,

I have scheduled you for a parent-teacher conference at the following time:
Date: <u>Friday, November 16</u>
Time: <u>1:45</u> to <u>2:15</u>

Please complete the information at the bottom of this form; then return the form to school tomorrow. If the time scheduled above is not convenient for you, please suggest several alternate times.

Sincerely,

<u>Mrs. Cox</u>
teacher's signature

Student's name: <u>Jake Willett</u>

✔ Yes, I will attend the conference at the time and date listed above.

____ No, I cannot attend a conference at that time.

I would rather schedule a conference for the following:
Date: _____
Times: (please list more than one) _____ to _____, or
_____ to _____, or _____ to _____

Parent's signature: <u>Mrs. Willett</u>
Daytime phone: <u>348-5645</u>
Evening phone: <u>348-8890</u>

☆ ☆ ☆ ☆   See you then!

Good-Neighbor Report

Keep track of today's activities for your absent classmates. Take careful notes on the chart below. Be sure to include page numbers, assignment directions, and any special instructions about an assignment given by your teacher.

Subject	Assignment
READING 	
WRITING 	
SCIENCE 	
SOCIAL STUDIES 	
MATH 	
OTHER ASSIGNMENTS/ ACTIVITIES 	

Note to the teacher: Use with "Good-Neighbor Reports" on page 255.

259

Trackin' Down Treasures

Dear Parent,

　We're trackin' down some hidden treasures—the skills and talents of our classroom parents! Please complete the information below and return it to school as soon as possible.

Your name: _____

Child's name: _____

Phone number: _____

Occupation: _____

Talents/interests: _____

_____

Convenient day and time for you to assist: _____

In what areas would you like to assist?

- art projects
- field trips
- holiday parties
- guest reader
- providing supplies and materials

- providing treats
- teaching a special interest/talent
- tutoring students
- special student projects
- other: _____

You're a Valuable Volunteer!

Dear _____,

　Thank you for volunteering to share your time and talents in our classroom—you're quite a gem! Keep this paper in a "treasured" spot as a reminder of the valuable time you will volunteer.

You have volunteered to assist on _____ from _____

to _____. You will assist with _____

_____.

Comments: _____

_____

_____

_____

WEEKLY REPORT

Here's a report on the progress your child has made in school this week!

Student name: _____   Date: _____

Total number of papers in report: _____

CLASSWORK

_____ Completed all assignments. Terrific work!
_____ Missing assignments (see below).

_____
_____
_____

HOMEWORK

_____ Completed all assignments. Great job!
_____ Missing assignments (see below).

_____
_____
_____

TEACHER COMMENTS

_____ Turns in all work on time.
_____ Needs to turn in all work on time.
_____ Follows classroom rules.
_____ Needs to follow classroom rules at all times.
_____ Pays attention in class.
_____ Needs to pay attention in class.
_____ Contributes to class discussions.
_____ Needs to contribute to class discussions.
_____ Great test scores!
_____ Needs to study for tests and quizzes.
_____ Always has necessary supplies.
_____ Needs to bring necessary supplies to class.
_____ Needs to control talking at inappropriate times.
_____ Needs to respect others and their belongings.

BEHAVIOR

_____ Excellent
_____ Good
_____ Fair
_____ Poor

Other Comments: _____
_____
_____

_____
teacher signature

Parent signature: _____   Date: _____
Comments: _____
_____
_____

Incomplete Work

_____ date

Dear Parent,

_____ needs to complete the following assignments:

_____

_____

_____

This work is due by _____

Your help and support are greatly appreciated.

Sincerely,

_____
teacher signature

_____
parent signature

Please sign and return.

©The Mailbox® • *Superbook*® • TEC61052

Missed Assignments

_____ date

Dear Parent,

_____ needs to complete the following assignments:

_____

_____

_____

This work is due by _____

Your help and support are greatly appreciated.

Sincerely,

_____
teacher signature

_____
parent signature

Please sign and return.

©The Mailbox® • *Superbook*® • TEC61052

Note to the teacher: Use with "Don't Forget Your Briefcase!" on page 257.

Rescheduled Conference Notification

As you requested, your parent-teacher conference has been rescheduled.

Student: _____

Teacher: _____

Room number: _____

Date: _____

Time: _____ to _____

See you then!

©The Mailbox® • Superbook® • TEC61052

Conference Confirmation

Don't forget your parent-teacher conference!

Student: _____

Teacher: _____

Room number: _____

Date: _____

Time: _____ to _____

See you then!

©The Mailbox® • Superbook® • TEC61052

Conference Request

Dear _____,

I have scheduled you for a parent-teacher conference at the following time:

Date: _____

Time: _____ to _____

Please complete the information at the bottom of this form; then return the form to school tomorrow. If the time scheduled above is not convenient for you, please suggest several alternate times.

Sincerely,

_____
teacher's signature

©The Mailbox® • Superbook® • TEC61052

Student's name: _____

_____ Yes, I will attend the conference at the time and date listed above.

_____ No, I cannot attend a conference at that time.

I would rather schedule a conference for the following:

Date: _____

Times: (please list more than one) _____ to _____, or

_____ to _____, or _____ to _____

Parent's signature: _____

Daytime phone: _____

Evening phone: _____

See you then!

©The Mailbox® • Superbook® • TEC61052

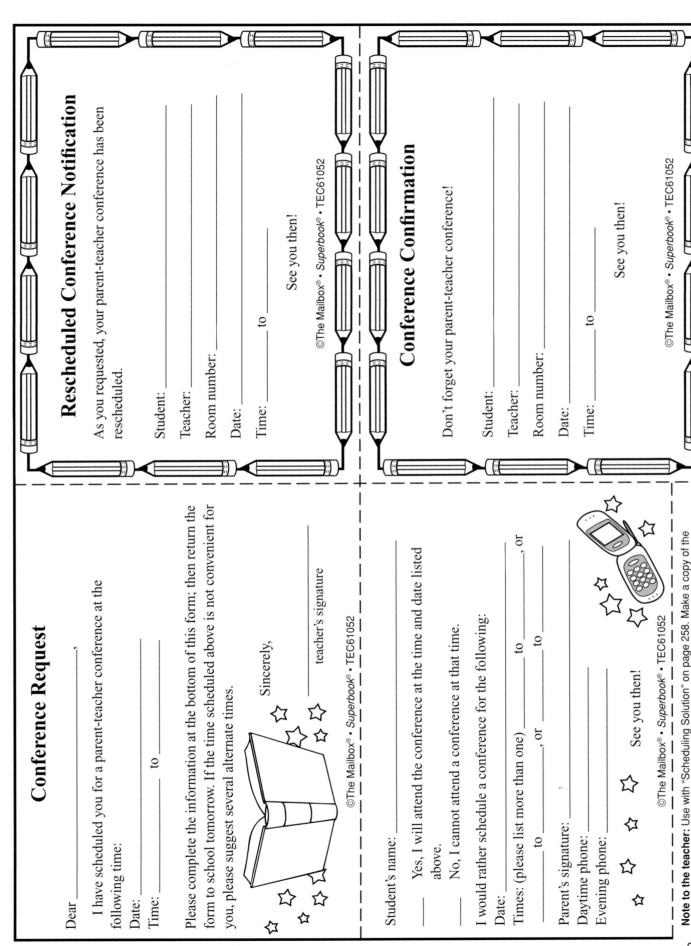

Note to the teacher: Use with "Scheduling Solution" on page 258. Make a copy of the appropriate form; then complete it and send it home.

Motivation & Positive Discipline

Quick Check

Use this quick tip to keep your students motivated to complete their work on time. When preparing for lunch, a special class, or recess, call students to line up using the names from the last set of papers that students turned in to you. Any student who has not turned in that assignment can turn it in to you then if it is complete or make a note to finish the work later. You should soon have students who are eager to turn in their work on time every time!

READY REINFORCEMENT

Have a supply of encouragement on hand with preprogrammed sticky notes. Use a rubber stamp to create a positive remark on each sheet of a small sticky-note pad. Keep the pad in your pocket or on your desk. When you see an opportunity to praise a student, hand her a sheet from the pad. The notes can also be attached to papers that show praise-worthy work!

YOU'RE A SUPERSTAR!

JOB WELL DONE!

We Really Did It!

Help your students remember to bring all the items they need for special classes with this idea. Use a computer program to design a banner that reads "We Really Did It!" Display the banner in the classroom. Each day that the entire class brings all the needed materials (including homework) to their special class, select a student to color one letter on the banner. When all the letters of the banner are colored, reward the class with a special treat.

We Really Did It!

Rising Above the Negative

Show your students the effects of positive and negative words with this unforgettable demonstration! Obtain several Ping-Pong balls, several small rocks, a permanent marker, and a clear fish bowl half-filled with water. Divide your class into groups. Instruct each group to generate two lists of words—one containing positive words that could encourage others and one with negative words that could discourage. Remind students that the listed words should be those that are allowed in a classroom. Allow each group to share their responses as you make two lists on the board. Circle any words that are repeated. Using the permanent marker, write each circled positive word on a different ball and each circled negative word on a different rock. Place all the labeled balls and rocks into the fish bowl; then have your students observe what happens. (The positive words float, and the negative words sink.) Ask your students to explain how this demonstration symbolizes the effect of positive and negative words on people. Guide students to realize that negative words can weigh a person down and make them feel low, but positive words can uplift. Your students won't likely forget the lesson provided by this image!

Student Accountability

Encourage good student behavior when you are absent. Have your substitute give each student a copy of the student behavior and assignment sheet on page 267. Then have her direct the child to fill out his assignments and rate his behavior for the day. Ask the substitute to collect each student's form for you and record any additional information she would like you to know. When you return, you will have a written record of each child's performance while you were out.

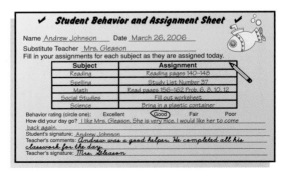

LEARNING BUDDIES

Initiate friendships and teach responsibility with learning buddies. Work together with a first- or second-grade teacher to pair each of your fifth graders with one of the younger students. Then schedule a class time each week for the learning buddies to work together. For each visit, plan an activity—such as reading a picture book, completing an art project, or playing an educational game—that the buddies can work on together. Your students' sense of responsibility will grow just as wide as their smiles!

Special Awards

The end of a grading period is often the time when achievement awards are handed out. Why not choose a special time to recognize students for nonacademic accomplishments? Set aside time in the middle of each grading period for a celebration of all the good qualities your students possess. Make copies of the invitation and award patterns on page 269. Have each student fill out an invitation to his family members for the ceremony. Then complete an award for each student, applauding characteristics such as a cooperative attitude, willingness to help others, improved behavior, and artistic ability. On the day of the awards ceremony, present each child with a certificate while his family and friends look on. Then toast your students with juice or punch and conclude the event with refreshments.

PUTTING IN YOUR TWO CENTS' WORTH

Make sure all your students get opportunities to contribute to discussions with this quick motivation tip! When working in cooperative groups, give each group member two pennies. Explain that when a student has something to add to the discussion, he must place one penny in the center of the group. After a student contributes both pennies, he cannot speak again until every other group member has put in his two pennies. This simple idea will help students become better listeners and ensure that every student always gets to put in his two cents' worth!

Conduct Record

Keep track of student behavior with this timesaving idea. Duplicate page 268 for each student. Keep the pages alphabetized in a binder or folder. When a student misbehaves or disrupts the class, have him fill in one row on the card. Then check the card to make sure the student's entries are appropriate. Briefly discuss the situation with the student; then add your initials under the student's. After two incidents, make a copy of the card and send it home with the student, asking the parent for assistance in correcting the inappropriate behavior. This method helps the student take responsibility for his actions as well as provides a means of documenting the incident and communicating with parents.

BEHAVIOR RECORD/NOTE TO PARENT

NAME _Doug Banks_
DATE

Conduct Card

Take a few moments to think about your actions, then fill in the chart below. Initial your entry and return the card to your teacher. After the second entry, the card will be sent home for your parent or guardian to sign. After the third entry, a conference will be scheduled with your parent or guardian.

Date	What I Was Doing	What I Should Have Been Doing	Initials
1. 10/22	I was talking to Jimmy about the birthday party.	I was supposed to be working quietly on my project.	THM DJB
2.			
3.			

✔ Student Behavior and Assignment Sheet ✔

Name____________________________ Date________________

Substitute Teacher____________________________________

Fill in your assignments for each subject as they are assigned today.

Subject	Assignment

Behavior rating (circle one): Excellent Good Fair Poor

How did your day go?____

____

Student's signature:____

Teacher's comments:____

____

Teacher's signature:____

✔ Student Behavior and Assignment Sheet ✔

Name____________________________ Date________________

Substitute Teacher____________________________________

Fill in your assignments for each subject as they are assigned today.

Subject	Assignment

Behavior rating (circle one): Excellent Good Fair Poor

How did your day go?____

____

Student's signature:____

Teacher's comments:____

____

Teacher's signature:____

Note to the teacher: Use with "Student Accountability" on page 265.

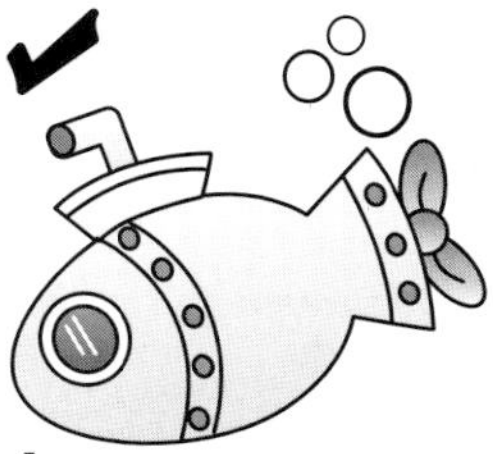

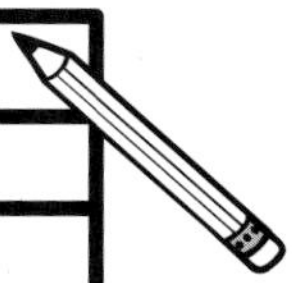

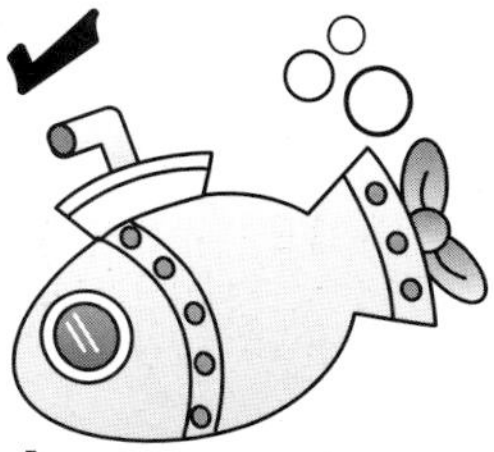

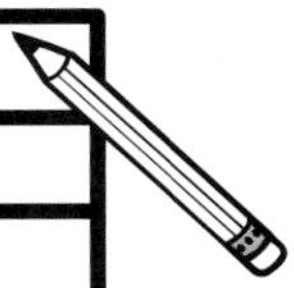

Conduct Card

Take a few moments to think about your actions, then fill in one row of the chart below. Initial your entry and return the card to your teacher. After the second entry, the card will be sent home for your parent or guardian to sign. After the third entry, a conference will be scheduled with your parent or guardian.

Date	What I Was Doing	What I Should Have Been Doing	Initials
1.			
2.			
3.			

Dear Parent,

We need your assistance to maintain a positive learning environment in our classroom. Please sign and return this card by ___/___/___ with any suggestions or comments you may have concerning the situation. Thank you in advance for your help.

Sincerely,

_____
teacher's signature

Parent suggestions/comments: _____

_____

_____

_____

_____

_____
parent's signature

©The Mailbox® • Superbook® • TEC61052

268 **Note to the teacher:** Use with "Conduct Record" on page 266.

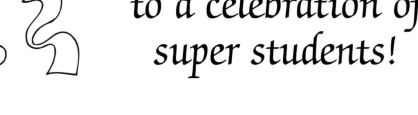

Please come to a celebration of super students!

Date:_____

Time:_____

Place:_____

In Recognition of

GREAT! FANTASTIC! HOORAY!

_____
student

for

_____

_____

_____

GREAT! FANTASTIC! HOORAY!

What a Super Student!

FIVE-MINUTE FILLERS

Question of the Day

Before students arrive each day, write a question on the board that requires students to do a little research. Upon finding the answer, a student writes the reply on a piece of paper along with her name and the source and page number of her answer. Then she places the folded paper in a shoebox with a slotted top. At the end of each day, draw a response from the box. Reward a correct answer with a valued classroom privilege.

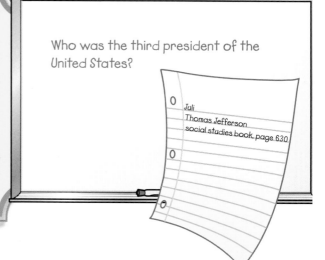

Who was the third president of the United States?

Juli
Thomas Jefferson
social studies book, page 630

Quick-Take Graphs

Draw the lines for a blank bar graph on poster board and laminate it for durability. Then, at a moment's notice, program the poster with a wipe-off marker. Give each student a self-stick note. Have him write his name on the note and post it in the correct column on the graph. Students can make observations and draw conclusions in no time flat!

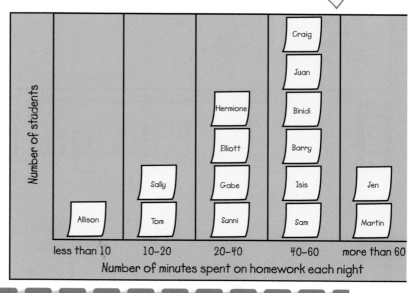

Twenty Questions

Get students using their brainpower with a game that is an old favorite. One child chooses an object, and other students ask questions that can be answered with a simple yes or no. If the object is identified before 20 questions have been asked, students offer facts about the object. If the object is not identified after 20 questions, clues are given until someone makes a correct guess.

Is it in this room?

Is it bigger than a refrigerator?

Multiplication Facts

Help students learn difficult multiplication facts with a simple guessing game. Fold several index cards in half. Program each half with a number as shown. Turn the card over and, on the left side, write the product of the two numbers and another clue. On the right side write the question, "Who are we?" Keep the cards folded with the numbers on the inside and place them in a resealable plastic bag. When a pair of students finishes work early, have the duo take the cards to a table and quiz each other quietly.

Our product is 56.
We are next-door neighbors on the number line.

Who are we?

8 7

Intermediate ABCs

Create these easy-to-use letters to have students practice alphabetizing words to the third or fourth letters. Trace one large capital letter onto a sheet of poster board and cut it out. On the front of the letter, list in random order about ten words that begin with that letter and have the first two or three letters in common. On the back of the letter, list the words in alphabetical order. When the class has a few minutes to spare, display the letter and have each student alphabetize the list. When all students have completed the list, turn the letter over so students can self-check. Over the year, use different letters until students become experts at alphabetizing more difficult words.

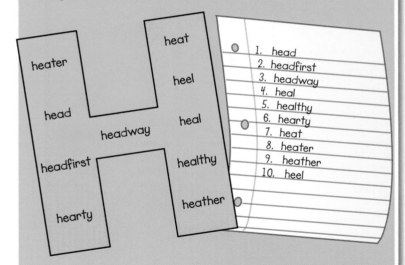

heater
heat
heel
head
heal
headway
healthy
headfirst
heather
hearty

1. head
2. headfirst
3. headway
4. heal
5. healthy
6. hearty
7. heat
8. heater
9. heather
10. heel

Word Wall

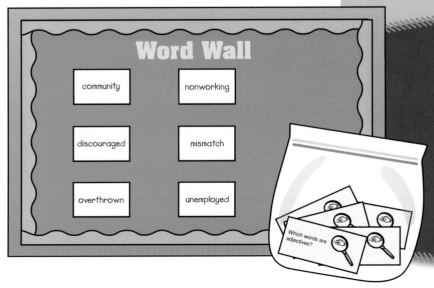

community   nonworking

discouraged   mismatch

overthrown   unemployed

Which words are adjectives?

Word Wall Investigations

Keep a copy of the word wall cards on page 272 close at hand for a quick whole-class review during transition times. If desired, make several sets of cards and place each in a resealable plastic bag. A student can practice quietly on his own when all his work is complete.

Word Wall Cards

Use with "Word Wall Investigations" on page 271.

Which words are nouns? TEC61052	Which words are verbs? TEC61052
Which words are adjectives? TEC61052	Which words are adverbs? TEC61052
Find two words that are synonyms. TEC61052	Find two words that are antonyms. TEC61052
How many words have three syllables? TEC61052	Create a sentence using three of the words. TEC61052
How many different prefixes can you find? TEC61052	List each word in alphabetical order. TEC61052

ARTS & CRAFTS

Back-to-School Pencil Toppers

Top off your students' first day of school with this art project.

Materials for each student:
1½" ball of no-cook modeling dough in a desired color,
  prepared without oil (see the recipe on page 280)
12" length of waxed paper
toothpick
pencil
plastic cup
clear nail polish

Steps:
1. Place the waxed paper on the desktop.
2. Push the ball of dough onto the eraser end of the pencil.
3. Lay the pencil on the waxed paper; then mold the dough into a desired shape, such as your initial, a heart, or a smiley face.
4. Use the toothpick for adding features to your design.
5. Stand the pencil in a plastic cup to allow the topper to dry overnight.
6. Paint the topper with clear nail polish for durability; then allow it to dry in a well-ventilated area.

First-Day Frames

Preserve your students' memories of the first day of school with this picture-perfect craft. During the first day of school, take a photograph of each student. Then give the student his developed photograph along with the materials listed below to create a framed first-day-of-school memory.

Materials for each student:
several old puzzle pieces that have been
  spray-painted different colors
three 3½" x 5" tagboard cards
glue
scissors
ruler
hot glue gun
black permanent marker

Steps:
1. Cut away the interior from one tagboard card to make a frame with a one-inch border.
2. Glue the puzzle pieces around the border's perimeter.
3. Hot-glue a second tagboard card to the back of the frame at the bottom and sides only, leaving the top open for inserting the photo.
4. Use the marker to write the date or other words, such as "Piecing Together the New Year" or "Picture-Perfect Student," on the frame.
5. Make a stand for the frame by cutting away a corner from the remaining tagboard card. Fold the card in half; then glue the uncut half to the back of the frame.
6. Insert your first-day photograph, cutting it to fit if necessary.

CORNY COBS

Kids love to hear and tell jokes—the cornier the better! Combine their love for jokes with this art idea for a great fall display.

Materials for each student:
copy of page 282
sheet of yellow construction paper
4 ½" x 6" piece of green construction paper
pencil
construction paper scraps
crayons or colored pencils
clear tape
scissors
stapler

Steps:
1. Fold the yellow paper in half vertically.
2. Cut out the corncob pattern; then position the pattern along the fold line of the yellow construction paper and trace it. Cut out the tracing.
3. Cut out the arm pattern; then trace it twice on the green paper. Cut out the tracings.
4. Tape the squared-off end of the corncob's left arm to the back of the top cob.
5. Tape the squared-off end of the corncob's right arm to the back of the bottom cob.
6. Decorate the corncob with kernels using scrap pieces of construction paper and crayons or colored pencils. Overlap and then staple the ends of the arms together in front of the cob.
7. Write a joke on the square pattern and tape it to the overlapped section of the cob's arms.
8. Open the corncob and write the answer to the joke inside.

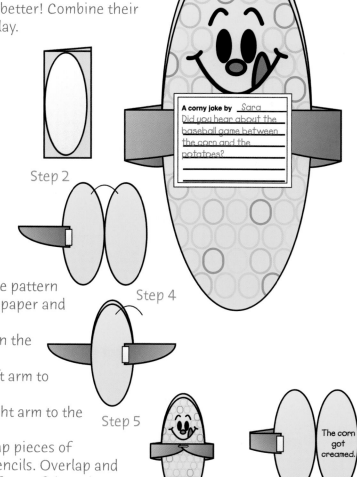

A corny joke by Sara
Did you hear about the baseball game between the corn and the potatoes?

The corn got creamed.

Step 7
Step 2
Step 4
Step 5
Step 6
Step 8

Two-Sided Mask

Target antonyms with this Halloween mask project. As a class, brainstorm several pairs of adjectives that are antonyms, such as *grotesque* and *beautiful.* List students' responses on the board. Instruct each student to select one adjective pair; then have him draw a rough sketch of two different faces—one that portrays each adjective—on drawing paper. Next, give each student an unmarked paper grocery bag. Instruct each student to refer to his sketches to draw and create faces illustrating his pair of adjectives, showing one face on the front of the bag and the second face on the back side. Have your students slip the bags over their heads and turn, one at a time, to share both sides of their masks with the class.

Native American Story Belts

What would Thanksgiving be without discussing Native Americans? Native Americans strung wampum, or polished shell beads, into belts. Some wampum belts were used by Native Americans to document information exchanged among tribes and important public events. Guide each student through the steps shown to make her own wampum belt that illustrates the important events in her life. Then allow each student to wear her belt while she shares the illustrated events with the class.

Step 1

Materials for each student:
two 3" x 18" strips of oaktag
hole puncher
assorted colored yarn
clear tape
colored pencils or markers
scissors
ruler

Step 4

Steps:
1. Tape together the two strips of oaktag end to end. Measure the oaktag strip to fit your waist, cutting away any excess.
2. Use colored pencils or markers to illustrate the important events in your life on the belt.
3. Punch holes about one inch apart along the outer edges of the belt.
4. Thread and wrap a length of yarn through the holes and around the edges to create an edging for the belt. Knot the ends.
5. Tie several lengths of yarn to both ends of the belt. Braid the lengths; then use them to tie the belt around your waist.

Hanukkah Stained-Glass Window

Step 7

Step 2   Step 5

Materials for each student:
copy of the star pattern on page 283
two 6" x 6" black construction paper squares
two 6" x 6" squares of waxed paper
old yellow or gold crayon
glue
scissors
plastic knife
hole puncher
string or yarn
tape
pencil

Setting up the pressing station: In a safe location, cover a tabletop with a towel; then place an iron and a supply of newsprint nearby.

Steps:
1. Cut out the star pattern; then trace the star in the center of one black square.
2. Cut out the interior of the star tracing so that the star's border is uncut.
3. Place that black square on top of the second black square and trace the star pattern. Repeat Step 2 with the second star tracing.
4. Trace the star pattern onto one waxed paper square.
5. Use the plastic knife to shave the crayon onto this star tracing (waxy side up). Place the shavings slightly beyond the star's border to ensure complete coverage when melted. Cover the shavings with the second waxed paper square waxy side down.
6. Melt the crayon shavings between the two waxed paper squares by placing a sheet of newsprint over them, then pressing the newsprint with a warm iron at the pressing station.
7. Glue the stained-glass window between the two black squares, making sure the star patterns are aligned.
8. Hole-punch the top corner and tie a length of string through the hole for hanging.

Tiny-Tree Trimming

Materials for each student:
copy of the treetop pattern on page 283
large paper or plastic cup
ten to twelve 1½" x 12" strips of green
  construction paper
6" x 9" piece of green
  construction paper
clear tape
glue
scissors
assorted decorative
  craft materials,
  such as glitter,
  trims, stickers, and
  beads
ruler
pencil

Step 1

Step 2

Step 6

Steps:

1. Cut approximately
   ¾-inch-long slits about
   one-fourth inch apart along one long
   edge of each strip of green paper.

2. Turn the cup upside down. Tape
   or glue one strip, cut edge down,
   around the bottom edge of the cup.
   Trim away any excess.

3. Tape or glue another strip above the
   first one, overlapping it slightly. Trim
   to fit.

4. Continue taping or gluing the strips
   in this manner until the entire cup is
   covered.

5. Cut out the treetop pattern and trace
   it onto the 6"x 9" piece of green
   construction paper. Cut out the
   tracing.

6. Form the treetop and secure it with
   tape. As in Step 1, cut slits in the
   base of the treetop.

7. Secure the cone to the top of the cup
   with tape. Then decorate the tree as
   desired.

Quilled Cards

Quilling will turn your students' plain Valentine's Day cards into masterpieces! Give each student a sheet of white construction paper; a supply of ¼-inch-wide red, pink, and purple construction paper strips; glue; scissors; and a toothpick. Have each student fold his white paper to form a greeting card. Provide craft scissors for each student to trim the edges of his card, if desired. Then demonstrate how to decorate the card by wrapping a strip of construction paper halfway around a toothpick, sliding it off, and gluing it—standing on edge—to the card to form different designs. Direct each student to hold each piece briefly after gluing until the glue starts to set. Have him experiment with wrapping the strips tightly and loosely around his toothpick. After the glue dries completely, have each student pen a Valentine's Day note to a friend inside his card.

KWANZAA COLLAGE

Have students celebrate Kwanzaa by making harvest collages. Discuss some of the fruits and vegetables grown in Africa, such as bananas, plantains, yams, cassava, coconuts, and dates. Give each student an 18" x 24" sheet of manila paper, scissors, glue, and magazines to cut up or a supply of paint chip samples from a local paint store. Instruct each student to draw a large basket containing outlines of African fruits and vegetables on his paper. Then direct the student to cover each fruit and vegetable, collage-style, by gluing on small colored squares cut from the magazines or paint chips. Suggest that students use different shades of color to give the effect of light and dark shadings.

BANK ON IT!

Every student needs a place to store his pot of gold, and these St. Patrick's Day banks will certainly fill the bill! Have each student bring in an empty can or other sturdy container. Then give each student a cup filled with green tempera paint, a paintbrush, different-colored paint pens, scissors, and one copy of the St. Patrick's Day patterns on page 284. Direct each student to paint the sides of his container green and cut out the patterns. After the paint has dried, have the student use the paint pens to trace the patterns on the sides of his bank, decorating them as desired. Then suggest to your students that the end of the rainbow must be your classroom!

Spring Paperweight

Provide each student with a small rock (about three or four inches long), acrylic paint, a paintbrush, craft glue, and assorted craft materials. Instruct the student to decide what kind of paperweight to design; then have her paint the rock accordingly. Allow the paint to dry. Next, have the student create three-dimensional details for her design and attach them with craft glue.

Mother's Day Planter

Materials for each student:

half-gallon plastic milk jug
live flowering plant
2 cups of potting soil
four 24" lengths of ¼-inch-thick
　macramé cord

scissors or an art knife
permanent markers
ruler
hole puncher

Steps:

1. Create a planter by using scissors or an art knife to cut off the bottom four inches of the half-gallon jug.
2. Punch a hole one inch below the top edge of each of the four corners of the planter.
3. Using the markers, decorate the outside of the planter with Mother's Day messages and illustrations. Set the planter aside until the marker ink has dried.
4. Place two cups of potting soil in the planter, and then plant the flower inside.
5. Water the plant.
6. Knot one end of each 24-inch length of cord; then thread each cord through a hole. Gather all the cords' ends together and tie them in a knot.

Decorative Bookmark

Motivate your students to read with these decorative bookmarks. Give each student a 2" x 6" piece of white poster board, an eight-inch length of ribbon, scissors, glue, and a hole puncher. Provide discontinued wallpaper books for your students to peruse. Instruct each student to cut out any interesting wallpaper designs that she sees and glue them on her blank bookmark in an attractive arrangement. After the glue has dried, laminate the bookmark for durability. Next, have each student punch a hole at the top of her bookmark and attach the ribbon as shown.

Bubble Art

These simple bubble pictures burst with color! Give each student a sheet of white construction paper and several different-size plastic lids. Instruct him to fill the construction paper with circles by tracing the lids, overlapping the circles in several places. Explain that the tracings should look as if bubbles have blown across their papers. Then have each student color the circles so that the colors blend where two or more bubbles overlap. Suggest adding depth to his picture by experimenting with light and dark colors.

CHIP CLIP

These homemade chip clips are perfect lunchbox companions! Each child uses acrylic paint to make a ¾" x 6" craft stick a solid color and then sets it aside to dry. Next, he uses paint or paint markers to decorate his stick as desired. After the paint dries, he glues a spring-type clothespin to the back of the decorated stick.

Cookie Cutter Magnets

These magnets will proudly help display students' work. Have each student trace a seasonal cookie cutter on a sheet of colorful craft foam and then cut out the resulting shape. Next, she uses scraps of craft foam and permanent markers to add details to her cutout. After attaching a self-adhesive magnet to the back, her craft is ready to be put to work!

COLLAGE PENCIL HOLDER

Materials for each student:
empty frozen juice can
old magazines
decorative ribbon
Mod Podge gloss (optional)
paintbrush (optional)
scissors
glue

Steps:
1. Cut out magazine pictures and words that describe you or represent the things you like.
2. Glue the cutouts to the can collage-style, overlapping them so that they cover the entire can.
3. After the glue has dried, use the paintbrush to apply Mod Podge gloss over the cutouts. Set it aside to dry.
4. Glue decorative ribbon around the top and bottom edges of the can.

ART ESSENTIALS

Easy-to-Do Recipes for a Variety of Art Supplies

Homemade Play Dough

Use homemade play dough in place of expensive store brands for your next class project.

1 cup flour
½ cup salt
2 teaspoons cream of tartar
1 cup water
1 teaspoon vegetable oil
food coloring

Mix the dry ingredients. Then add the remaining ingredients and stir. In a heavy skillet, cook the mixture for two to three minutes, stirring frequently. Knead the dough until it becomes soft and smooth. Stir up several colors and store them in icing tubs.

No-Cook Modeling Dough

Begin your next modeling project with a batch of this no-cook dough that's a snap to make!

2 cups flour
1 cup salt
water
food coloring or tempera paint
2 tablespoons vegetable oil (optional)

Mix the ingredients together. Add oil if you do not want the dough to harden.

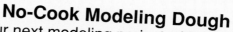

Baking Dough

Bake this dough in the oven after your students use it to create their art projects.

2 cups flour
1 cup salt
water

Mix enough water with the dry ingredients to make a dough. Give each student a portion of the dough with which to work. After students create their masterpieces, bake the dough at 300° for about an hour—longer for thicker objects.

To-Die-for Dye

Use this simple method of dyeing to yield an abundance of bright and colorful art materials.

⅓ cup rubbing alcohol
food coloring
items to be dyed (beans, rice, macaroni, seeds, etc.)
waxed paper

Pour the rubbing alcohol into a container; then add food coloring to obtain the desired color. Drop the materials to be dyed into the liquid and let them soak for a few minutes. Finally, spoon the mixture onto waxed paper to dry. The alcohol evaporates quickly, leaving the dyed objects ready for art.

Papier-Mâché

Stir up a quick and easy batch of papier-mâché to fan your students' 3-D creativity!

1 part liquid starch
1 part cold water
newspaper strips

Mix equal parts of liquid starch and cold water. Tear strips of newspaper, and dip each strip into the mixture before applying it to a form of chicken wire, rolled newspaper, or an inflated balloon.

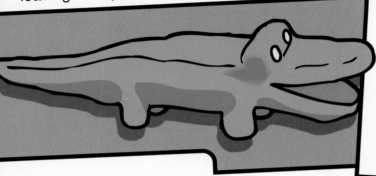

Salt Paint

Add an icy touch to winter pictures with salt paint.

2 teaspoons salt
1 teaspoon liquid starch
several drops of tempera paint

Mix the ingredients together and apply with a paintbrush. Then allow the painting to dry.

Shiny Paint

Give your next painting project a wet look with this easy recipe.

1 part white liquid glue
1 part tempera paint

Mix equal parts of liquid glue and tempera paint; then apply with a brush. Shiny paint provides a wet look even when its surface is dry.

Corn Patterns
Use with "Corny Cobs" on page 274.

A corny joke by _____

_____

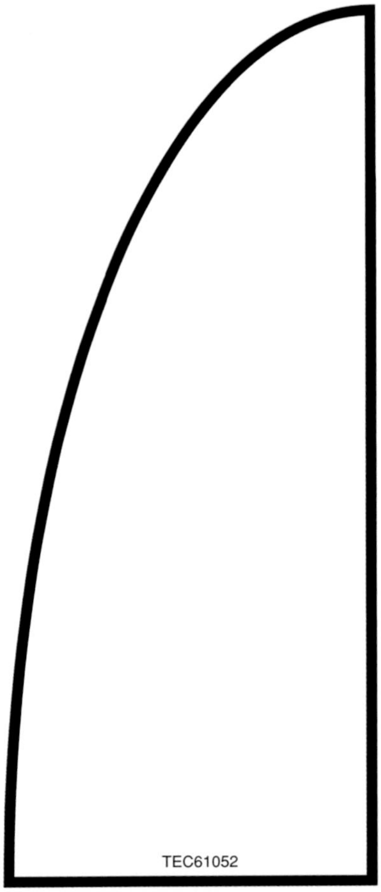

cob

TEC61052

arm

TEC61052

Star Pattern
Use with "Hanukkah Stained-Glass Window" on page 275.

TEC61052

Treetop Pattern
Use with "Tiny-Tree Trimming" on page 276.

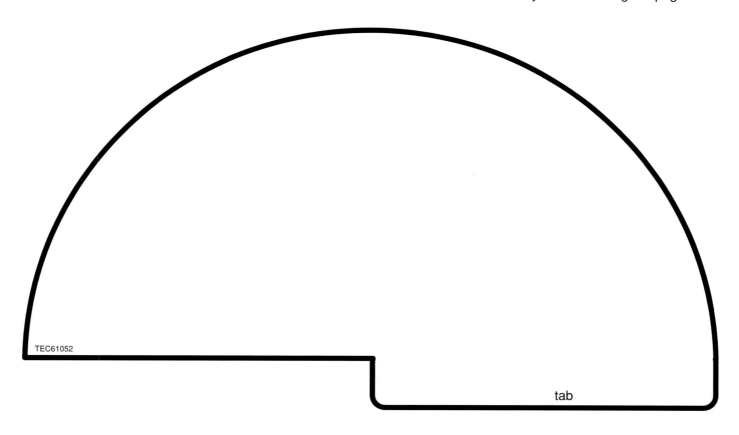

TEC61052

tab

St. Patrick's Day Patterns
Use with "Bank on It!" on page 277.

Dress to Impress

Involve your students in celebrating the season by having a custom-made costume contest. Direct each student to choose a real or an imaginary character who's school- or study-related, such as a teacher, an administrator, a book character, a scientist, or an explorer. Require costumes to be made from materials found at home or school. (Supply materials to any student needing them.) Also supply each student with a 4" x 6" index card, directing him to write a speech from his character's point of view that explains who he is and why he should win the contest. Enlist staff members to judge the costumes and speeches. After the judging, give each student a small treat and announce the top three most impressive characters.

Some Big Thank-Yous!

What are your students most thankful for? Find out by creating a gigantic thank-you card for your school. Fold a six-foot sheet of white bulletin board paper in half, greeting card–style. Open the paper and then write the title "Thank You, [your school's name]!" across the top. Place the card on a classroom table along with a supply of colorful markers and crayons. Have each student write a brief message on the card to someone in the school she wishes to thank for a kind deed. Suggest that each student draw a decorative illustration next to her message. After each student has added her thanks, display the card on a wall at the front of the school. If desired, invite other faculty members and students to add to this gigantic Thanksgiving Day thank-you.

Thanksgiving Dinner Guests

Have students imagine that they can invite anyone they'd like to Thanksgiving dinner at their home. Each student selects one person and writes a paragraph explaining who he would choose as a dinner guest and at least three reasons why. He writes the final copy on a large index card and glues it to a paper plate to make a turkey body. He adds a construction paper head, feathers, and feet. Post students' paragraphs on a bulletin board titled "You're Invited!"

Check out the skill-building reproducibles on pages 286–290.

Treat Bags

Which bag will hold the most treats? Find the volume of each bag. Color the bag with the largest volume.

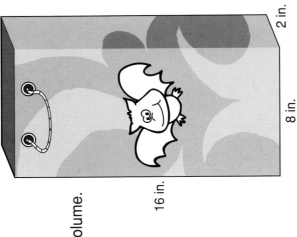

16 in.

8 in.

2 in.

7 in.

7 in.

3 in.

7 in.

10 in.

2 in.

9 in.

5 in.

4 in.

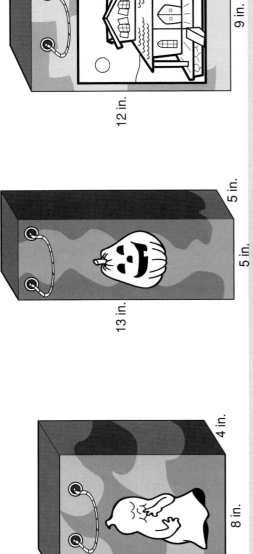

12 in.

9 in.

3 in.

13 in.

5 in.

5 in.

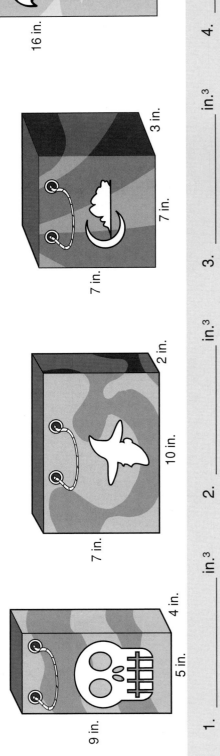

10 in.

8 in.

4 in.

6 in.

3 in.

3 in.

1. _____ in.³

2. _____ in.³

3. _____ in.³

4. _____ in.³

5. _____ in.³

6. _____ in.³

7. _____ in.³

8. _____ in.³

Weighty Words

Each boldfaced word or phrase below can be associated with Halloween, but one of the descriptive words that follows it does not fit with the others. Circle the word that does not belong; then explain why not on the line provided. Use a dictionary or a thesaurus for help.

1. **pumpkin:** orbicular edible ambitious harvested

_____

2. **monster:** hulking frolicsome brawny threatening

_____

3. **bat:** swift felicitous fanged nocturnal

_____

4. **candy:** delectable unsavory appetizing palatable

_____

5. **trick:** homely shocking mischievous ingenious

_____

6. **graveyard:** eerie isolated somber finicky

_____

7. **haunted house:** lonesome dilapidated cozy austere

_____

8. **skeleton:** skinless clattery modish frail

_____

9. **mummy:** malodorous aged cadaverous fragrant

_____

10. **night wind:** empathetic clamorous gusting wintry

_____

11. **costume:** prompt realistic inventive ghastly

_____

12. **black cat:** titanic svelte ebony agile

_____

NAME _____

DATE _____

NOT JUST TALKIN' TURKEY

Combining two or more shorter sentences into a longer, more detailed sentence makes your writing smoother. Use the examples below to combine each set of sentences. Write new combined sentences on a separate sheet of paper. In the turkey beside each number, write the number of the example that you used for help.

How to combine two or more shorter sentences:

1. **Use an adjective.**
   My mom made a fabulous pie. It was coconut cream.
   My mom made a fabulous coconut cream pie.
2. **Use an adverb.**
   We are going to roast the turkey. We will roast it tomorrow.
   We are going to roast the turkey tomorrow.
3. **Use a series of words.**
   The turkey weighs 20 pounds. The turkey is golden brown. The turkey smells delicious.
   The turkey weighs 20 pounds, is golden brown, and smells delicious.
4. **Use an appositive phrase.**
   Ms. Reichart makes the best apple strudel. Ms. Reichart is our German neighbor.
   Ms. Reichart, our German neighbor, makes the best apple strudel.
5. **Use a compound subject or predicate.**
   Joe watched the football game on TV. Jim watched the game too.
   Joe and Jim watched the football game on TV.
6. **Use *and, but,* or *or.***
   I love to go outside after eating Thanksgiving dinner. I won't go outside if it's raining.
   I love to go outside after eating Thanksgiving dinner, but I won't go outside if it's raining.

---

 1. Aunt Myra ate too much food. The food was rich.

 2. Our next-door neighbor is coming over for dinner. Dinner is at noon.

 3. Thanksgiving is a time for family. It is a time for food and fun.

 4. Ruff is my dog. Ruff likes sweet potatoes.

 5. My brother Waldo started a food fight. My sister Wilma started one too.

 6. My dad heaped my plate full of stuffing. My dad heaped my plate full of mashed potatoes. My dad also heaped my plate full of cranberry sauce.

 7. My five-year-old cousin got the wishbone. He gets the wishbone every year.

 8. Thanksgiving is my favorite holiday. Christmas is my favorite holiday too.

9. Bob is my friend. Bob can crack walnuts with his teeth.

 10. My uncle Al loves fresh corn. He doesn't like corn-on-the-cob.

 11. Our cat curls up on top of the table. Our cat goes to sleep right in the middle of dinner.

 12. We have a turkey named Terrell. He is a pet.

It's a Turkey's Life

Have you ever wondered what a turkey would say if it could talk? Imagine that the turkey below has human qualities. Fill in each blank with information about the turkey. Then use colored pencils to add creative details to the turkey according to the responses. For example, if your turkey likes sports, you might show him or her holding a basketball and wearing sneakers.

Name: _____

Nickname: _____

Address: _____

Place of birth: _____

Family members: _____

Job description: _____

Pets: _____

Favorite TV show: _____

Favorite hobby/sport: _____

Favorite snack food: _____

Favorite song: _____

Favorite book: _____

Favorite holiday: _____

Use mental math to estimate how much money each friend will spend and how much he or she will have left. Then use paper and a pencil or a calculator to find the exact amounts. Record your answers in the table below.

Ticket Information
All Tickets $0.25 Each
Gonzo's Guess-Your-Weight ....2 Tickets
Fanny's Fabulous Face-Painting ....4 Tickets
Zigfield's Zany Zoo ....3 Tickets
Babette's Balloons, each balloon ....2 Tickets
The Twister ....5 Tickets
Harry's Hair-Raising Haunted House ...5 Tickets
Madame Zelda's Fortune-Telling ....3 Tickets
Ferris Funkweller's Ferris Wheel ....4 Tickets
Go-for-It Game Room, each game........2 Tickets

Concession Stand
Super-size a soft drink for just $0.25 more!
Hamburger...$1.65
Hot dog $1.30
Corn dog $1.50
Popcorn $1.25
Cotton candy $0.75
Caramel apple $0.55
Soft drink $0.95

	Estimated Amount		Exact Amount	
	Cost	Change	Cost	Change
1. Tommy has $15.00 to spend on tickets. He wants to buy enough tickets to try all seven activities at the carnival one time, buy a balloon, and play one game in the game room.				
2. Debbie's friends sent her to the concession stand with $15.00. They told her to buy three hot dogs, two hamburgers, two caramel apples, and three drinks.				
3. Marcos had $7.00. He bought 16 tickets, then headed for the concession stand.				
4. Josh and Janet were given $10.00 to spend at the fair. Josh bought tickets for the haunted house and the Twister; then he bought six more tickets for the game room. Janet bought tickets to have her face painted and to visit the zoo.				
5. Missy wants to spend her $5.00 on tickets for the Ferris wheel and the fortune-teller. She also wants to get some cotton candy and popcorn.				
6. Albert had $20.00 in his pocket. He bought tickets to ride the Twister three times; then he lost $5.00.				
7. Paco has $3.00, and Maria has $1.75. They plan to pool their money and purchase 12 tickets.				
8. Marvin was really hungry. With his $6.50 he purchased two corn dogs, popcorn, cotton candy, and a soda.				
9. Zelda's throat is parched after telling so many fortunes. With the $18.75 she earned, she bought super-size soft drinks for herself, Ferris, and Harry.				
10. Trina loves balloons! She has $4.75 and wants to get nine balloons.				

Winter

Holiday Economists

Give students a little insight into the cost of holiday gift giving with this real-life activity. First, have each child write on a sheet of paper a list of ten gifts he'd like to receive along with each item's estimated cost. Then divide students into small groups and give each group several store catalogs or newspaper sale pages. Each student searches the catalogs for each item on his list and records its actual price on his sheet. Finally, have the student calculate an estimated and an actual total for his ten items. As a class, discuss the differences between the totals. Extend the activity by posing problems such as those in the illustrations, having each student calculate an answer for each one. Students will quickly develop an understanding of holiday economics and an appreciation for gift giving.

$ Circle the most expensive item on your list. If the gift were on sale for 20% off, what would the sale price be? How many hours would you have to work at $5.00 an hour to purchase the item?

$ If you earned $5.00 an hour working after school, how many hours would it take to save enough money to buy each gift on your list? How long would it take to buy all the gifts?

$ Rank your gifts in order of importance—1 being the most important and 10 being the least important. Choose the top five items and calculate their total cost.

In Pursuit of Holiday Trivia

Gather reference materials on the season's various holidays, such as Christmas, Kwanzaa, and Hanukkah. Then divide students into groups of four or five. Direct each group to research 15–20 interesting facts about the holidays. Next, give each group a sheet of poster board, about twenty-five 4" x 6" index cards, markers, and scissors. Instruct the group to design a trivia game that includes a gameboard, game cards, game markers, an answer key, and a rules sheet. Afterward, place each completed game in a different area of the room; then assign each group to a game other than the one it designed. Direct each group to appoint one member as moderator and then follow the rules for playing the game. After about 15 minutes, have each group rotate to the next game. Continue in this manner until each group has played every game except its own.

Name That Resolution!

Have each student brainstorm a list of resolutions for the upcoming year. Ask several volunteers to share their resolutions; then lead a discussion about how some resolutions aren't accomplished because they are unrealistic and too difficult to achieve. Direct each student to scan her list and cross out any resolutions that aren't realistic. Next, provide each student with a 12" x 18" sheet of light-colored construction paper and colorful markers or crayons. Instruct the student to write her name vertically in large, decorative letters down the 18-inch side of her paper. Challenge the student to write a different, realistic resolution that begins with each letter in her name. Have each student share her goals; then display them on a wall or bulletin board titled "Name That Resolution."

Poetry Readers' Theater

Lead your students in a celebration of Black History Month with a series of dramatized poetry readings. Write on the board a list of famous African American poets. Pair students; then direct each pair to find a poem of interest written by one of the people on the list. Give students time to gather props or musical selections to dramatize the poem and then to rehearse it. On the day of the presentations, hang a large sheet of bulletin board paper from the ceiling to the floor as a backdrop. Invite parents, staff members, or another class to the presentation or videotape it for a later viewing. Students will delight in adding their own creative touches and interpretations to their poetry presentations.

Electronic Valentines

Enlist the aid of your media specialist in searching the Internet for names of schools and specific classrooms in other cities, states, or countries. Pair students; then assign each pair an email address. Direct the pair to send a special Valentine's Day message via email to its assigned class or school. Students will eagerly await their replies, and who knows? It could be the beginning of some interesting friendships!

Check out the skill-building reproducibles on pages 293–301.

St. Patrick's Day Puzzle

Help students recognize facts about St. Patrick's Day with the following activity. Obtain ten different interlocking pairs of puzzle pieces from an old puzzle. Pairs should not connect to one another. On each pair write one question and its answer from the list below, with the question on one piece and the answer on the matching piece. Separate and mix the pieces; then place them in a bag. Have each student draw a puzzle piece from the bag and find the classmate with the matching question or answer. Instruct student pairs to double-check that the question and answer match by interlocking the pieces. After all matches have been found, have each pair share its question and answer for a fun-filled trivia session about St. Patrick's Day!

 Who was St. Patrick? He was a priest who brought Christianity to Ireland.

 Why is St. Patrick honored by the Irish? He performed many brave and kind deeds for the people.

 In Irish lore, what happens if you catch a leprechaun? He is supposed to lead you to a pot of gold.

 What is special about a four-leaf clover? It is supposed to bring good luck to its finder.

 By the end of the 1850s, how was St. Patrick's Day often celebrated? With parades held each year in cities across the country.

 What does the Irish flag look like? It is divided into three equal sections of orange, white, and green.

 What is Ireland often called? The Emerald Isle.

 What are some of the many symbols associated with St. Patrick's Day? Shamrocks, leprechauns, harps, gold coins, and the color green.

 What does one legend about St. Patrick state? He drove out all the snakes in Ireland.

 What is a shamrock? A trifolium, or clover.

The Magic of Eight

For each clue, write a word that rhymes with the word *eight*. The first one has been done for you.

1. You don't have to ask a sleepy bear to do this during the winter. h i b e r n a t e

2. Do this if you want to stretch a story to make it funny. __ __ __ __ __ __ __ __ a t e

3. This is uite the opposite of crooked. __ __ __ a i __ __ __ __

4. This object is definitely not a Frisbee disk. __ __ a t e

5. These wheels will get you where you want to go. __ __ __ __ __ __ __ __ __ __ a t e __

6. Beat the clock or you'll be this. __ a t e

7. Artists do this every day. __ __ __ __ __ __ __ __ a t e

8. Blood and air may do this. __ __ __ __ __ __ a t e

9. A fisherman would say you can't fish without this. __ a i t

10. You do this when you give a little dough away. __ __ __ a t e

11. You do this if you put off doing something until another day. __ __ __ __ __ __ __ __ __ __ __ __ a t e

12. Mimes often do this to you. __ __ __ __ a t e

13. Water does this when it vanishes into thin air. __ __ __ __ __ __ __ a t e s

14. It's all part of a detective's job. __ __ __ __ __ __ __ __ __ a t e

15. Every sentence must have its mark. __ __ __ __ __ __ __ a t e

16. A ship's captain must know how to do this. __ __ __ __ __ __ a t e

Just in Time for Christmas!

Find out how much time each reindeer spent on the activity described.

_____ 1. Comet started weight training at 12:35 PM and ended at 2:50 PM.

_____ 2. Dasher attended nutrition classes from 10:10 AM to 1:37 PM.

_____ 3. Blitzen got on the treadmill 2 hours and 10 minutes before 3:00 PM and then stopped at 1:16 PM.

_____ 4. Prancer sure put in a long day. After starting practice at 8:22 AM, he didn't quit until 5 hours and 13 minutes before midnight.

_____ 5. Rudolph started landing practice 7 minutes before 11:09 AM and finished 48 minutes after noon.

_____ 6. Vixen took an early morning walk from 5:18 AM to 11:05 AM.

_____ 7. Cupid began his 20 laps in the heated pool 17 minutes before 2:10 PM and finished at 2:44 PM.

_____ 8. Dancer took a much-needed break from take off practice at 11:56 AM. His break ended at 12:29 PM.

_____ 9. Donner was in the gym for 8 hours and 27 minutes, but part of that time he spent on his lunch break. His break lasted one hour and 14 minutes.

_____ 10. Cupid spent one hour and 32 minutes in a step aerobics class and two hours and 33 minutes in the weight room.

_____ 11. Buttercup, Santa's newest recruit, ended his classroom training at 1:00 PM. Then he studied until 3:37 PM.

_____ 12. At a quarter to four in the afternoon, the whole herd—except for Prancer and Donner—got together for a dodgeball game. They played until 20 minutes after five in the evening.

The Great Gift Exchange

Match each gift to the elf who receives it. Read the clues and complete the logic chart. Put a ✔ in each box that is true and an **X** in each box that is not true.

Gifts:	fruitcake	toy-making tools	hot-chocolate maker	bunny slippers	art book	antique ornament
Elves:						
Egbert						
Englebert						
Erwin						
Ethel						
Edna						
Elvira						

Clues:

1. Erwin's gift is edible.
2. Ethel is not interested in art.
3. Elvira receives neither the hot-chocolate maker nor the art book that her sisters receive.
4. Egbert knows his sister's favorite animal is a bunny.
5. Englebert's twin brother collects antiques.

Nguzo Saba (en–GOO–zoh SAH–bah)

The Seven Principles of Kwanzaa

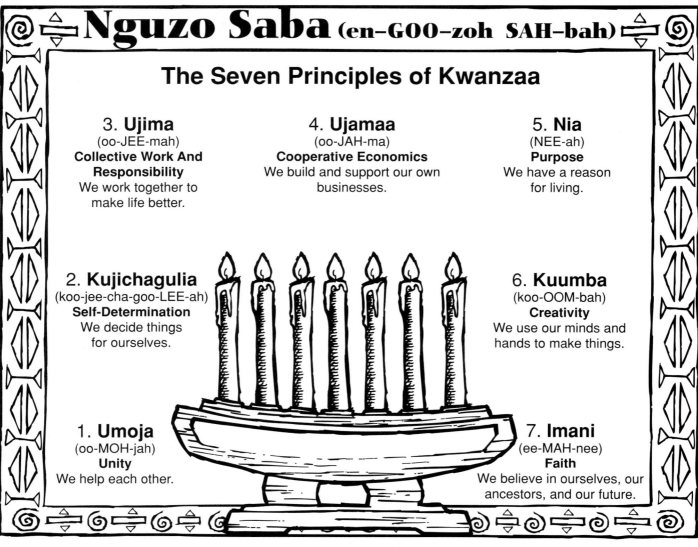

3. **Ujima**
(oo-JEE-mah)
Collective Work And Responsibility
We work together to make life better.

4. **Ujamaa**
(oo-JAH-ma)
Cooperative Economics
We build and support our own businesses.

5. **Nia**
(NEE-ah)
Purpose
We have a reason for living.

2. **Kujichagulia**
(koo-jee-cha-goo-LEE-ah)
Self-Determination
We decide things for ourselves.

6. **Kuumba**
(koo-OOM-bah)
Creativity
We use our minds and hands to make things.

1. **Umoja**
(oo-MOH-jah)
Unity
We help each other.

7. **Imani**
(ee-MAH-nee)
Faith
We believe in ourselves, our ancestors, and our future.

Read each of the 12 statements. In the blank next to each statement, write the number of the principle or principles that action matches. Explain each of your answers on the back of this sheet.

_____ 1. Katrina decided to spread the word about the holiday by creating posters and displaying them throughout her neighborhood.

_____ 2. Randy made a Kwanzaa greeting card for his parents.

_____ 3. Shenika decided that she wants to go to college and become a doctor.

_____ 4. Alex studied his family's history and labeled a genealogy chart with the information he found.

_____ 5. Nicole, along with her brother Tomario and sister Shonda, prepared a traditional meal of catfish, collard greens, and sweet potato pie for her family.

_____ 6. The members of the Saunders family created special gifts for one another.

_____ 7. Kimberly interviewed several African American businesspersons and prepared a report for her social studies class.

_____ 8. A *bendera*—a flag with black, red, and green stripes—was displayed at the local Kwanzaa festival.

_____ 9. Tomeka shared an African folktale with a kindergarten class at her school.

_____ 10. Marcus created a poem about his life and his plans for the future.

_____ 11. Kinara's mother made long, colorful dresses called *bubas* for Kinara and her sisters.

_____ 12. Marian and her brother kept a scrapbook of special family events.

The Season Is the Reason

In order to survive the winter months, animals must adapt to their environments. Match each adaptation with an animal. Then cut out each animal's picture and paste it in the box next to its description.

1. Its body temperature drops, its blood circulation slows, and it falls into a deep sleep.

2. It spends the northern summer in the Arctic and then migrates 12,500 miles to the Antarctic during the southern summer.

3. It spends its summer thousands of feet above sea level. When winter weather arrives, this animal walks down into a valley.

4. It migrates 2,100 miles south from the northeastern United States to Mexico.

5. It spends the southern summer in the Antarctic and then travels 5,000 miles toward the equator to its breeding ground.

6. Its brown coat turns white in winter; then it turns brown again for summer.

7. It has feathers that cover its toes to protect it against extreme cold.

8. It eats as many wooded plants as it can in the summer, storing this food as fat on its humped body for the harsh months ahead.

9. It has a thick fur coat to keep it warm. The fur on it's throat and chest is a yellowish color.

10. It has a thick oily coat and lives in a lodge to stay warm.

11. During severe storms, it scoops out a hollow shelter in the snow and sleeps until the storm is over.

12. It often stores large supplies of seeds and nuts in the ground, under fallen leaves, or in stockpiles near its nest.

pine marten   beaver   squirrel   brown bear   humpback whale   polar bear

mountain quail   arctic tern   monarch butterfly   snowshoe hare   moose   snowy owl

297

DATE

Kingly Words

Read each definition. Write a word or word combination that has the letters *k-i-n-g* in it.

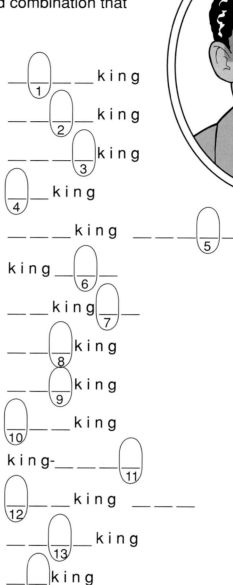

1. banging ___ (1) ___ ___ k i n g

2. sock ___ ___ (2) ___ k i n g

3. pondering ___ ___ ___ (3) k i n g

4. an early pirate from Scandinavia (4) ___ k i n g

5. a moving chair ___ ___ ___ k i n g ___ ___ ___ ___ (5)

6. land ruled by a king or queen k i n g ___ (6) ___

7. in a kidding manner ___ ___ k i n g (7) ___

8. searching ___ ___ (8) k i n g

9. going under the water ___ ___ (9) k i n g

10. preparing food (10) ___ ___ k i n g

11. unusually large k i n g-___ ___ ___ (11)

12. a place for cars (12) ___ ___ k i n g ___ ___ ___

13. collapsing ___ ___ (13) ___ k i n g

14. coming out of sleep ___ (14) k i n g

15. piling ___ ___ ___ (15) k i n g

16. pulling sharply ___ (16) ___ k i n g

Write each circled letter from above to a matching number below. The letters will spell two words for an idea in which Dr. Martin Luther King Jr. strongly believed.

___ ___ ___ ___ ___ ___ ___ ___ ___ ___ ___ and ___ ___ ___ ___ ___
1 2 3 4 5 6 7 8 9 10 11   12 13 14 15 16

PARTY PACKAGES

You are planning a party for 30 guests. Complete the chart to show the exact number of packages needed. The first one has been done for you.

Item	Number of Items Per Package	Number of Items Each Guest Will Receive	Number of Packages Needed
1. balloons	10	2	6
2. marshmallow hearts	5	2	
3. Valentine's Day cards	10	1	
4. lollipops	12	2	
5. sugar cookies	6	3	
6. chewing gum	8	4	
7. party hats	5	1	
8. conversation hearts	50	20	
9. cinnamon sticks	9	3	
10. stickers	15	8	
11. pretzels	20	10	
12. party favors	5	3	
13. paper cups	15	1	
14. noisemakers	3	2	

Sweetheart Acronyms

For each valentine word below, think of a title or group of words that the acronym could represent. (Your answer does not have to relate to Valentine's Day.) The first one has been done for you.

1. HEARTS Henry's Edible and Really Tasty Sweets _____

2. LOVE _____

3. CUPID _____

4. ROSES _____

5. PARTY _____

6. CARDS _____

7. CANDY _____

8. SWEETS _____

9. FLOWER _____

10. FRIEND _____

11. SECRET _____

12. COOKIES _____

Shamrock Shake-Up

Use only three straight lines to divide the box below into six parts. Each part must contain three shamrocks and one pot of gold. Move three long pencils, straws, or sticks around on the diagram below until you find the solution. Then draw three lines on the diagram to show your final answer.

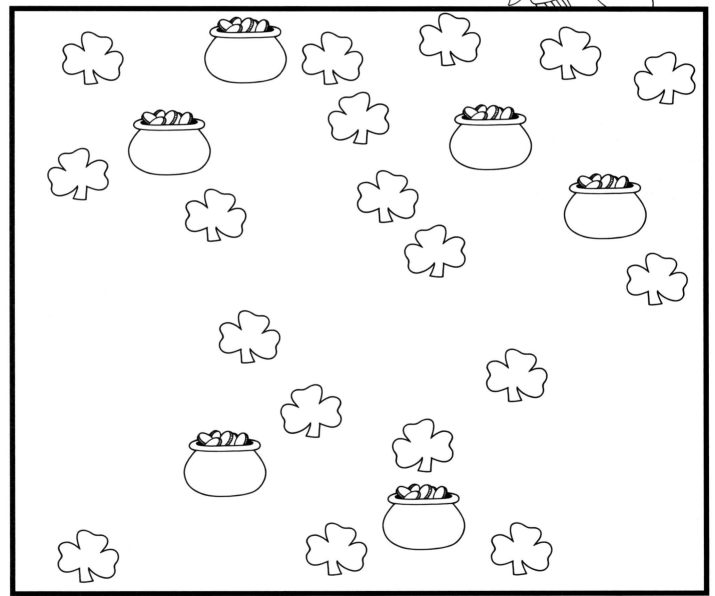

Note to the teacher: Provide each student with three long pencils, straws, or sticks.

Spring

EASTER EGG SURPRISE

Spring is viewed as a time of new beginnings. Discuss the season with your students and have them give examples of events and activities that they associate with this time of year, such as the birth of animals, the blooming of flowers, and the onset of warm weather. Record their responses on the board. Next, provide each student with a plastic egg and a strip of light-colored construction paper. Direct each student to write a sentence on his strip that describes a favorite seasonal event using nouns, verbs, and descriptive adjectives. Have the student place the strip in his egg. Afterward, collect all the eggs and place them in a decorative basket. Pass around the basket and have each student choose one egg, open it, and read the description inside. If desired, replace the eggs in the basket and share the surprise messages with other classes.

The sun's warm rays reflect off the dewy green grass in the first light of dawn.

The average American produces almost 4.5 pounds of trash each day. Where does all the trash go? Most of it just keeps piling up in already overflowing landfills.

Earth Day Envelopes

Help your students understand and appreciate the importance of protecting the earth and its quickly dwindling resources. On strips of paper, write different problems facing the earth today, such as the need for recycling; the overflowing of landfills; acid rain; the depletion of the ozone; and air, water, and land pollution. Make a strip for each group of four students. Place each strip in a different envelope. Then, after discussing the meaning behind Earth Day, divide students into groups of four and give each group an envelope. Direct each group to research the causes and effects of the problem contained in its envelope and devise a plan for solving that problem. Afterward, instruct the group to write a letter to a local government official or an environmental agency explaining its findings and plan. Have each group share its letter with the class. Finally, if desired, mail each letter to the official or agency indicated.

A Day at the Beach!

9:00–10:00

Room 202: Sand Painting—Mrs. Ferrell's Class
Room 203: Shell Study—Mr. Davis's Class
Room 204: Ocean Animals—Ms. McDole's Class

10:00–11:00

Room 202: Sand Painting—Ms. McDole's Class
Room 203: Shell Study—Mrs. Ferrell's Class
Room 204: Ocean Animals—Mr. Davis's Class

11:00–12:00

Room 202: Sand Painting—Mr. Davis's Class
Room 203: Shell Study—Ms. McDole's Class
Room 204: Ocean Animals—Mrs. Ferrell's Class

SEE YOU AT THE BEACH!

When the end of the year rolls around, everyone is yearning for sunshine and sandy beaches. Create a warm day at the beach for your students with this fun-filled idea. Ask other teachers of your grade level to plan a beach-related lesson of a particular length. Suggest lessons and activities such as sand painting, learning to identify seashells, and studying interesting ocean creatures. Then devise a schedule like the one shown that rotates each class to a different classroom and lesson. If desired, have students dress in touristy attire. Culminate the day with an outside beach party that includes beach towels, beach balls, good food, and music.

Welcoming Advice for the New Crew

Get your current class involved in welcoming and helping next year's students! Cover a bulletin board with white paper, and add the title "How to Survive Fifth Grade!" Also provide a supply of colorful markers and crayons. Each student uses the markers to write a brief, positive message or a tip for a successful year. Invite each student to share her words of wisdom; then save the dynamic display for the upcoming school year.

Naming Special Memories

End the school year by having students share feelings of friendship and good wishes with one another. Arrange students in a circle; then give each child a sheet of light-colored construction paper. The student writes her first and last names in decorative block letters in the center of the paper. Then she passes her sheet to the classmate to her right. Each child receiving a paper uses a colorful marker to write a positive comment about the person whose name is on the paper. Encourage students to write positive comments related to that person's skills, talents, or friendliness, or simply have them write good wishes for a great vacation. Instruct the student to sign her comment and then pass it on to the next student. After all students have signed one another's papers, return each paper to its owner. If desired, laminate each student's page to create a long-lasting memory of a special year.

Check out the skill-building reproducibles on pages 304–308.

Hot on the Trail of an Easter Egg!

Use the directions below to find the hidden egg. Use a ruler and a colored pencil to lightly trace your path on the map. Then mark the spot where you find the egg with a decorative Easter egg.

1. Walk west 20 steps.
2. Wander north 20 steps.
3. Amble east 15 steps.
4. Gallivant north 10 steps.
5. Travel west 35 steps.
6. Go south 10 steps.
7. Take 10 steps east.
8. Journey north 15 steps.

9. Saunter east 30 steps.
10. Proceed south 20 steps.
11. Push west 15 steps.
12. Trek south 10 steps.
13. Traipse east 30 steps.
14. Wend north 25 steps.
15. Meander southwest 55 steps.
16. Mark this spot with a colored egg.

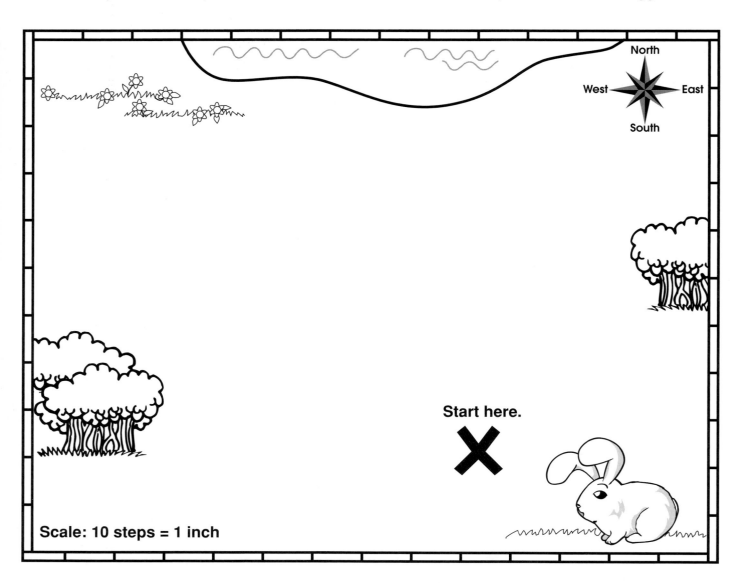

Scale: 10 steps = 1 inch

Start here.

X

NAME _____

DATE _____

SPRING-CLEANING

The Tidy family is busy with its annual spring-cleaning. One item in each group doesn't belong. Write a category title on the blank above each group. Then cross out the item that does not belong.

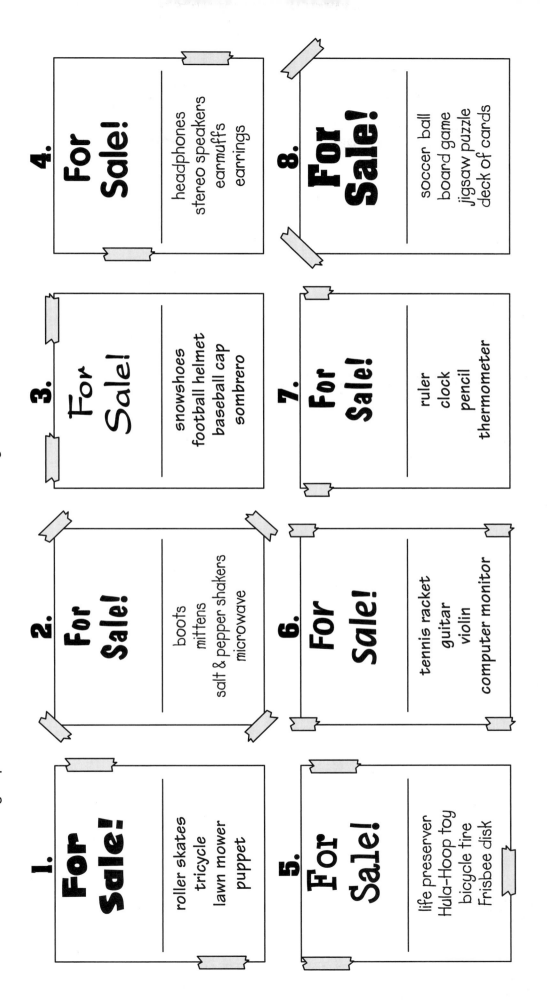

1. For Sale!

roller skates
tricycle
lawn mower
puppet

2. For Sale!

boots
mittens
salt & pepper shakers
microwave

3. For Sale!

snowshoes
football helmet
baseball cap
sombrero

4. For Sale!

headphones
stereo speakers
earmuffs
earrings

5. For Sale!

life preserver
Hula-Hoop toy
bicycle tire
Frisbee disk

6. For Sale!

tennis racket
guitar
violin
computer monitor

7. For Sale!

ruler
clock
pencil
thermometer

8. For Sale!

soccer ball
board game
jigsaw puzzle
deck of cards

©The Mailbox® • Superbook® • TEC61052 • Key p. 316

A Perfect Pair

Why are the words *heart* and *earth* a perfect pair? These two words are *anagrams*—a word pair formed by rearranging the same letters. Write an anagram for each word below.

1. taste _____

2. petal _____

3. crate _____

4. resign _____

5. groan _____

6. early _____

7. melon _____

8. horse _____

9. scent _____

10. bread _____

We make a perfect pair!

11. teach _____

12. teams _____

13. steam _____

14. hears _____

15. plane _____

16. reams _____

17. spear _____

18. pools _____

19. angle _____

20. stale _____

Year-End Calculations

How Much Time Have You Spent in School?

1. Write the number of days school has been in session so far this year. (Most schools are in session about 180 days.)

   _____

2. Subtract the number of days you missed due to illness, doctors' appointments, vacations, etc., from the number of days spent in school (see Number 1).

   _____ – _____ = _____

3. Write the starting and ending times of your school day. Then calculate how many hours and minutes you spend in school each day. Use this to determine the number of minutes you spend in school each day.

   starting time _____ ending time _____

   hours _____ minutes _____

   minutes you spend in school each day _____

4. Calculate the number of minutes you spend at lunch, at recess, and on other breaks each day. Subtract this number from the minutes you spend in school each day (see Number 3) to see how much time you spend working in school each day.

   minutes spent during break times _____

   _____ – _____ = _____

5. Multiply the number of days you've spent in school (see Number 2) by the number of minutes you spend working in school each day (see Number 4). This gives you the total number of minutes you've spent working in school this year.

   _____ x _____ = _____

6. Divide the number of minutes spent working in school (see Number 5) by 60 to find the total number of hours you've spent working in school this year.

   _____ ÷ _____ = _____

7. Divide the number of hours spent working in school this year (see Number 6) by 24 to find the total number of 24-hour days you've spent working in school this year.

   _____ ÷ _____ = _____

8. Divide the number of 24-hour days spent working in school (see Number 7) by 7 to find the total number of weeks you've spent working in school this year.

   _____ ÷ _____ = _____

The End Is Near!

Before heading off for summer vacation, put your brain to work one
last time to solve this set of puzzles!

List as many words of four or more letters as
possible using only the letters in the title of this
sheet. There are at least 28 words. Write any
extra words you find on the back of this sheet.

1. _____
2. _____
3. _____
4. _____
5. _____
6. _____
7. _____
8. _____
9. _____
10. _____
11. _____
12. _____
13. _____
14. _____
15. _____
16. _____
17. _____
18. _____
19. _____
20. _____
21. _____
22. _____
23. _____
24. _____
25. _____
26. _____
27. _____
28. _____

See how many words from
your list can be found in this word
search. Circle each word that you
find. There are 28 words.

H	N	R	H	H	E	D	I	N	D
T	I	E	E	T	A	N	E	A	I
A	E	N	A	R	S	E	E	A	A
E	R	N	D	A	T	R	A	H	R
D	E	I	E	E	E	T	T	E	I
E	E	D	E	E	R	E	N	A	S
E	N	H	R	A	N	I	I	R	E
N	S	E	E	I	D	R	A	I	N
I	H	H	N	R	E	T	S	E	R

Write the words from your list that you did not
find in the word search.

Homophones are words that are pronounced alike
but are spelled differently and have different meanings.
The words *blue* and *blew* are homophones. Write
the homophones that are in your list of words.

Bonus Box: Find another way to group the
words from your list. For example, the words can
be grouped by parts of speech or the sounds with
which they begin. Write your grouping on the back
of this sheet.

Answer Keys

Page 26
1. C
2. E
3. A
4. D
5. B

Page 28
1. H
2. C
3. I
4. D
5. F
6. J
7. B
8. G
9. A
10. E

Sentences will vary.

Page 31

February
1. The students in Ms. Adams's class are helping her prepare for the upcoming month's holidays. They've put up red heart cutouts, pictures of Abraham Lincoln and George Washington, and posters of famous African Americans.
Question: For which month are the students decorating?

give a speech
3. With her heart thumping, Leslie stepped up to the podium and arranged the notecards in her hands. The people quietly waited for her to begin.
Question: What is Leslie preparing to do?

a bouquet of flowers
5. John knew he'd have to hide his mother's present. But where would he hide it? His mother would be able to identify the floral fragrance. He couldn't put it in a drawer—it would get crushed. Besides, he needed to keep it in water so it wouldn't wilt.
Question: What present does John have for his mother?

research or medicine
7. The man in the lab coat adjusted the lens of the microscope so he could clearly see the specimens wriggling on the slide. He told his assistant to hold all his calls so he could finish his work.
Question: What kind of work does this man do?

scuba diving or snorkeling
2. Jason was very excited about his new adventure. He quickly put on his goggles and fins; then he jumped into the crystal-clear water.
Question: In what kind of adventure is Jason participating?

a library
4. The only sounds in the quiet room are the opening and closing of books, the shuffling of papers, and at times the cough of an occupant. The rows of shelves are filled with many books, magazines, and reference materials.
Question: What type of room is this?

babysit
6. "I can't believe your parents stuck you with that job again!" Chris said to his friend. "Think of all of the things you have to do—feeding, changing diapers, and reading a bedtime story. Yuck!"
Question: What job does Chris's friend have to do?

on an airplane
8. As the young girl rested her head on the cushioned seat, she was offered a drink and a snack. Suddenly there was an abrupt jerking movement, and she noticed a flashing sign that warned her to fasten her seat belt.
Question: Where is the young girl?

Page 58
Order within each column may vary.

Nouns	Verbs	Adjectives	Prepositions	Conjunctions	Pronouns
gerbil	eat	furry	under	or	he
scientist	crash	exciting	over	but	her
computer	write	grumpy	through	yet	she
month	jump	new	behind	and	mine

Page 59

Nouns:
mouse
staircase
librarian
bus driver

Verbs:
sang
purrs
fell
ate

Adjectives:
beautiful
lazy
easy
short

Adverbs:
swiftly
loudly
quietly
quickly

Pronouns:
they
We
she
you

Page 61
1. The bad weather forced disney world to close for the first time in many years.
2. The cookies for the party were bought at The Cookie cutter Bakery.
3. At the soccer game, i cheered each time our team scored a goal.
4. My sister's favorite book is *The view from Saturday.*
5. Dad asked mom, "what time is Carly's piano recital?"
6. In july, our family went to yellowstone national park.
7. Mom has an appointment with dr. fields on friday.
8. when it started raining, she let the cat inside.
9. A french chef won the cooking contest.
10. The wreck occurred on highway 311.

Page 63
1. Yes
2. Yes
3. No
4. No
5. No
6. Yes
7. No
8. Yes
9. No
10. Yes
11. Yes
12. Yes
13. No
14. Yes

Car 1 wins!

Bonus Box: Answers will vary.

Page 77

Answers will vary but may include the following answers:

1. The ~~big~~ massive bag of goodies was stuffed with cookies, candy, and snacks.
2. We stopped and picked up the ugly ~~thing~~ object.
3. They ~~want~~ require the kids to help clean the park.
4. I ~~like~~ enjoy stopping by the store each weekend.
5. My parents gave me an ~~interesting~~ intriguing gift to open.
6. The ~~pretty~~ attractive shirt had many colors and designs.
7. The class was ~~happy~~ overjoyed about Friday's field trip.
8. Ms. Smith asked me to ~~take~~ choose a pencil from the can.

Page 104

1. 24,000
2. 45.6
3. 0.64
4. 800,000
5. 300
6. 18
7. 3,000
8. 44,700
9. 600,000
10. 45
11. 20
12. 46,000
13. 28.4
14. 1.3
15. 1,000
16. 70,000
17. 1

PET SHOP

Page 112

Answers may vary.

1. multiples of 3: 3, 6, 9, ⑫ 15…
   multiples of 4: 4, 8, ⑫ 16, 20…
2. multiples of 7: 7, 14, 21, 28, 35, 42, 49, 56, 63, ⑦⓪…
   multiples of 10: 10, 20, 30, 40, 50, 60, ⑦⓪…
3. multiples of 2: 2, 4, 6, 8, 10, 12, 14, 16, 18, 20, 22, 24, 26, 28, ㉚…
   multiples of 15: 15, ㉚ 45, 60, 75…
4. multiples of 5: 5, 10, 15, 20, 25, ㉚…
   multiples of 6: 6, 12, 18, 24, ㉚…
5. multiples of 8: 8, 16, ㉔ 32, 40…
   multiples of 12: 12, ㉔ 36, 48, 60…
6. multiples of 9: 9, 18, 27, 36, 45, 54, 63, 72, 81, 90, ㊙…
   multiples of 11: 11, 22, 33, 44, 55, 66, 77, 88, ㊙…
7. multiples of 10: ⑩ 20, 30, 40, 50…
   multiples 5: 5, ⑩ 15, 20, 25…
8. multiples of 7: 7, 14, 21, 28, 35, 42, 49, ㊌…
   multiples of 8: 8, 16, 24, 32, 40, 48, ㊌…
9. multiples of 3: 3, ⑥ 9, 12, 15…
   multiples of 6: ⑥ 12, 18, 24, 30…
10. multiples of 4: 4, 8, 12, 16, 20, 24, 28, 32, ㊱…
    multiples of 9: 9, 18, 27, ㊱ 45…

Page 107

1.
```
  4 9 4
+ 3 2 8
-------
  8 2 2
```

2.
```
  5 7 2
+ 3 2 8
-------
  9 0 0
```

3.
```
1, 7 3 9
+  8 5 6
--------
2, 5 9 5
```

4.
```
  2 9 6
+ 5 7 3
-------
  8 6 9
```

5.
```
3, 4 3 5
+ 1, 3 7 2
--------
4, 8 0 7
```

6.
```
7, 8 5 1
+ 2, 1 3 6
--------
9, 9 8 7
```

7.
```
5, 9 3 4
+ 2, 2 1 5
--------
8, 1 4 9
```

8.
```
  3 0 3
+ 3 9 8
-------
  7 0 1
```

9.
```
1, 2 9 6
+ 3, 1 0 4
--------
4, 4 0 0
```

10.
```
  8 4 8
+ 3 2 3
-------
1, 1 7 1
```

11.
```
  5 6 1
+ 2 2 3
-------
  7 8 4
```

12.
```
7, 1 7 3
+ 1, 7 9 8
--------
8, 9 7 1
```

13.
```
  6, 4 3 7
+ 7, 1 9 8
---------
1 3, 6 3 5
```

14.
```
  8, 9 4 2
+ 6, 3 7 4
---------
1 5, 3 1 6
```

310

Page 113

A. 1,504
B. 1,988
C. 3,388
D. 3,312
E. 391
F. 3,468
G. 4,116
H. 4,636
I. 5,040
J. 656
K. 7,372
L. 1,073
M. 7,832
N. 1,079
O. 1,925

Winning car key: 6,323

Page 114

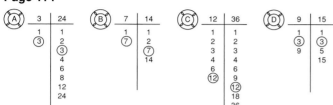

A) 3 | 24 — 1, ③ | 1, 2, ③, 4, 6, 8, 12, 24
B) 7 | 14 — 1, ⑦ | 1, 2, ⑦, 14
C) 12 | 36 — 1, 2, 3, 4, 6, ⑫ | 1, 2, 3, 4, 6, ⑫, 18, 36
D) 9 | 15 — 1, ③, 9 | 1, ③, 5, 15

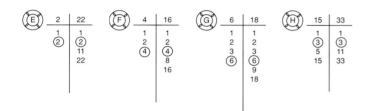

E) 2 | 22 — 1, ②, 5, 10 | 1, ②, 11, 22
F) 4 | 16 — 1, 2, ④ | 1, 2, ④, 8, 16
G) 6 | 18 — 1, 2, 3, ⑥ | 1, 2, 3, ⑥, 9, 18
H) 15 | 33 — 1, ③, 5, 15 | 1, ③, 11, 33

I) 10 | 38 — 1, ②, 5, 10 | 1, ②, 19, 38
J) 5 | 30 — 1, ⑤ | 1, 2, 3, ⑤, 6, 10, 15, 30
K) 8 | 36 — 1, 2, ④, 8 | 1, 2, 3, ④, 6, 9, 12, 18, 36
L) 14 | 40 — 1, ②, 7, 14 | 1, ②, 4, 5, 8, 10, 20, 40

Page 115

A. 201 R2
B. 236 R1
C. 1,270
D. 301
E. 112 R7
F. 1,007 R2
G. 1,533
H. 1,052
I. 1,601 R3

Page 116

A. 58 R5
B. 173 R3
C. 17 R6
D. 9 R9
E. 34 R6
F. 47 R2
G. 52 R1
H. 586 R10

Page 117

1. A = 200
2. A = 200, B = 40
3. B = 40, C = 120
4. C = 120, D = 1,440
5. D = 1,440; E = 360
6. E = 360, F = 60
7. F = 60, G = 120
8. G = 120

Page 122

Answers may vary.

1. $\frac{1}{2}$, $\frac{2}{4}$, $\frac{4}{8}$, $\frac{8}{16}$
2. The red boxes cover the same amount of space as the green box.
3. The blue boxes cover the same amount of space as the green and the red boxes.
4. The orange boxes cover the same amount of space as the green, the red, and the blue boxes.
5. yes
6. $\frac{1}{2}$, $\frac{2}{4}$, $\frac{4}{8}$, $\frac{8}{16}$
7. The numerator of each fraction is half the denominator. To get the next fraction, multiply the numerator and denominator of the previous fraction by two.
8. The five colored boxes would represent $\frac{5}{8}$, which would cover more space than the green or red boxes.

Page 123

1. 5 miles
2. $6\frac{1}{10}$ miles
3. $1\frac{1}{10}$ miles farther
4. $13\frac{3}{10}$ miles
5. $8\frac{17}{20}$ miles
6. $4\frac{6}{10}$ or $4\frac{3}{5}$ miles
7. Camper group B hiked farther
8. $11\frac{1}{20}$ miles
9. $8\frac{17}{20}$ miles
10. Answers will vary.

Page 124

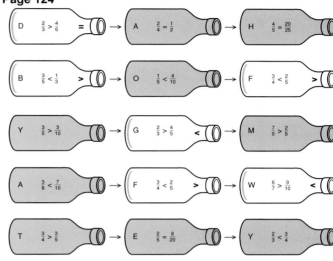

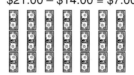

Row 1: D $\frac{2}{3} > \frac{4}{6}$ = → A $\frac{2}{4} = \frac{1}{2}$ → H $\frac{4}{5} = \frac{20}{25}$
Row 2: B $\frac{3}{5} < \frac{1}{3}$ > → O $\frac{1}{5} < \frac{4}{10}$ → F $\frac{3}{4} < \frac{2}{5}$ >
Row 3: Y $\frac{3}{5} > \frac{3}{10}$ → G $\frac{2}{3} > \frac{4}{5}$ < → M $\frac{7}{9} > \frac{2}{5}$
Row 4: A $\frac{3}{8} < \frac{7}{10}$ → F $\frac{3}{4} < \frac{2}{5}$ > → W $\frac{6}{7} > \frac{9}{10}$ <
Row 5: T $\frac{3}{4} > \frac{3}{5}$ → E $\frac{2}{5} = \frac{8}{20}$ → Y $\frac{2}{3} < \frac{3}{4}$

AHOY, MATEY!

Page 125

1. $18.00 − $12.00 = $6.00

2 of 3 rows = 6 + 6 = 12
$\frac{2}{3}$ of 18 = 12

$18 \times \frac{2}{3} = \frac{18}{1} \times \frac{2}{3} = \frac{36}{3} = 12$

2. $21.00 − $14.00 = $7.00

2 of 3 rows = 7 + 7 = 14
$\frac{2}{3}$ of 21 = 14

$\frac{2}{3} \times 21 = \frac{2}{3} \times \frac{21}{1} = \frac{42}{3} = 14$

3. $15.00 − $5.00 = $10.00

1 of 3 rows = 5
$\frac{1}{3}$ of 15 = 5

$\frac{1}{3} \times 15 = \frac{1}{3} \times \frac{15}{1} = \frac{15}{3} = 5$

4. $16.00 − $12.00 = $4.00

3 of 4 rows = 4 + 4 + 4 = 12
$\frac{3}{4}$ of 16 = 12

$\frac{3}{4} \times 16 = \frac{3}{4} \times \frac{16}{1} = \frac{48}{4} = 12$

Bonus Box: Roley's offers a bigger fraction off the regular price than Bull's-Eye Toys and Games. Roley's regular price is also lower than the regular price at Bull's-Eye, so the sale price for the games is better at Roley's.

Page 128
1. $39.99
2. $24.99
3. $8.99
4. $37.99
5. $12.99
6. $9.99
7. $29.99
8. $19.50
9. $34.99

Page 129
1. Possible answers:

750.4	5407.
754.0	5470.
4057.	5704.
4075.	5740.
4507.	7045.
4570.	7054.
4705.	7405.
4750.	7450.
5047.	7504.
5074.	7540.

2. 540.7 or 547.0
3. Possible answers:

0.457	04.75
0.475	4.057
0.547	4.075
0.574	4.507
0.745	4.570
0.754	4.705
04.57	4.750

4. 70.45
5. 0.457 or 0.475
6. 5.047 or 5.074
7. Possible answers:

4.507	5.047
4.570	5.074
4.705	5.407
4.750	5.470

8. 40.57
9. 0.457
10. .0457

Page 130
1. $6.09
2. $2.99
3. $6.98
4. $5.01
5. $14.49
6. $5.05
7. $14.15
8. $6.75
9. $61.51
10. Ireland, $3.38; Denmark, $5.67

Page 135
1. 2 hours
2. 3 hours and 10 minutes
3. 3 hours and 20 minutes
4. 1 hour and 15 minutes
5. 5 hours and 38 minutes
6. 2 hours and 15 minutes
7. 55 minutes
8. 1 hour and 40 minutes
9. 5:30 PM
10. 7:00 AM
11. 11:25 PM
12. 12:40 PM
13. 10:40 PM

Bonus Box: Answers will vary.

Page 136
1. 16 sq. cm
2. 12 sq. cm
3. 7 sq. ft.
4. 10.5 sq. yd.
5. 975 sq. mm
6. 9 sq. cm
7. 9 sq. cm
8. 11.5 sq. ft.

Page 140

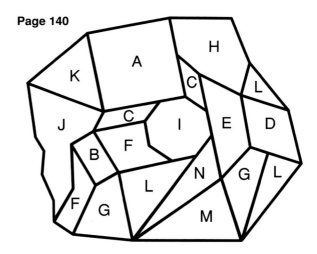

Page 141
1. CUBE
2. SPHERE
3. PRISM
4. CYLINDER
5. CONE
6. PYRAMID

RED-HANDED RUBY

Page 144

1.

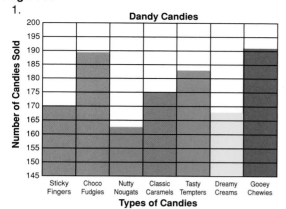

Dandy Candies

(Bar graph: Number of Candies Sold vs. Types of Candies)

- Sticky Fingers: 170
- Choco Fudgies: 189
- Nutty Nougats: 162
- Classic Caramels: 175
- Tasty Tempters: 182
- Dreamy Creams: 167
- Gooey Chewies: 190

2.

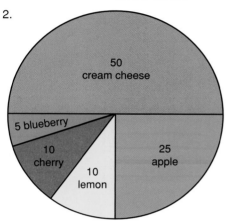

- 50 cream cheese
- 5 blueberry
- 10 cherry
- 10 lemon
- 25 apple

Papa Pete's Pastries

Page 145

Answers about the fairness of each game will vary.

1. ⅕
2. ⁸⁄₁₂ or ⅔
3. ½
4. ⁶⁄₇, ³⁰⁄₃₁, ¹¹⁄₁₂
   The player should choose dates in January.

Page 146

= 7	= 8	= 9	= 10	= 11	= 12
= 6	= 7	= 8	= 9	= 10	= 11
= 5	= 6	= 7	= 8	= 9	= 10
= 4	= 5	= 6	= 7	= 8	= 9
= 3	= 4	= 5	= 6	= 7	= 8
= 2	= 3	= 4	= 5	= 6	= 7

1. ¹⁄₃₆
2. ¹⁄₁₈
3. ¹⁄₁₂
4. ⅑
5. ⁵⁄₃₆
6. ⅙
7. ⁵⁄₃₆
8. ⅑
9. ¹⁄₁₂
10. ¹⁄₁₈
11. ¹⁄₃₆

PASCAL and Fermat

Page 149

Identity
21,345 + 0 = 21,345
987 x 1 = 987
918,273,645 x 1 = 918,273,645

Associative
12 + (6 + 6) = (12 + 6) + 6
58 x (2 x 3) = (58 x 2) x 3
(100 x 5) x 2 = 100 x (5 x 2)

Distributive
879 x (3 + 7) = (879 x 3) + (879 x 7)
137 x (2 + 4) = (137 x 2) + (137 x 4)
555 x (5 + 5) = (555 x 5) + (555 x 5)

Commutative
6 x 7 = 7 x 6
10 x 45 = 45 x 10
135 x 456 = 456 x 135

Page 150

A.	12	I.	9
B.	42	J.	8
C.	10	K.	23
D.	104	L.	15
E.	88	M.	178
F.	73	N.	275
G.	9	O.	2,557
H.	70	P.	3

Page 157

1.	R	6.	K
2.	G	7.	L
3.	T	8.	F
4.	E	9.	M
5.	U	10.	Z

MELTING and FREEZING

Page 160

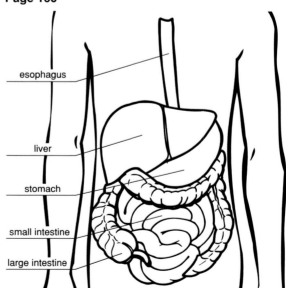

- esophagus
- liver
- stomach
- small intestine
- large intestine

Page 163

Cell Talk

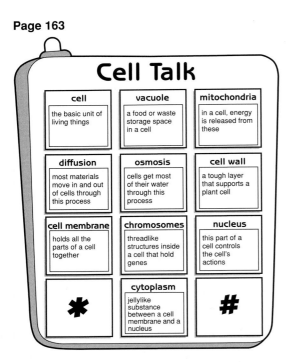

cell	vacuole	mitochondria
the basic unit of living things	a food or waste storage space in a cell	in a cell, energy is released from these

diffusion	osmosis	cell wall
most materials move in and out of cells through this process	cells get most of their water through this process	a tough layer that supports a plant cell

cell membrane	chromosomes	nucleus
holds all the parts of a cell together	threadlike structures inside a cell that hold genes	this part of a cell controls the cell's actions

✳	cytoplasm	#
	jellylike substance between a cell membrane and a nucleus	

Page 165

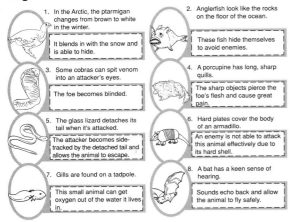

1. In the Arctic, the ptarmigan changes from brown to white in the winter.
   It blends in with the snow and is able to hide.
2. Anglerfish look like the rocks on the floor of the ocean.
   These fish hide themselves to avoid enemies.
3. Some cobras can spit venom into an attacker's eyes.
   The foe becomes blinded.
4. A porcupine has long, sharp quills.
   The sharp objects pierce the foe's flesh and cause great pain.
5. The glass lizard detaches its tail when it's attacked.
   The attacker becomes sidetracked by the detached tail and allows the animal to escape.
6. Hard plates cover the body of an armadillo.
   An enemy is not able to attack this animal effectively due to its hard shell.
7. Gills are found on a tadpole.
   This small animal can get oxygen out of the water it lives in.
8. A bat has a keen sense of hearing.
   Sounds echo back and allow the animal to fly safely.

Page 172

Newton's third law of motion was tested.

Page 175

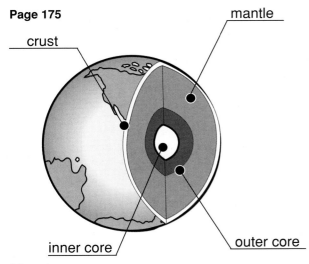

crust, mantle, inner core, outer core

lithosphere

Page 176

1. wind
2. water
3. ice
4. water
5. ice
6. ice
7. water
8. wind
9. water
10. wind

Page 181

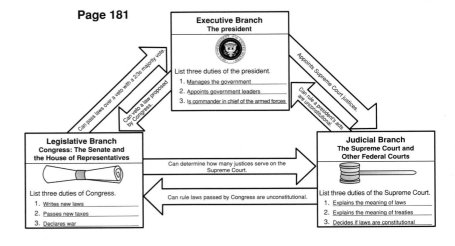

Executive Branch
The president

List three duties of the president.
1. Manages the government
2. Appoints government leaders
3. Is commander in chief of the armed forces

Can pass laws over a veto with a 2/3s majority vote

Can veto a law proposed by Congress.

Appoints Supreme Court justices.

Can rule a president's acts are unconstitutional.

Legislative Branch
Congress: The Senate and the House of Representatives

List three duties of Congress.
1. Writes new laws
2. Passes new taxes
3. Declares war

Can determine how many justices serve on the Supreme Court.

Can rule laws passed by Congress are unconstitutional.

Judicial Branch
The Supreme Court and Other Federal Courts

List three duties of the Supreme Court.
1. Explains the meaning of laws
2. Explains the meaning of treaties
3. Decides if laws are constitutional

Page 183

M. 1787
I. 12
N. 55
D. 7
R. 3
W. 39
E. 2
O. 81
A. 1791
J. 27
L. ⅔
S. ¾

JAMES MADISON

Page 193

1. New York
2. Georgia
3. New Hampshire, Massachusetts, Connecticut, Rhode Island
4. Pennsylvania, New York, New Jersey, Delaware
5. Maryland, Virginia, North Carolina, South Carolina, Georgia

Page 286

1. 180 in.³
2. 140 in.³
3. 147 in.³
4. 256 in.³
5. 54 in.³
6. 320 in.³
7. 325 in.³
8. 324 in.³

Number 7 should be colored.

Page 287

1. ambitious
2. frolicsome
3. felicitous
4. unsavory
5. homely
6. finicky
7. cozy
8. modish
9. fragrant
10. empathetic
11. prompt
12. titanic

Answers will vary. Accept reasonable explanations.

Page 288

1. Aunt Myra ate too much rich food. (1)
2. Our next-door neighbor is coming over for dinner at noon. (2)
3. Thanksgiving is a time for family, food, and fun. (3)
4. Ruff, my dog, likes sweet potatoes. (4)
5. My brother Waldo and my sister Wilma started food fights. (5)
6. My dad heaped my plate full of stuffing, mashed potatoes, and cranberry sauce. (3)
7. My five-year-old cousin gets the wishbone every year. (2)
8. Thanksgiving and Christmas are my favorite holidays. (5)
9. Bob, my friend, can crack walnuts with his teeth. (4)
10. My uncle Al loves fresh corn, but he doesn't like corn-on-the-cob. (6)
11. Our cat curls up on top of the table and goes to sleep right in the middle of dinner. (5)
12. We have a pet turkey named Terrell. (1)

Page 290

Answers may vary. Accept reasonable estimates.

	Estimated Amount Cost	Estimated Amount Change	Exact Amount Cost	Exact Amount Change
1.	$7.00	$8.00	$7.50	$7.50
2.	$11.00	$4.00	$11.15	$3.85
3.	$4.00	$3.00	$4.00	$3.00
4.	$7.00	$3.00	$5.75	$4.25
5.	$4.00	$1.00	$3.75	$1.25
6.	$9.00	$11.00	$8.75	$11.25
7.	$3.00	$2.00	$3.00	$1.75
8.	$6.00	$0.50	$5.95	$0.55
9.	$4.00	$15.00	$3.60	$15.15
10.	$5.00	$0.00	$4.50	$0.25

Page 293

1. hibernate
2. exaggerate
3. straight
4. plate
5. roller skates
6. late
7. illustrate
8. circulate
9. bait
10. donate
11. procrastinate
12. imitate
13. evaporates
14. interrogate or investigate
15. punctuate
16. navigate

Page 294

1. 2 hours and 15 minutes
2. 3 hours and 27 minutes
3. 26 minutes
4. 10 hours and 25 minutes
5. 1 hour and 46 minutes
6. 5 hours and 47 minutes
7. 51 minutes
8. 33 minutes
9. 7 hours and 13 minutes
10. 4 hours and 5 minutes
11. 2 hours and 37 minutes
12. 1 hour and 35 minutes

Page 295

Gifts:\nElves:	fruitcake	toy-making tools	hot-chocolate maker	bunny slippers	art book	antique ornament
Egbert	✗	✗	✗	✗	✗	✔
Englebert	✗	✔	✗	✗	✗	✗
Erwin	✔	✗	✗	✗	✗	✗
Ethel	✗	✗	✔	✗	✗	✗
Edna	✗	✗	✗	✗	✔	✗
Elvira	✗	✗	✗	✔	✗	✗

Page 296

Answers may vary. Accept all reasonable responses.

1. Principles 6, 7—She is using her creativity to share knowledge of a holiday that celebrates her heritage.
2. Principles 6, 7—He is using his creativity to share and celebrate his heritage.
3. Principles 2, 5—She is deciding for herself what career path she will follow.
4. Principle 7—His research shows his belief in his ancestors and heritage.
5. Principles 1, 3, 6, 7—They work together to share a traditional meal of Kwanzaa.
6. Principles 1, 6—The family is showing its unity through creative gift giving.
7. Principle 4—She is showing support for African American businesses.
8. Principle 7—It is a display of cultural pride.
9. Principles 1, 7—She is helping the children understand the holiday by way of a traditional tale.
10. Principles 2, 5, 6, 7—He shows purpose and self-determination through a creative poem.
11. Principles 1, 6, 7—She uses her creativity to share her cultural heritage with her family.
12. Principles 3, 6, 7—They work together to create a history of their family.

Page 297

1. brown bear
2. arctic tern
3. mountain quail
4. monarch butterfly
5. humpback whale
6. snowshoe hare
7. snowy owl
8. moose
9. pine marten
10. beaver
11. polar bear
12. squirrel

Page 298

1. knocking
2. stocking
3. thinking
4. Viking
5. rocking chair
6. kingdom
7. jokingly
8. seeking
9. sinking
10. cooking
11. king-size
12. parking lot
13. breaking
14. waking
15. stacking
16. jerking

<u>nonviolence</u> and <u>peace</u>

Page 299

1. 6
2. 12
3. 3
4. 5
5. 15
6. 15
7. 6
8. 12
9. 10
10. 16
11. 15
12. 18
13. 2
14. 20

Page 301

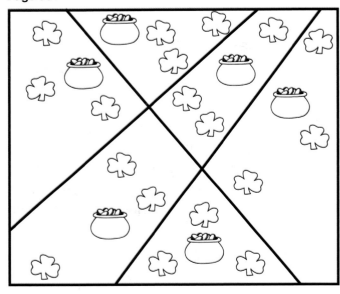

Page 304

Drawings for the southwest path may vary.

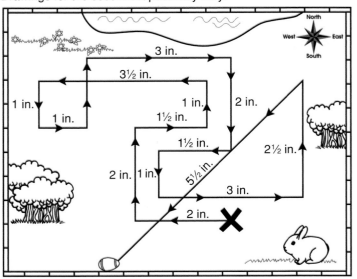

Page 305

Answers may vary.

1. Things with wheels, puppet; Toys, lawn mower
2. Things that come in pairs, microwave
3. Things worn on the head, snowshoes; Sports equipment, sombrero
4. Things worn on the ears, stereo speakers; Things that affect hearing, earrings
5. Things with holes in their centers, Frisbee disk
6. Things with strings, computer monitor
7. Things used to measure something, pencil
8. Playthings with more than one piece, soccer ball

Page 306

Answers may vary.

1. state
2. plate
3. trace
4. singer
5. organ
6. relay
7. lemon
8. shore
9. cents
10. beard
11. cheat
12. mates, tames, steam, meats
13. meats, teams, mates, tames
14. share
15. panel
16. mares, smear
17. pares, pears, spare
18. spool, loops
19. glean, angel
20. least, steal, tales, slate

Page 308

The following is a possible list of words, each of which is found in the word-search puzzle. Accept other reasonable answers.

1. arise
2. dinner
3. hear
4. nine
5. rest
6. teen
7. dear
8. earth
9. heart
10. raid
11. saint
12. trend
13. death
14. eastern
15. here
16. rain
17. sheet
18. reed
19. deer
20. hart
21. hinder
22. read
23. sneer
24. diner
25. head
26. need
27. rein
28. stern

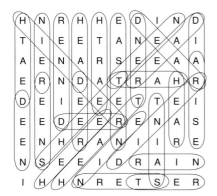

The words from each student's list that are not found in the word search will vary. Accept all reasonable answers.

Homophones: heart/hart, dear/deer, hear/here, rain/rein, read/reed

Index